robert m. newcomb

50/-

D1179728

DATE DUE

1A - 9 74			

DEMCO 38-296

Århus

6-68

PLATE I

St. Martin casting half his cloak to the beggar. Bronze, by Sebald Hirder the
elder, *circa* 1525; Bayerisches Nationalmuseum, Munich.

CHRISTIAN ANTIQUITIES

OF

CAMBORNE

CHARLES THOMAS

H. E. WARNE LTD

1967

Printed in Cornwall by
H. E. WARNE LTD., ST. AUSTELL

IN MEMORIAM

DONALD WOODROFFE THOMAS
1891-1959

Clerk to the Camborne Urban District Council, 1922-34; Clerk to the East Penwith Magistrates; County Councillor for Camborne (South), 1937-55; County Alderman, 1955-59; a Trustee of the Royal Institution of Cornwall; President of the Royal Cornwall Geological Society, 1959; first Chairman of the County Records Committee, 1952-59

and

GEORGE FREDERICK SANDFIELD
1903-1965

Rector of Camborne, 1945-1965,
and Honorary Canon of Truro Cathedral

CONTENTS

ILLUSTRATIONS IN THE TEXT

PLATES

PREFACE

IN ANOTHER PREFACE, written exactly a hundred and fifty years ago, Charles Sandoe Gilbert, the literary-minded chemist who sensibly employed his travellers in collecting local information as well as in peddling his wares, rose to heights of eloquence which I cannot hope to emulate. I can, however, borrow certain of his phrases, which in themselves well merit repetition today. 'No knowledge, we conceive, is more useful, or more becoming the natives of any country, than an intimate and exact knowledge of it', he remarked, and the present enthusiasm for local history seems to bear him out. He also observed that 'local attachment ranks among the best feelings of our nature', and that it was 'an irresistible impulse of this kind' which led to the publication of his *Historical Survey of Cornwall*. Poor Gilbert! he managed to bankrupt himself in the process, but no-one may doubt either his patriotism or his field-work; as he rightly claimed 'During several years . . . (he) indulged himself in pedestrian excursions through this county, to which he owes his birth, and for which, he hesitates not to avow a decided predilection.'

The present book is also the work of a native, in this case of the parish which forms its subject, and is also the outcome of many years of pedestrian excursions and of a decided predilection for local attachment. It is a common failing of the Cornish writer to assume that his own parish is more interesting than anyone else's; but, in the particular field with which this study is concerned, the claim does have some basis. The (pre-1840) ecclesiastical parish of Camborne is a large one—in size, it comes thirty-fifth of the 209 ancient parishes in Cornwall—and a populous one (in 1841, it had the fourth highest population). It constitutes a big wedge across the north coast of west Cornwall, and since most of the parishioners are concentrated in the town of Camborne (see fig. 32), the parish contains over twelve square miles of countryside, arable or croft. The northern tip of Camborne parish has long been known to be exceptionally rich in prehistoric remains; the complex of Bronze Age, post-Roman, and medieval sites loosely referred to in archaeological circles as 'the Gwithian area' is, for example, actually just within Camborne and not really in the parish of Gwithian at all. The remainder of Camborne parish proves, upon detailed examination, to be equally productive of ecclesiastical antiquities, some of them (like the two pre-Conquest altar slabs) of unique interest. A detailed account of these Christian remains not only merits a book to itself; it can usefully serve, as our knowledge of this period is now so rapidly increasing, as a cross-section of, and as a kind of interim account of, the Christian archaeology of Cornwall as a whole.

I use the word 'detailed' advisedly. A recent review in a Devonshire journal reproached another local historian with having provided too *much* detail. Who wants to know what X saw in 1794, or what A wrote about B in 1865? But this level of documentation is essential when, as here, one deals with classes of monuments like stone crosses, the majority of which can be and have been moved from their original stances; or with a county like Cornwall, where there is a very long-standing tradition of publishing primary sources (often the only sources) in the local newspapers rather than in learned journals. Again, Cornwall has only constituted its central archive, in the shape of the County Record Office, since the last war, which means that previous generations of local historians never had access to a mass of material which still remains unpublished. The value of the approach in detail, and the value of its outcome, should be obvious; to take the instance of stone crosses in Camborne alone, one can now be fairly sure where most of them originally stood, and this allows (from the contexts) a better estimate of their date and function, which in turn materially assists us in dating and describing the many hundreds of such monuments in Cornwall.

In the sphere of early Christian (that is, pre-Norman) archaeology, one can at last through field-work, excavation, and comparative studies, go rather further than the archaeological horizon represented by such former classics as Canon Taylor's book of 1916, or Dr. Hugh Hencken's of 1932. This is a specialist's field, and local histories in Cornwall have yet to draw upon it. Without claiming unusual expertise in this direction, I have tried to demonstrate, in chapters III and VII especially, how much more meaningful such sites or remains can be when they are viewed in the wider framework of Britain—or, where necessary, western Europe—at this period.

The compilation of this book, a labour of love and an act of piety toward a parish where my family have lived for centuries, has occupied me off and on for a great many years. I am consequently grateful to an enormous number of people for their kindness and help, beginning with the late Canon J. S. Carah, whose museum-like vicarage, fascinating to a boy of six, inevitably led to further antiquarian interest. At a later stage, I was aided by the late Mr. R. Morton Nance ('Mordon'), who never failed to help me with his great store of knowledge. For years, too, I enjoyed (without at the time really appreciating it) the encouragement and understanding of my late father, not least during times when I should have been otherwise employed. The debt which I owe him for this, as to my immediate family circle, need not be further particularised, but is apparent in the fact that this study has appeared at all.

Within Camborne, I would wish to thank all those who have lent me, given me, or let me copy and use here, maps and manuscript sources; who allowed themselves to be interrogated about the recent past; or who contributed so much in discussions and ideas. They include the late Mr. William Blewett, the Misses Carah, Mr. T. R. Harris, Dr. K. F. G. Hosking, Mrs. Gladys King, the late Mr. Peter Pendray, Mr. W. E. Wallace, the late Mr. Ernest Williams, and the successive Secretaries of Tehidy Minerals Ltd., the late Captain Bernard Kelly, M.C., J.P., and Mr. J. E. Hooper. Mr. J. F. Odgers, the social historian of Camborne and a family friend over five generations, has consistently helped and encouraged me. Mr. Burrell (Camborne Public Library), Miss E. M. Rule, Mr. S. C. Wilson, M.B.E. (Clerk to the Camborne-Redruth U.D.C.), and a wide range of fellow-Cambornians who have let me wander around, and even to excavate, their properties, must also be mentioned with gratitude.

For various kindnesses, I must also thank Canon J. G. Adams (St. Goran), Mr. A. K. Hamilton Jenkin, F.S.A. (Redruth), Mr. Langman (Redruth Public Library), Mr. Michael Tangye (Redruth), and fellow-members of the Cornwall Archaeological Society. I have been aided for years by the kindness and efficiency of the staff of the Royal Institution of Cornwall (Mr. H. L. Douch, the late Mrs. Knott, and Mr. Roger Penhallurick) and of the County Record Office, Truro (Mr. P. R. Hull, County Archivist, and Miss Hawkridge). My old friend Mr. P. A. S. Pool was good enough to read this whole book in draft, and to make numerous helpful criticisms. I am particularly indebted to Dr. C. A. Ralegh Radford, not only for many years of advice concerning this difficult period, but for his views on St. Ia's chapel (chapter V), which we are able to visit and discuss together.

The photographs, as far as possible chosen to avoid any previously-published items or views, were taken, supplied, or otherwise processed by my brother (Mr. N. D. Thomas) and by my friends and colleagues Messrs. P. J. Fowler, F.S.A., J. V. S. Megaw, F.S.A., Malcolm Murray, Kenneth White, and Charles Woolf. In the case of older photographs, where the photographer is not always known and where the copyright may or may not have lapsed, I have given what I believe to be the correct attributions, but must apologise in advance to their present representatives in case of error. The line-drawings, except where otherwise indicated, are my own.

Finally, I would record my especial gratitude to the other person mentioned, with my father, in the dedication; the late Canon G. F. Sandfield, Rector of Camborne from 1945 to 1965. To describe him, as one of his many obituaries did, as 'an outstanding and devoted churchman of the Evangelical school' is perfectly correct, but he was far more than this. In an age where the differences between Anglicanism and Method-ism are rapidly eroding, Canon Sandfield (who often preached from Methodist pulpits) exemplified the kind of priesthood which transcends such doctrinal labels. The standard of pastoral care which he brought to his years in our midst was reflected in the deep affection in which he was held by all. It is not, perhaps, so widely known that he was also keenly interested in the Christian history and antiquities of his parish, and indeed on a number of occasions he urged me to compile a work along these lines. His personal encouragement and kindness to me, and to anyone engaged in local studies, was characteristic of an incumbent who will long be remembered.

Feast of St. Martin, 11th November, 1966.

ACKNOWLEDGEMENTS

I am grateful to the following for permission to reproduce the works mentioned; the Bodleian Library, Oxford (Appendix A, from Rawlinson MS. D. 997), the Trustees of the British Museum (Appendix B, from Egerton MS. 2657), the Royal Institution of Cornwall (fig. 19, from MS. Borlase 41, extracts from the Henderson MSS., and (chap. II) the translation by Nance and Smith from *Bewnans Meryasek*), the County Record Office, Truro (documents cited in Appendices C and H), the Cornwall Archaeological Society (figs. 2 and 8, which first appeared in *Cornish Archaeology*), and the Bayerisches Nationalmuseum, Munich, for permission to reproduce the photograph which forms the frontispiece. Details in figs. 3, 11, 26, 29 and 30 are taken from maps and plans in the possession of Tehidy Minerals Ltd., Camborne, and are reproduced with their permission; the parish maps (figs. 1, 10 and 18) which are primarily designed to show patterns of settlement and communication, are based mainly on the 1838-1842 Tithe Apportionment Survey for the parish. Pl. IV below, left, is reproduced by kind permission of Messrs. W. J. Bennetts and Sons, Camborne. Every effort has been made to see that excerpts and quotations in the text have been duly acknowledged or identified in the footnotes.

THE SPELLING OF CORNISH NAMES

To avoid undue confusion, the numerous place-names cited have been given in the forms most widely current today, e.g. as painted on farm-gates, or as printed in the most recent Electoral Registers. Even this system has some latitude, as spellings can change quite rapidly (see Appendix G), but where alternatives exist, that which is linguistically correct (e.g. *Penpons*, rather than *Penponds*) has been preferred.

In transliterating Cornish words, whether they may be MC (Middle Cornish—from the 14th century), or ModC (Late Cornish, or 'Modern Cornish', the 17th and 18th centuries, when a number of place-names were still being formed), I have given the unified spelling followed in current Cornish writing and in the current dictionaries. The only accents employed are the circumflex ($\hat{a}$) to mark vowel-length (in unified spelling, a length-sign, so: $\bar{a}$ is often used for this), and the diaresis ($\ddot{u}$) for the umlaut sound of *u*, normally written *ee*, *e*, or *i*, in place-names according to stress. An asterisk (*) before any name or word implies that it is not actually attested in any surviving source, but can be legitimately inferred from comparison of cognate forms or from the known action of phonetic rules.

I

THE PARISH OF CAMBORNE

'CAMBURNE. A churche standinge among the barrayne hills' wrote
John Norden in 1584[1]. So it must have been then; and so it remained for
another two centuries. In 1750, an aged lady of Wendron assured Dr.
Richard Lanyon, the churchtown hamlet contained only seven houses[2].
Another of the doctor's informants, a man of ninety-two—he would have
been born about 1745—could recall when there had been thirteen houses,
all near the church. By 1800, this figure had risen to 'about 120 houses'
(Lanyon), and a count of the detailed 1805 Tehidy Estate Map[3], here
shown in fig. 26, suggests this is approximately correct. In 1840, the total
had leapt up to some four hundred dwellings. The hamlet had become a
town, and a directory of 1830 could comment[4] 'From a very insignificant
place, this town is fast rising into opulence, and consequently importance,
from the valuable mines of copper and tin surrounding it; and is becoming
a serious rival to the neighbouring town (Redruth) in its trade, etc. Several
new streets have been added within these few years, and there are other
projected . . .' while the accompanying columns in the same work list
seven inns, three milliners, a cabinet-maker, and even two boarding-
schools for young ladies. 'A thriving town, surrounded by mines' wrote
the editor[5] of the first edition of John Murray's famous *Hand-Book for
Travellers* (1850), further describing the church as[6], 'a fine Perp. structure
of granite'. Alas for Camborne! the sleepy rustic village, at whose parish
pump the news of Waterloo had been duly announced[7], was now all
set to become what Mr. John Betjeman has aptly called[8] 'a large brown
two-storey town to the west of the doleful hill of Carn Brea'.
   The very name of Camborne seldom appears in any topographical
literature, Cornish or otherwise, before the 19th century, and there would
seem to be no surviving depictions of any part of the town prior to the
invention of photography. This obscurity, relieved only by the construction
of the main turnpike road (the A.30) in 1839, was well explained by Canon
J. Sims Carah[9]. 'This is readily understood when we realize how small
a village Camborne was . . . and how *recessed* it was from the highways
through the county. There was no such thing as passing through Camborne
on the way to anywhere else. Those who came to Camborne were those
who wanted to come to the place, and Camborne Church Town was then
only one village and a very small village in a large country parish where
villages abounded.'
   Outside the town, the last sentence is still true; Camborne is to some
extent a large country parish full of villages, or rather of those agglomera-
tions of dwellings which represent villages in Cornwall. The old
ecclesiastical parish, the geographical unit with which this book is
concerned, lies in Penwith, most westerly of the nine Cornish hundreds[10],

and with an extent of 6,598 acres it ranks as a fairly large one. It is bounded on the east of Illogan, on the west and south-west by Gwithian, Gwinear and Crowan, and at its south-east corner (just) by Wendron. As usual in Cornwall, the parish bounds themselves are natural ones. On the west side there is the stream sometimes called[11] Connor or Conor River, or Dour Conor, from its source at Boswin down to Gwithian Bridge. On the east, the Red River—whose original name is lost, and which has been discoloured by mine waste for centuries—runs from Bolenow moors to another bridge at Coombe or Bell Lake[12]. Short land-bounds, indicated by banks or hedges (see below), run from both Bell Lake and Gwithian Bridge to the northern sea cliff, and the southern edge of the parish is defined by a road, presumably a trackway of great age, across the high moors.

The circuit of the entire parish (on foot or horseback) would not be far short of fifteen miles, and it is therefore scarcely surprising to find that these bounds do not appear to have been beaten very often. In 1710, the sum of 15s. 0d.—for refreshment?—was 'pd for exspences vewing the pish bouns' (Churchwardens' accounts) and in the next year, when 'the bounses of the parish was Renewd by Mr. William Smith, Rector' together with some leading parishioners, only a partial circuit was undertaken[13]. A deleted note states that the bounds 'hathe not been Renewed many yeares before us' (see Appendix C, a statement of the parish bounds in the 17th century).

The shape of the parish (fig. 1) is that of a wide strip, over five miles long and in places over two miles across. It is the north-south length which always strikes one; the antiquary Edward Lhuyd, who visited Camborne in 1700, estimated the breadth correctly at about two miles, but otherwise thought the parish was '7^m long from Gwidhian p^{sh} to Gwendan' (Wendron)[14]. The exclusion of the small area in the north-west corner, at Godrevy, which lies north of the Red River and might geographically be expected to form part of Camborne, is probably due to some now-irrecoverable tenurial arrangement of the late 12th or 13th century. This area is the extinct Manor of Crane Godrevy, a subsidiary of the vast manor of Tehidy (Domesday *Tedinton(e)* or *Tedenton*) which covered part of Camborne, most of Illogan, and more beside; and it would appear to have been counted with Gwithian parish, possibly because of its proximity to Gwithian church and its remoteness from the church at Camborne. The land bound which cuts off Crane Godrevy from Tehidy is of great interest, as the central part of it is a constructed bank with a ditch either side. Fig. 2 shows a diagrammatic view[15] of a section excavated across this bank in 1963. It may originally have been made to delimit Crane Godrevy from the parent manor, but has for many years served additionally as the Camborne-Gwithian parochial bound.

Camborne parish, as fig. 1 makes clear, is physically divisible into three parts. The northern third, from the high North Cliffs down to the Red River, has never been very intensively settled, and like the northern third of the neighbouring Illogan parish, was maintained for years by the Bassets as a kind of large-scale game preserve. It contains a number of

Fig. 1
Camborne parish, showing settlements first mentioned before A.D. 1600,
roads (double lines), lanes and tracks (single lines), and land over 500 feet
(stippled area).

medium-sized farms—Pencobben, Reskajeage, Gwealavellan, Callean, Menadarva, Ash-hill, New Downs, Goonzoyle—and once had others (Hellowe, Balrose, Tolgarrack, Carlenno, Roseluwy) which have subsequently vanished or which have been incorporated in the existing ones. Most arable land here lies between the 50 and 250 ft. contours, facing south or west, on a stony or sandy soil overlying 'killas' (slate). Isolated patches of scrub in the Red River valley, and marginal land along the cliff edge, show what this area must have looked like prior to the great post-medieval clearance and intakes.

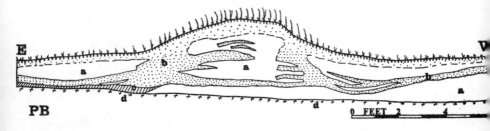

Fig. 2

Section across the Camborne-Gwithian parish boundary bank, 1963. Key: (d), undisturbed stony surface, (c), a buried plough-soil, probably last cultivated in the Iron Age, (b), medieval land-surface, stripped of turf to build the bank, and (a), sterile blown sand. (See CA 3 (1964), p.53 and fig. 16.)

The central third of the parish, stretching south from the Red River to (approximately) the east-west course of the main railway line, lies between 250 and 350 ft., has a certain amount of woodland (particularly in tributary valleys), and contains igneous or metamorphic rocks intersected by SW-NE elvan dykes[16]. This is the heart of the parish, off the granite, and sheltered from the salt-laden air of the coast; advantages which are reflected in the fact that this third contains not only the church-town, but four of the six settlements whose names bear (or bore) the prefix *tre-* or *tref-*, the usual element (meaning, very approximately, 'a homestead, a land-holding', and usually loosely translated as 'farm') in the names of major arable holdings of medieval or pre-Norman origin.

The remainder of the parish lies south of the main railway line, and was once generically known as 'South Country', a name not yet altogether obsolete. The area shelves upwards to the granite, which outcrops from 400 ft. and over, and is marked by the three main hill-spurs of, from west to east, Carnwynnen or Carwynnen, Carn Camborne, and Carn Entral. Around and to the south of these hills lie the remains of uneven moorland between 400 and 700 ft., seamed by numerous tiny valleys which still support a surprising weight of deciduous growth. The focus of the South Country is Troon, older Trewoon (*tre*(*f*), plus *gun*, 'downs, level upland') which has been aptly called the largest village in west Cornwall; and another *tref*, Treslothan, was once spread on the western flank of this high ground. The basic farming pattern here still tends to be that of the small-holding, as small as ten to fifteen acres[17], with little fields resulting from preliminary clearance of the surface granite ('moorstone') into the dry-stone walls or earth-cored stone-faced banks known throughout Cornwall as 'hedges'.

The parish of Camborne thus offers a fair cross-section, north to south, of the northern sea-board of west Cornwall, from the high slate cliffs to the central watershed. To the archaeologist no less than to the historian, this parish teems with interest. Despite the surprising lack of any major parish history, in a county where the parish history has been a popular and established literary *genre* for over a century, the steady development of the town could be fairly fully documented, and a wealth of pre-1850 social, tenurial and mining records awaits proper analysis and treatment at such places as the County Record Office, the Royal Institution of Cornwall, the Probate Registry, and Tehidy Minerals Ltd., the firm which took over the far-ranging mineral rights (with many of the records) from the Basset family of Tehidy. Camborne is exceptionally rich in the remains of antiquity, and the writer's own modest campaign of excavations in the last fifteen years merely serves to indicate how much could still be done[18]. In this context it is easier to understand how the parish, far from being an eroded waste of industrial debris, is also quite unusually rich in the remains of early Christianity, and may be used to illustrate all the phases through which, prior to the Industrial Revolution, Christian life and archaeology have passed in this part of Britain.

The name 'Camborne'

Since the 16th century, most writers have tried to interpret this name as a compound of C.*cam*, 'crooked, bent, curved' and OE.*burne*, 'river, stream, fountain, well'. So William Borlase, who should have known better, wrote in 1750 (Appendix B) that Camborne was so named from 'a crooked Spring or brook wch. gives rise to the principal river of the parish . . .' and William Hals, who knew little Cornish, repeated this idea[19].

The early forms of the place-name show conclusively that OE.*burne* does not, and never did, enter into it. We find *Camberon* in 1181; *Cambron* in 1294, 1329, and 1427; *Cambrone* in 1371, 1384, 1387, 1426, 1448, and 1449; *Camborne* (as now) as early as 1431, and *Cambron* as late as 1780;

and the form *Camburne*, which gave rise to the spurious etymology cited above, not until 1515[20]. The earliest instances of each of these forms, taken together, and reading the 1181 (Pipe Roll) example as *Camb(e)ron*, give a fully consistent series. The first element is C.*cam*, 'curved, bent', and the second is OC.**bron*[20], MC. and ModC.*bron*, ModW. *bron*, ModB.*bronn*, 'breast', here used in the transferred topographical sense of 'front of a hill, hill-slope'. The metathesis of *bron* to *born* is found in a lenited form in such place-names as Talverne (*tal vorn*, 'top of the hill-front' (*lit.* 'brow of the hill-front') and the house on the side of the hill at Roseworthy, Camborne, now called 'The Ferns' or 'Rosehill in the Ferns' (1884 *Fern*, 1688 *The Vearne*, from (*an*) *vorn*, for (*an*) *vron*, 'the hill-front'); also, perhaps, the lost Camborne tenement of Vorner or Trevornow, with its alternate Treverna, on the hill-side by Roskear (1588 *Trevornow*, 1838 *Treverna*, *tre(f)* + *vornow*, for *vronnow*, or else *vyrnow* for *vrynnow*, a doublet form[21]), embodying the plural of this word.

Camborne is thus 'curved hill-front', and local geographical considerations suggest that the feature so named, visible from the medieval church-town, was not (as has been suggested) Carn Brea, several miles to the east, but the hill called 'Carn Camborne'. This is the now built-over hill-front crowned by the village of Beacon, or Camborne Beacon, which takes its name from the ornamental engine-house stack of the former Carn Camborne mine.[22]

It is difficult to escape the conclusion that the name *Cambron* is not only probably pre-Norman, but also originally the name of some independent land-holding, transferred to the church and churchtown in a secondary phase—presumably the 12th century. The evidence for this is rather complicated. To start with, many west Cornish place-names commencing with 'Carn' may take the second element, not from the hill, but from a land-holding below it, or the name of a prominent land-owner of early times. Carn Entral has a former tenement of Entral (1380 *Entrall*) below it, where the second element *hal*, 'low ground, moor (in the Cornish sense of 'marsh overgrown with furze and willow')' suggests that this name must refer to the tenement and not the hill-top. Carwynnen, 1838 and earlier *Carnwynnen*, *Carnwinin*, may contain the personal name **Uuinan*, and the farm of Boswin just below it may embody the same (OC. *bot* **Uuinan*, MC. *bos Wynan*—*bos*, 'homestead'). Was there a 'Camborne' on the slopes of Carn Camborne? This, too, can be demonstrated. The road ascending the hill, from the railway station to Beacon, is still 'Camborne Hill', a name fossilised in the local song 'Going up Camborne Hill' which recalls Richard Trevithick's epoch-making road locomotive trial of 1801[23]. On the east side of the road is the former tenement of Camborne Vean; on the west, Camborne Veor. These, as quite late farms, unequal halves of a still earlier tenement of Camborne or Cambron (Camborne Vean, from C.*byghan*, means 'Little Camborne', and Camborne Veor, from C.*mur*, *meor*, means 'Great Camborne'), are shown on the Tehidy estate maps of 1805 and on the Tithe Apportionment Survey of 1840. Today (1966), part of the 1800-period Camborne Vean farm-house and a good few of the original fields, sub-divided from the

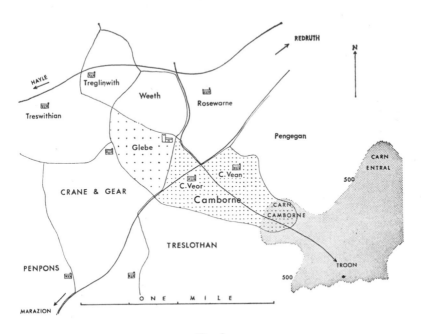

Fig. 3
Medieval land-holdings in the central part of the parish, showing the putative tenement of 'Cambron' (Camborne Veor, Camborne Vean, and the Glebe). Names in capitals are those of manors; all boundaries are to a limited extent conjectural.

medieval arable enclosures, can still be traced, and the remains of Camborne Veor farm have been, aptly, incorporated in the yard behind what are now the Council Offices of Camborne-Redruth U.D.C.

This is shown in the sketch map, fig. 3. The reconstructed tenement has a strong claim to represent the original *Cambron* of the 11th century, if not earlier. Where the original homestead lay is bound to be a matter of some conjecture, but the site of the successive houses called 'Camborne Veor' naturally suggests itself. It is also probable that the Glebe, an irregular area of forty Cornish acres[24], was detached from *Cambron* (in the 13th century?) to form an endowment for the Rectory by the Bassets, as owners of the tenement in question and as patrons of the living. Camborne church, which lies within the Glebe, would then have actually stood on *Cambron*. It is just conceivable that, like St. James' chapel at Treslothan (p.64), the church site originated in an 11th-century vill chapel—dedicated in honour of the Blessed Virgin and St. Anne—standing in what was later to become the churchyard (p.56).

Further than this, one cannot safely go. Any attempt to reconstruct the manors and land-holdings of medieval Camborne, as in fig. 3, will bear some correspondence to reality if it follows the outlines detectable in 18th- and 19th-century deeds and estate maps, and the general pattern is clear; a series of principal tenants' holdings within a superior manor, almost certainly Tehidy, some of which may have been elevated to subordinate manors (e.g., Crane and Gear, Crane Godrevy), while others (Treslothan, for instance) may have been nominally independent. Many of these holdings gave rise to surnames[25], a good few of which persisted until the 17th century, as the parish registers witness. Whether there was ever a family who styled themselves 'de Cambron' is, however, doubtful[26].

A note on early roads through Camborne

The present main road across the parish, the A.30 from Redruth to Hayle and Penzance, is essentially the Turnpike Road. This particular stretch was constructed, at the instigation of (and with the heavy subventions of) certain local landowners, under an Act of May 14th, 1839, and toll-gates existed at the bottom of Tuckingmill, the head of Trelowarren Street (somewhere short of Centenary Chapel), and Treswithian, just east of the 'Cornish Daws' or 'Three Choughs' Inn.

This involved the making of entirely new stretches of road, particularly on either side of Camborne churchtown. College Row or College Street, so called from at least 1819[27], came to a dead end about the present Fire Station, and had to be extended to Treswithian. The short western extension of the churchtown, known as Bakers' or Bakehouse Lane[28] as an alternative to 'Trelowarren Street' (which first appears in 1833[29]) had to be driven through to Roskear.

Prior to this activity, the churchtown was, as we have seen, isolated in the angle between two older roads, both of which must go back to early medieval times. The detailed sources for these are, firstly, Joel Gascoyne's map of 1700[30], the Camborne part of which is shown here as fig. 4; secondly, Thomas Martyn's map, in its various editions[31] from 1748 (fig. 5); and thirdly, the pioneer edition of the Ordnance Survey 1-in. sheets for Cornwall in 1813, with subsequent revisions[32]. All these can be compared, as Gascoyne's and some versions of Martyn's are also at (approximately) one inch to the mile scales. The evidence from early Itineraries and Road-books is not quite so useful, since these are by their nature selective.

Gascoyne's map is the most interesting. The main road, on the line of the A.30, comes west from Redruth past *Trevanson* (Trevenson—now Cornwall Technical College), crosses the Red River, and then divides. The northern road goes past (Higher) *Rosewarn* and *Rosewarn the Lower*, through *Tresothan* (Treswithian), and on to Roseworthy, where it crosses the Connor stream into Gwinear parish.

This northern road is also shown by Martyn, adding side roads, in particular one at *Rosewarne* and *Wheal Kitty* (which was roughly where Rosewarne House and its enclosed grounds lie), which goes due south

Fig. 4
The parish of Camborne in 1700, extracted from Joel Gascoyne's map of Cornwall.

to join the other main road by *Camborne Vean*. This side-road, omitted by Gascoyne, who probably found it as a small muddy lane, is now (from north to south) Tehidy Road, Fore Street, and Cross Street, and provides the link between the major roads and the churchtown.

The northern road has had several names. The junction with the side road to the churchtown has always been Parkenbowen ('Beef Close'; C.*parc bowyn*). From here west to Treswithian runs 'Gilly Road' or 'Gilly Lane'; and beyond Treswithian, prior to 1839-40, the road made several detours which have subsequently become forgotten. One, a little way west of Treswithian, curved north through the hamlet of Croon at Croon Corner[33]. Croon was more or less destroyed by the building of the Turnpike. Opposite Polstrong gates, at 'Cuckold's Roost'[34], the pre-1839

road went down the hill, north of the present A.30, to Roseworthy, and
the central part of this stretch is of some interest as still preserving what
must be the pre-1839 cobbled surface.

East of Parkenbowen, the road runs between Lower Rosewarne and
Higher Rosewarne (finally demolished in 1955)[35] on its north, and
Rosewarne House and grounds on its south, to the former hamlet of
Gerry. This part may be the 'Rosewarne Lane' of 1828[36]. From Gerry to
Tuckingmill, and indeed from Parkenbowen, the most common local
term for this road has always been 'Eastern Lane', though the Rosewarne
stretch of it is marked 'North Lane' on the large-scale O.S. sheets.

The southern road represents the main east-west highway to Marazion,
and thence to Penzance, with a fork off to Helston south-west of the
churchtown district. Gascoyne's map (fig. 4) rather curiously shows it on
conventional lines as far west as this fork—which is still in the same place,
just over the railway bridge in Pendarves Road—but then takes it to run
north of *Penpons* (the present 'Higher Penpons' by Trevithick's cottage)
and then, through somewhere in Gwinear parish called *Cosurne*, which
the writer cannot identify, on to Gwinear churchtown. This line can now
be traced but has never been more than a customary footpath, noteworthy
in that it still crosses the Connor stream by a granite clapper bridge
of apparent antiquity, practically unknown outside the village (see
pl.IX). Martyn, whose work in most respects must be seen as derived
from Gascoyne's, shows the correct road; passing just *south* of 'Higher
Penpons', and through Baripper, along the line of the present road
through Carnhell Green, Wall, Fraddam, Relubbas and Goldsithney
to Marazion. This has claims to be the last portion of the medieval pilgrim
way to the Mount; and within Camborne, the early 15th-century references
in Bishop Lacy's Register to Baripper (e.g. 1430 *Beaurepper*), implying
possibly a hostel, and the traditional antiquity of the site now occupied
by the St. Michael's Mount Inn, tend to confirm this.

From the junction with the churchtown side road at Camborne Cross—
a junction now marked by Richard Trevithick's statue—this road was
known for an undefined distance eastward as 'Redruth Row'[37]. West
from Camborne Cross, up to the fork, it appears as 'Helston Road' on
the 1805 Tehidy map. In earlier sources, such as the 17th century Glebe
Terriers (Appendix C), it is simply 'the Highway'.

The minor roads of the parish, for example the very long one running
south from the churchtown to Camborne Cross, up 'Camborne Hill'
to Beacon and Troon and beyond, originate in a network of trackways,
some of which were customary churchways marked here and there by
crosses (chapter VI), while others merely served to link the medieval
tenements with each other and with the two main thoroughfares. Not all
of these have survived, and it would be a well-nigh impossible task to
discuss them all in detail at this remove in time.

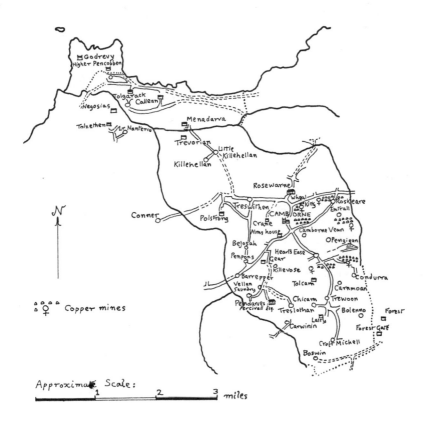

Fig. 5
The parish of Camborne in 1748, extracted from Thomas Martyn's 'New and Accurate Map of the County of Cornwall'.

NOTES

1. John Norden, *Speculi Britanniae Pars. A . . . description of Cornwall, etc.*, Chr.Bateman, London 1728.
2. Lanyon 1841, 112.
3. One of series at Tehidy Minerals Ltd., Camborne (map roll 6).
4. Pigot 1830, 138.
5. T. C. Paris, of Penzance, who edited the first four editions in respect of Cornwall.
6. *Op.cit.*, 121.
7. Information from the late Mr. William Carlyon, Camborne, 1945; his grandmother, as a very small girl, witnessed this event. The pump was somewhere opposite the church: cf. Carah 1927, 15.
8. John Betjeman, *Cornwall; Shell Guide* (1964), 27.
9. Carah 1927, 4.

10. These, originally six in number, are much larger than normal English hundreds and may represent some kind of pre-Norman division—cf. *CA* 3 (1964), 70.
11. So, e.g., John Leland, writing about 1540; C.*dour*, 'water, stream'.
12. Both names are corrupted from an older *Combellack* (still a local surname), C.*cum helyk*, 'willow valley'.
13. 'From between Illugan and Cambren, Round to Brepor Bridge', that is, about two-thirds of the way.
14. MS. Bodl. Rawlinson D.997, fol. 2 r; see Appendix A for text.
15. See *CA* 3 (1964), 53-4, and fig. 16.
16. For the geology, cf. J. B. Hill and D. A. MacAlister, *Falmouth and Truro and the mining district of Camborne and Redruth* (*Mem. Geol. Survey*), H.M.S.O., 1906; Henry Dewey, *British Regional Geology: South-West England* (2nd edn., H.M.S.O., 1948); and the Geological Survey (over-printed) O.S. 6-in. sheets, 2nd edn., 1908, Cornwall, squares 62 and 63.
17. Cf. particulars of a holding for sale at Carn Entral, 1966; ten hedged fields, average size 1.3 acres, total area of farm 13.4 acres! It was described as 'healthy and elevated . . . very suitable for dairying'.
18. Thomas 1958, which describes some of the main prehistoric discoveries in the northern tip of the parish; and subsequent entries in the (annual) Cumulative Index in *CA*.
19. Hals 1750, 21.
20. Graves 1962, 49.
21. R. M. Nance, *Cornish-English Dictionary* (Marazion, 1955) s.v.*bron, bryn*.
22. Collins 1912, 441.
23. Inglis Gundry, *Canow Kernow: Songs and Dances from Cornwall*, FOCS (1966), 53—the unidentified 'she' who wore 'white stockings' was surely Lady Basset, the traditional passenger?
24. Cf. the Glebe Terrier of 1680, in which the rector states that he 'hath been informed that the whole parcell of land given to the church at first was 40 acres'. It is worth noting that the Terrier of 1680 also mentions a 'Camborne Moor'; Mr. T. R. Harris kindly informs the writer that the Tehidy Accounts for 1781 refer to 'Camborne Upper Wastrel als. Camborne Moor', showing that this 'moor' (waste land) must have been that part of the Weeth adjoining the Glebe, now College Row.
25. E.g. Penpons, Killihellan, Gear, Crane, Tolcarne, etc. A few examples—Combellack, Newton, Rosewarne—still survive in the district as surnames.
26. The 'Arnand (?Arnaud) de Cambron' who heads the list of rectors (Vincent 1949, 21; presumably 13th century) cannot be traced. William of Worcester (1478) mentions 'Willelmus Chambron' as a benefactor of Bodmin Priory in 1353.
27. *RPC* II, under 'Burials', s.a.
28. *Cornishman*, 7 October 1954 ('Camborne's Century as a Shopping Centre').
29. Pamphlet, *Valuation of the Town and Parish of Camborne; The Old Rate made A.D. 1806 and the New Rate 1833* (*penes* Mr. T. R. Harris, Camborne).
30. *A Map of the County of Cornwall, Newly Surveyed*, by Joel Gascoyne (London 1700). There is a photocopy now at CRO, Truro.
31. *A New and Accurate Map of the County of Cornwall*, by Thomas Martyn: 1748, 1749 (repr. 1784), and 1784. See now R.C.E. Quixley, *Antique Maps of Cornwall and The Isle of Scilly* (Penzance, 1966).
32. The western sheet is published as 1839, the central and eastern as 1813, but all appear to be the same survey; there is a revision with railways to 1887.
33. *Kerroone* 1679, *Carroon* 1761: *ker un*, 'camp on the down', with reference to a (destroyed) earthwork just to the south.
34. So named, Cary's *Itinerary* (1815), 67.
35. *Cornishman*, 20 October 1955 ('Memories Recalled by Demolition', etc.).
36. *RPC* II, under 'Burials', s.a.
37. *Cornishman*, 7 October 1954 ('Camborne's Century as a Shopping Centre').

II

THE PATRON SAINTS

The original patron of Camborne church and parish was Meriadoc or, as he is usually called in Cornwall, Meriasek, bishop and confessor[1]. The following extracts from various early records show, however, a change in the parochial dedication which will be discussed below.

1329   *Ecclesia sancti Meriadoci de Cambron*[2]
1343   'The church of St. Martin or Meredoc Martin'[3]
1426   *Ecclesia Parochialis Sancti Mereadoci de Cambrone*[4]
1447   'To the church of the parish of Meriadoc . . .'[5]
1448   The church of *Sancti Martini in Cambrone*[6]
1501   The rectory of St. *Meriadoc de Cambron*[7]

In the century and a half between 1350 and 1500, then, the popular universal saint Martin of Tours replaced the much more localised Meriadoc or Meriasek, a figure not elsewhere found as a parochial patron. It must be stressed that this is not, as at Phillack (where St. Felicitas replaced the obscure Irish virgin St. Piala) or at St. Dennis (where St. Denis or Dionisius was adduced in error because of a local place-name *C.dinas*, 'fortress'), a shift of Norman times. There is no evidence that it commenced before the 14th century. There is also no evidence from chapels, wells, or any other kind of source, of an interest in St. Martin within the parish, and apart from the very widespread cult of this French saint in medieval Europe, the precise reasons for this change of patronage remain obscure.

St. Martin himself is of course in no sense an unworthy patron. Most people will know the story of how this complex man, born in Pannonia (now Hungary) about A.D. 330, aspired to the service of God from a tender age and was forced, against his will, to enter the Roman army. The event for which he is best known (see Frontispiece) can be told in the words of Martin's near-contemporary biographer, Sulpicius Severus, writing about A.D. 400[8].

'So it came about that one day when he (Martin) had nothing on but his weapons and his uniform, in the middle of a winter which had been fearfully hard beyond the ordinary, so that many were dying of the intense cold, he met at the city gate of Amiens a coatless beggar. This beggar had been asking the passers-by to take pity on him, but all had gone by the unfortunate figure. Then the God-filled man understood, from the fact that no one else had had pity, that this beggar had been reserved for him. But what was he to do? he had nothing with him but the cape he had on, for he had already used up what else he had, in similar good works. So he took the sword he was wearing and cut the cape in two, and gave one half to the beggar, putting the rest on himself again. This raised a laugh from some of the bystanders, for he looked grotesque in the mutilated garment; but many had more sense, and sighed to think they had not done something of the kind; indeed, having more to give, they could have clothed the beggar without stripping themselves.

And that night, in his sleep, Martin saw Christ wearing the half of his cape with which he had clothed the beggar. He was told to look carefully at Our Lord and take note that it was the garment that he had given away. Then he heard Jesus say aloud to the throng of angels that surrounded Him: "Martin is still only a catechumen" (that is, one under instruction in the faith) "but he has clothed Me with this garment".'

The very origin of the word 'chapel' is bound up with this incident; what was alleged to be the actual half-cape became a special relic of the Merovingian kings, and from the shrine of this little cape, or *capella*, the Old French word *capele*, whence our *chapel*, was derived.

On Whit-Sunday, 1958, the Bishop of Truro declared that the parish church of Camborne should henceforth be known as the Church of St. Martin and St. Meriadoc. It is especially pleasing that this ancient association should have been publicly restored during the Rectorship (1945 to 1965) of the late and much-loved Canon George Frederick Sandfield, under whose guidance the parish church of Camborne has regained much of its former character as a centre of corporate life and worship in the town.

Bewnans Meryasek

Though there exists a surprising quantity of supposedly biographical writing concerning St. Meriasek, none of it can be shown (even by inference) to be earlier than the 12th century, and most of it is several centuries later. The major source is the lengthy verse drama or miracle play *Bewnans Meryasek*, 'The Life of Meriasek', cited here as *BM*. This is written (save for stage-directions and a very occasional interpolation in Latin or English) in a late form of Middle Cornish, contains a lengthy episode set in Cornwall with numerous local references, and was almost certainly designed for public performance in the Camborne area.

The only known manuscript, fortunately complete, was in the library at Peniarth, Merioneth, in 1869, when it appears to have been recognised (by Mr. W. W. E. Wynne of Peniarth and by Canon Robert Williams, the author of *Lexicon Cornu-Britannicum* (1865)) for what it actually was[9]. It is now in the National Library of Wales, Aberystwyth (Peniarth MS.105). *BM* was published, with a parallel but sometimes confusing English translation and various notes, by Whitley Stokes in 1872[10]. A preferable edition, correcting many of Stokes' misreadings of the MS., with full notes on the actual scripts, and the Cornish text given also in the standardised system of orthography known as 'unified spelling', was prepared by the late R. Morton Nance and the late A. S. D. Smith[11], but save for three short extracts[12], none of this has yet been made available in a printed form.

The Peniarth copy of *BM* is a working copy, an *Ordinale* or book of words for use in an actual performance. The actors who played in this, and similar, miracle plays seem to have been local amateurs, cajoled into service for the occasion, and they were not expected to learn their (often very long) parts by heart. A prompter, armed with just such a text, moved around behind them reading out the play in a low voice, the actors repeating their parts after him in louder tones[13].

The colophon at the end of the MS. reads, expanded, *Finitur per dominum RADTON anno domini* $M^L . V^C . iiij;$ 'This is finished by master Rad. Ton in the year of our Lord 1504'. Nance has commented that Master Ton, who mis-spells certain names and can in a variety of ways be shown to have been copying a text in front of him (save for the first ten pages, which are in another hand), is not likely to have been the original author or compiler. Indeed no one is quite sure who Master Ton was. One 'Richard Ton' was curate of the neighbouring parish of Crowan in 1537—Ton or Todn is a possible, but most uncommon, Cornish surname—but *Rad.* is the normal contraction for Ralph or *Radulphus* rather than for *Ricardus*, Richard. 'Sir Ric. Tone, *prest*', was buried at Camborne[14] in 1547; he may have been a Camborne man. If *BM* was written or (more accurately) compiled in the late 15th century, its author is likely to have had some connection with the great collegiate church of Glasney at Penryn, the main intellectual centre of west Cornwall and a known focus for the production of such miracle plays[15]. Now a connection about this time between Camborne and Glasney *is* known. Dr. John Nans, who had been collated as Provost of Glasney in 1497, went to Camborne as Rector in 1501, exchanging positions with Master Alexander Penhylle or Penhale, who left Camborne to go to Glasney. Penhylle had been Rector of the next-door parish of Illogan from 1493 to 1500, had only been at Camborne for a year, and had been a Prebend of Glasney since 1495[16].

Bewnans Meryasek is 4568 lines overall, and was intended to be performed in successive parts on two days. Most medieval mystery or miracle plays disregard the classic unities of the theatre, but the structure of *BM* is not just a simple sandwich; on this analogy, it would be a ten-tiered layer cake. It is based partly on a Breton Life of Meriasek, but a number of well-defined episodes have been added to this core. Some of these are for light relief; others derive from popular (if in this case not wholly relevant) collections of medieval legends and stories; and one episode in particular—lines 621 to 1024—is of the very greatest interest to the student of medieval Cornwall since, unique in the five surviving medieval Cornish plays, it deals with the visit of the saint to Camborne.

The late Canon G. H. Doble discussed at some length[17] the nature of the postulated Breton sources for *BM*. He concluded that the author or compiler began by drawing on a written Breton Life which, not unnaturally, made no reference whatsoever to Cornwall, let alone any visit to the associated parish of Camborne, and that it proved necessary to provide this whole Cornish episode. There can be little doubt that a cleric of Glasney, whether he was John Nans, Alexander Penhylle, or some anonymous figure, would have had the chance of seeing an appropriate Breton Legendary. One such existed; Doble has printed[18] the text of

a Latin Life of Meriasek or Meriadoc, which he regarded as being derived
from an older (lost) Life of the saint contained in a Vannes legendary.
The 1589 Breviary of Vannes seems to have drawn on this postulated
lost Life for the lections for the feasts of Sts. Gobrien and Mériadec.

On the other hand, such references as that to a church of *St. Meriadoc(us)
de Cambron* in *1329*, at least a century and probably a century and a half
before *BM* was put together, afford the strongest possible evidence for an
older cult of Meriasek in Cornwall, wholly independent of any contemporary Breton tradition. An obvious off-shoot of this cult is the fact
that it was thought *necessary* to add a Cornish episode to the Life taken
from a Breton source, and thus as it were to provide the written counter-
part of an existing oral tradition. Whether the local traditions concerning
Meriasek in Camborne were entirely oral or not, we have no means of
ascertaining. Had something been worked up into a Lectionary used at
Camborne? Doble thought[19] that there had been a pre-Reformation 'Book
of the Miracles of Meriasek' at Camborne, containing all the necessary
material, in the same way that we know from John Leland's notes, *circa*
1540, that written Lives (probably late, and in Latin) of St. Ia, St. Breaca,
St. Gwinear and St. Elwin were still in existence in west Cornwall when
he visited it[20]. Unfortunately Doble had been misled on this score by
Whitley Stokes, who printed[21] one of the *BM* stage-directions as 'Here
the son of a certain woman (*as is found in 'the Miracles of Blessed
Meriasek'*) shall parade, saying . . . etc.', a passage which (as Nance and
Smith showed) actually reads, not *de beato mereadoco*, but *de beate marie*—
'(The Miracles) of Blessed *Mary*'—and the Marian episode which follows
proves to have been borrowed directly from some such standard 15th-
century source as the *Miracles de Notre Dame*. The evidence for any
medieval written traditions of Meriasek at Camborne cannot thus be
sustained.

Three possibilities are involved. The compiler of *BM* constructed the
entire Camborne episode out of his head, hoping that it would be
accepted in the district; or else he used a series of local traditions about
Meriasek, which he had gathered in the locality at first-hand or (less
probably) had found in some unidentified written context; or, finally,
he pirated the Life of some other west Cornish saint, presumably a late
written Life like the ones seen by John Leland, and re-fashioned it to
refer to St. Meriasek.

The first of these explanations is the least likely. The reference to a
place-name, a rock called '*Carrek Veryasek*', implies an existing aetiolo-
gical tale of earlier date, just as such west Cornish, or specifically Camborne, features as 'Wesley's Rock', 'Wesley's Oak', and 'Wesley's Pulpit',
are still widely explicable in terms (often very detailed) of John Wesley's
activities[22]. No audience would have stood for a fictitious or entirely
novel version of well-known episodes about their patron saint, and in any
event there is little else in *BM*, read purely as literature, which marks its
compiler as the author of much fresh material. The second and third
possibilities given above are pretty evenly balanced. The third one—that
the Life of another saint was pirated for the occasion—had the support

of the late Henry Jenner. Jenner, in an important but little-known paper[23], argued at some length that the Camborne portion of the *BM* narrative had been immediately modelled on a set of stories connected with a saint from a neighbouring parish—'possibly St. Illogan, or perhaps St. Uny in the Redruth part of his work'. These are not very helpful as examples, since nothing is known of St. Illogan and very little of St. Uny, but St. Fingar or Gwinear, patron of Gwinear parish which adjoins Camborne to the west, is the subject of a surviving Life which does offer support to Jenner's hypothesis. To start with, it is a 13th-century Life, and therefore earlier than *BM*[24]; and in certain respects, admittedly such stock features as royal origin, persecution by the Cornish tyrant Teudar, causing a well to spring up from the ground, and the saint being the source of miraculous cures, it allows direct comparison with the Cornish aspects of *BM*. There are also reasons—to the present writer's mind, of a somewhat less compelling kind—for assuming a connection between Gwinear and Meriasek apart from this possible literary link, as Doble pointed out[25]; in particular, the propinquity in both Cornwall and Brittany of churches and chapels dedicated in honour of these two saints.

On balance, none the less, the second possibility is the most reasonable one, and perhaps the most attractive; that the author drew upon a group of Camborne traditions about Meriasek, just possibly in written form, more probably oral and linked to such visible features as the saint's chapel, well, rock, and other appurtenances. The broad resemblance to the traditions enshrined in the Life of Gwinear is explicable if one supposes that the Camborne traditions had, by the 15th century, been influenced by those of nearby saints and owed something to the general run of similar saints' written Lives or oral legends then current in west Cornwall. If this is so, and granting that Master Ton was simply engaged in making a 'prompt copy' of the drama, either Johns Nans or Alexander Penhylle may have been the compiler-author of *BM*, and the compilation would have occurred between 1493 (when Penhylle came to Illogan) and 1504 (when Ton was able to make a copy of it).

Text of the Cornish episode in BM

In this extract, some irrelevant material (available in Stokes 1872, and in the items listed under note 12 above) has been omitted. The late R. Morton Nance's notes are distinguished by the letters *R.M.N.* His translations of the stage-directions are given in brackets [ ], and some necessary explanatory matter has been added in parentheses ( ) and in italics. The marginal numbers refer to the lines as printed by Stokes in his original edition.

MERIASEK

587   A blessing on you, sailors!
                   If you are going to Cornwall, truly,
                   I should like to go with you.
                   I have not much to give,
                   but I will pray Christ Jesus
                   to assist you at all times.

SHIPMASTER

593   Thou are welcome with us, good man!
We will take thee to the Land's End,
by God's will, before the week is out.
                      [He goes up into the ship]
Come straight aboard here:
and, my seamen, forthwith hoist
up the sail for me now.
                   (*The ship sails to Cornwall*)

621   Go thou ashore, good man,
in Cornwall, thanks to Jesus;
thou hast come according to thy wish.
                [He disembarks in Cornwall]
                     (*Scene; Cornwall*)

MERIASEK

624   Thanks be to Jesus!
I have arrived at a strange
country here.
I will go on shore.
May Jesus, dear-hearted Lord,
guide me to a good place,
where I might worship dear Christ
and the surpassing Virgin Mary.
         (*Supposedly some little time later*)

632   I have come on land,
and I am tired of walking.
Mary, Mother and Maiden,
if thou hast a house or place
near here,
do thou direct me to it;
for much would I like, indeed,
to make myself an oratory
in association with a house of Mary.
Good man, joy to you!
What chapel is that?
             SERVING MAN

643   I will tell thee straight,
the Chapel of Mary of Camborne
that same house is called.
From what place dost thou ask it?
Tell me that in return,
good fellow.
               MERIASEK

649   From Brittany indeed to this country
I have come over the sea,
as God willed to instruct me;
and here I wish to make,
beside the Chapel of Blessed Mary,

an oratory for myself.
Is there water here at hand?
For never any other drink
shall enter my mouth indeed.
SERVING MAN
658   Water is very scarce here;
one must go a good way from here
in fact to fetch it.
If I could get ale or wine,
I would not drink water, I am sure;
nor would it be to my profit.

MERIASEK
664   To the north-east of the chapel here
I will go and roam,
To seek for myself water surely.
       [Let him go over to the meadow; he kneels]
Jesus, Lord, I pray thee,
Jesus, grant water shortly,
Jesus, to me by thy grace,
as thou didst once to Moses
from the hard rock.
       [Here the well springs up water]
SERVING MAN
(who has followed him to the meadow)
672   Good man, blessed be thou,
for bringing water here to us
to relieve us so pleasantly!
Thou art indeed beloved by God,
it is manifestly proved here
before us in this place.

(686-717 *An ague-ridden patient and a cripple now appear, and are
duly healed by Meriasek*)
MERIASEK
718   Give thanks to Christ, good men,
without anything to me.
Found a place here now,
by the will of Jesus of mercy,
surely I will
hereafter; a church
for worshipping Christ day and night.
As I intend, it shall be here,
beside the Chapel of Holy Mary.

(727-758 *Meriasek next heals a leper, who goes off rejoicing*)
       [Here Meriasek waits at Camborne]
(Note by *R.M.N.;* 'He (Meriasek) is next seen in line 822 coming from the
chapel. *Camborne* in the stage-direction above, seems to refer to this.')
       [Here Teudar shall parade]

TEUDAR

759   Teudar I am called,
              reigning lord in Cornwall.
              That Mahound be honoured
              is my charge without fail,
              near and far;
              any who worship another god
              shall have sharp pains
              and also a cruel death.

                          (*A messenger for Teudar arrives*)

MESSENGER

767   Hail to you, Sir Lord Teudar!
              I have tidings . . .
783   There is here in Penwith
              a little to the west of Carn Brea
              a priest making a practice of
              healing in this world the blind,
              the deaf and the crippled,
              and every disease on earth.
              He will not that a god be spoken of
              except Christ, Who suffered death,
              that when he was dead was raised
              again, he says, to life.

(793-812   *Teudar rages, and calls for his soldiers, who appear*)

TEUDAR

                     [Descends]   (*i.e., from his 'tower'*)

813   Let us start off
              in great force,
              my knights.
              Where he is living
              let me be told
              straightway.

                     (*Teudar and his band march to Camborne*)

MESSENGER

819   I surely see him,
              royal Lord,
              yonder in the plain:
              out from the chapel
              right certainly
              he is coming, in truth!

(825-949.   *Meriasek appears from 'the chapel', where he has been since
             line 758 above. He and Teudar now engage in a theological
             argument about the Immaculate Conception, the Redemption
             of Sins, etc.*)

TEUDAR

              [Ascends]   (*i.e., into his 'tower'*)
                     (*Meriasek meanwhile leaves the stage*)

950 Executioners, come into the plain!
Executioners, if you are faithful,
Executioners, come at once to me!
Hi, hi, hi! What, you pay no heed?
[He descends]
(*The Torturers, who are comic buffoons, now appear*)
965 Go, I say, to Camborne,
to the west of Carn Brea, forthwith.
There you will truly find
an audacious fellow; without question
he is a limb of the wicked angel.
He is called Meriasek.
He believes in Christ.
Let him be seized by you:
torture him diligently.
[Teudar goes away home]
(*The Torturers go off, supposedly to Camborne. Meriasek
now re-appears on the stage*)
(*Scene; Camborne*)
MERIASEK
983 Thanks be to the Lord,
I am warned by a vision
that I should go out of this country
back again to Brittany speedily,
and evade the false Teudar.
The plan is thought out,
yet shall he fail of it.
990 Here have I founded a place
beside Mary of Camborne.
Jesus Christ, bestow thy grace
upon this same house at all times
so that always the Trinity Father may be
honoured in it readily,
and Mary;
and the seven Sacraments
alike on feast-days and working-days
administered hereafter.
1000 If a faithful Christian shall have
the complaint and disease of ague,
and remember me in this place,
Jesus, dear-hearted Lord,
do thou relieve his complaint.
1005 Likewise the water from my well,
I pray that it may be a cure
for a man gone out of his mind
to bring him back to his wits again.
Jesus, Lord of Salvation,
grant this through thy mercy.

1011   My blessing with thee, O Place!
         I must begone shortly:
         my enemies are near.
         I will keep to the open country
         and rest here forthwith
         beneath the Rock, verily.
              [Here Meriasek shall hide himself under the Rock]
         (*The three Torturers now re-appear; the scene is supposed to
         be 'the open country'* (an gun) *near Camborne*)
                       SECOND TORTURER
1017   Hast thou seen Meriasek?
         The sharp-eyed fellow is not
         in Camborne, devil a bit!
                       THIRD TORTURER
1020   Mayest thou never sup!
         He has gone away to the open country:
         may he have his mother's curse
         (*A Drudge—Latin* calo, '*a soldier's servant, a low fellow*'—
         now appears and joins them)
                           DRUDGE
1023   Let us keep an eye on the bushes
         and on the Rock too
         in case he has gone into hiding.
         Leave him alone. He won't be found!
         Let us go home from here.
                  (*They cross the stage or 'plain' to Teudar's 'tower'*)
                       THIRD TORTURER
1034   Hail, Teudar, in your tower!
         Meriasek has gone from this country
         completely, that's all we know.
         In towns and in downs
         we have surely sought him indeed:
         nobody is able to speak of him.
         (*Teudar rages, descends, and beats them; and they leave the
         the stage. Meriasek now re-appears*)
                  (*Scene: the open country*)
                          MERIASEK
1066   Thanks be to Jesus!
         Here have I rested
         indeed beneath this rock.
         My enemies have gone away.
         They could never come at me:
         God so willed.
         'Meriasek's Rock' this
         shall be called henceforth.
         I will keep towards to sea
         to seek myself a passage.

(*Meriasek crosses the 'plain' and is assumed to have arrived at the coast again*)

1076   God's blessing on you, best of skippers,
        may God guard your vessel
        from harm!
        If you intend to go to Brittany
        I would beg indeed
        to go with you, without ado.
                (ANOTHER) SHIPMASTER
1082   Thou wouldst seem a worthy man.
        Come, in God the Father's name,
        aboard now with us.
        Hoist up the sail, mate!
        The wind has come fair for us.
        We have Brittany full in sight

(*At this point the MS. has the direction 'Finit', which must indicate the end of this episode. The various structures on the 'plain' were probably now re-arranged to suit the subsequent episode, which commences with Meriasek disembarking in Brittany*)

Discussion

In order to understand this long extract, it is essential to appreciate the conventions and the mechanics of the Cornish miracle plays. From the 14th century, if not before, these were performed in the open air; ideally within a circular earthwork known as a 'plain-an-gwarry' (C.*plen an gwary*, lit. 'plain of the play') which was not unlike a smaller circular version of a modern football ground, offering some form of raised seating all around for the audience. Some of these may have been laboriously constructed for this specific purpose, but accumulating evidence suggests that others, if not the majority, were prehistoric earthworks adapted to this end[26].

The actors generally remained somewhere in the central arena, the 'plain' (C.*plen* of line 820 above; Latin *placea* in stage-directions, e.g. lines 456, 525, etc.), and when not actually speaking their parts, must either have sat around the edge of it, or concealed themselves in various tents, wooden pavilions, turrets, or similar make–shift structures. Out of these they could appear at the appropriate moment, announcing who they were (e.g., Teudar in line 759), and Teudar's tower, which he ascends and descends, must have had a few steps inside it to allow him to appear looking out of the top of it. The positions of the major characters and their structures, if any, were allotted according to a system which, it has been plausibly argued, derives from earlier and less ambitious performances in a church. Thus 'Heaven', usually a tiered affair, had to be on the east (corresponding to a raised chancel), 'Hell' on the north or north-west (north transept), and worldly dignitaries on the west (west door or tower arch). Fig. 6 shows an actual plan of a plain so arranged, from the MS. of *BM*.

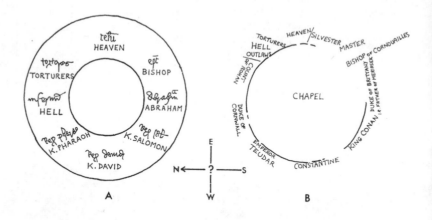

Fig. 6
Medieval plans for positioning the actors in miracle plays. A, from the
'Origo Mundi' (copied c.1400-1450), after Norris, with English equivalents
added; B, 'Bewnans Meryasek', the first day's setting (transliterated into
English), after Stokes 1872, 144-5 (copied in 1504).

Since this play was obviously designed to be performed in Camborne,
where-ever else it might also have been produced, there could have been
no really glaring inconsistencies in the references to local topography.
The text, allowing for the limitations of space imposed by the area available, is probably a reliable guide to what is meant. A close study does
allow a number of simple conclusions to be drawn, without any additional
suppositions as to the mechanics of the performance. Line 632, 'I have
come on land, and I am tired of walking', shows that Meriasek is assumed
to have come ashore in Mount's Bay, or that area (line 594 'We will take
thee to the Land's End'), and has approached Camborne along the
pilgrim route from St. Michael's Mount; it is about ten miles. He sees a
chapel, and a serving-man tells him it is the chapel of Mary of Camborne,
and is surprised at anyone not recognising this famous shrine. Meriasek
asks for water; there is none. He then goes north-east of the chapel, and
the stage direction is 'Let him go over to the meadow' (*tranceat ad
pratum*). The use of this specific word *pratum*, in contrast to *placea*, the
term employed for the plain generally, is significant, especially because of
its relationship to the Cornish word *pras*, 'common meadow, pasturage'.

Having caused a well to spring up, Meriasek heals several people, and then (line 718 ff.) announces his intention of building 'a place' (C.*plas*). In line 723 there is a probable copyist's error. Instead of reading 'Found a place here *now*/by the will of Jesus of mercy,/surely I will/ *hereafter*:' which contains a temporal contradiction, the colon should be placed after 'surely I will', allowing the rest of the verse to read 'Hereafter a church for worshipping Christ day and night (as I intend) shall be here, beside the Chapel of Holy Mary'. The word used for 'church' is C.*eglos*, which is distinguished from *chapel*, applied to Mary of Camborne's chapel in lines 642, 644, 653, 664 and 822, and from *oratry*, used by Meriasek of his original intention (lines 639, 653). Both *oratry*, implying saintly modesty, and *plas*, with an undertone of endearment or affection (lines 720, 990, 1001), refer to the same structure—the house of worship built by Meriasek next to the Chapel of Mary—which, the saint prophesies, shall become a full church in which 'the seven Sacraments/alike on feast-days and working days' (lines 997, 998) will be administered, again ' . . . hereafter' (line 990).

As it is extremely doubtful whether the word *eglos* could be used after the 12th century to refer to anything less than a full parochial church, this part of the play looks like an attempt to provide a retrospective prophecy concerning the foundation of the parish church of Camborne.

The passage dealing with Meriasek's flight from Teudar (lines 1014 to 1079) shows us Meriasek, having left Camborne, keeping to the downs or open country (line 1014, *My a vyn gwytha dhe'n wun*—'I will keep to the *gun*'). Here he hides under some very large and prominent rock, described as *Garrek* ('The Rock') in line 1016, 1024, and as *Carrek Veryasek* in line 1072. From here, too, he reaches the coast, but as it is intended to be a different boat and a new shipmaster, who does not know the saint (line 1074), presumably he is at some place other than Mount's Bay—Penryn is a possibility, the south coast a certainty. These clues all show that the downs or *gun* in question are those south of Camborne, centred on Troon (older Trewoon, *tre(f) wun*), the only area where large isolated rocks (of granite) would be found. 'Carrek Veryasek' should therefore be sought in this area.

In short, the references in the play indicate the following, still in existence and locally well-known about 1500;

(1) A chapel known as the Chapel of Mary of Camborne.
(2) Another place of worship alongside St. Mary's Chapel (line 991, *ryp Marya a Gambron*, 'beside Mary of Camborne'), founded by Meriasek, who describes it as both *oratry* and *plas*, which has become something that can be called *eglos*.
(3) A meadow (*pratum*) north-east of (1) and (2).
(4) A well (*fenten*, line 1004, 'a natural spring') somewhere at or in the meadow (3).
(5) A great rock called *Carrek Veryasek* somewhere on the granite in the Troon area, under which the saint is supposed to have hidden.

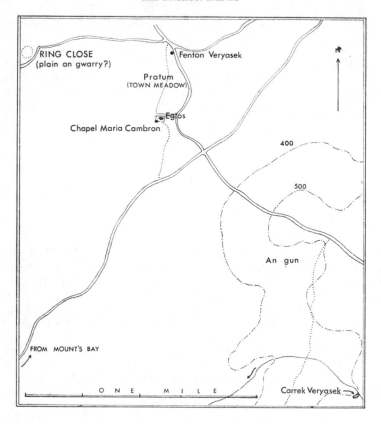

Fig. 7
The topography of the Camborne episode in 'Bewnans Meryasek', showing the sites to which reference seems to be made in the text and (top left) where Camborne's plain-an-gwarry may have been.

There is actually no difficulty in identifying these, and they are (with page-references to the present study)

(1) The chapel of St. Mary (and St. Anne) in the original Camborne churchyard (p. 55).

(2) Camborne parish church (p. 137).

(3) The original 'Town Meadow' north of the church (p. 35).

(4) St. Meriasek's well and well-chapel (Fenton-Veryasek) in Tehidy Road, Camborne (p. 54).

(5) Probably the Reens Rock, Newton, Troon (p. 36).

Figure 7 shows their relative positions.

Significance of the play

Is it a mere coincidence that this drama—a most powerful piece of medieval propaganda in favour of the sanctity and respectability of St. Meriasek—was written and no doubt widely performed towards the end of the prolonged period when Martin was ousting Meriasek (p. 21) as the patron saint of Camborne? Assuming that there had been rival factions on this score, it would be said by the advocates of St. Martin that St. Meriasek was a most negligible fellow, about whom nothing was known save for idle gossip and peasant superstition about a well and a rock. Is the whole drama, which (unlike the other four medieval Cornish plays) is the biography of a saint, and not a portion of inspired or apocryphal Scripture, an answer to this charge, offering the appropriate *cursus vitae* of the patron saint and stressing, as it does unceasingly, his devotion to the Virgin Mary, who seems to have been the subject of a very strong cult at Camborne? It may be significant that John Nans, when he came to the Rectory of Camborne from Glasney in 1501, managed to get his institution recorded in the episcopal register as being to the church of *sancti Meriadoci de Cambron* and not, as one would expect at this late date, *sancti Martini*. Were John Nans and Alexander Penhylle, successive rectors of Camborne and clerics of the drama-writing centre of Glasney, anxious to push the claims of the local saint? Were the Bassets, patrons of the living, equally anxious to invoke St. Martin, perhaps as a reflection of the ultimate Norman ancestry[27] of which this family was so conscious? The problem is a fascinating one, though it must remain nothing more than an enigma.

The pratum *and* Carrek Veryasek

The area immediately north of the pre-18th century church-town of Camborne was open ground; indeed, a little piece of it, fossilised as a small field, is still (1966) to be seen behind Camborne School of Mines. North-west lay two not always distinguishable tenements, The Weeth (1727 *Withe*) and Treglinwith (1495 *Treylenwer*, 1517 *Treglenwere*—the final -th-, from the 17th century, is by affection from 'Weeth'). The Weeth was wooded, and traversed by a little stream going down to the Red River (*gwyth*, coll.pl. of *gwedhen*, 'tree'), but Treglinwith seems to have been open ground (*tref* plus *clünwer*, 'green pasture' (*clün*, *gwer*)). This area may have been the customary grazing, on Tehidy land, for the churchtown tenants. The last surviving portion was what is now Wellington Road, appearing as 'Town Meadow' on the 1840 Tithe Map (nos. 1147-8-9), with 'The Meadow' as the triangle between Trelawney, Gustavus, and Tehidy Roads (no. 1109). Anyone going from the parish church to St. Meriasek's holy well would go north-east (as the play states —strictly, north-north-east) and would have crossed the area of these fields. In 1500, it was probably called just *Pras*, 'The Meadow' (pronounced something like English 'praise'), and the term *pratum* in *BM* must have been deliberately chosen to translate this, perhaps because of the visual similarity between the words[28]. A good parallel is to be found in the neighbouring parish of Crowan, where the main village is called

Praze, or, in full, Praze-an-Beeble (*pras an bobel*, 'the people's meadow'),
originating in a road-junction hamlet on the customary grazing of the
manor of Clowance.

The rock beneath which St. Meriasek hid himself must have been
a local landmark; very few specific place-names occur in any of the
Cornish miracle plays. There are a number of isolated granite carns in the
Troon district, but by far and away the most likely candidate is the
massive pile called 'Reens Rock', only a furlong or so from the middle
of Troon village, and therefore close enough to the early trackway south-
wards from Camborne to the Channel coast. Reens Rock is on the bank of
the stream opposite St. Ia's Chapel and Holy Well (p. 75), and would
of course have been well-known in the middle ages. The carn is seamed
with numerous fissures and has plenty of overhanging spaces; quite a
number of people could hide there, as local children still do today.
'Reens' (C.*ryn*, 'slope') is the name of the actual valley, which is now
rather overgrown.

Meriasek's nationality

The most fervent supporters of the saint could not, and did not, claim
that he was Cornish. *BM* admits him to be a foreigner; not only does he
come from and return to Brittany, features which are consistent with the
postulated origin of the drama in a Breton Life (p. 23 above), but in line
4297, there is an admission (as Doble pointed out) that Camborne possessed no corporeal relics of St. Meriasek. In both *BM* and the Breton
Life, Meriasek is of course the son of a duke and a relative of king Conan,
but this royal status, which need not reflect reality, is a normal convention
in such late Lives.

Doble believed[29] that Meriasek, if he really existed, might have been a
missionary saint from Wales. Doble located a township of *Meiriadog* in
Flint, and pointed to the medieval Welsh romance entitled, confusingly
for us, *Vita Meriadoci*, which deals with the adventures of a north Welsh
prince in the Snowdon region. The same name occurs in early British
tradition as the second element of Cynan (or Conan) Meriadoc, the ruler
who is alleged to have led the first colonists to Armorica in the late 4th
century A.D.[30]. Doble also drew attention[31] to the geographical con-
nections between sites honouring Meriadoc or Meriasek (as the saint of
the drama) and sites honouring Gwinear or Guinier, patron of Gwinear
parish. He thought that 'the two saints . . . after founding churches in
Cornwall, may have then gone on to the south coast of Brittany.' What this
distributional evidence really means is a matter of some conjecture, and
Doble's custom of personifying all such foundations as the indices of a
given saint's actual wanderings must be accepted with some reserve. In
this specific case, too, the very scanty evidence we have tends to link
Gwinear (as Fingar) with a group of west Cornish saints whose origins
seem to be Irish (p. 70). The most one can say is that occurrences of the
name Meriadoc, in one form or another, in Wales, Cornwall and Brittany,
and the associations in Brittany of the saint, do not rule out his having
been a post-Roman (Welsh?) colonist in Armorica, where he became a

bishop, or his having at some time visited west Cornwall in one capacity or another.

Remains of the cult of St. Meriasek

The evidence for the fairly late survival of an interest in St. Meriasek's holy well will be discussed in another chapter (p.125), but an alleged survival of worship of the saint into Victorian times must be briefly examined here. In a footnote, Canon Doble stated[32] that 'Mr. F. J. Stephens . . . says that within the last generation it was the habit of old miners to place a little image of clay over the first set of timbers on the entrance to a level, and that when the level was begun, a curious formula was uttered beginning "Send for the merry curse and the priest". Mr. R. Morton Nance suggests that this may represent the beginning of a prayer addressed to Camborne's patron saint in Cornish—*Sen Meryasek, ny a'th pys*—Saint Meriasek, we pray thee . . .'

This, if factual, would be an almost unparalleled survival, but Mr. F. J. Stephens' own words[33] allow another interpretation:

> 'I remember that in 1885, I was working in the 30 at Bangup' (i.e., at the 30-fathom level in a shaft, or part of a mine, so named) 'in the extreme west of West Frances, talking about an old adit which we had laid open. An old tributer said that it was much older than we had imagined, for it was a "holy adit", and he recollected his grandfather telling him of the ceremony when a new piece of work started, that it was a great occasion. The youngest miner was sent to fetch the priest and "Merry Kurse" and then a small procession would come, and the priest would sprinkle the setts, and the men would place a small figure made out of candle clay on the 10th sett. For a while the miners would sprinkle the 10th sett every time they passed. "Merry Kurse" baffled me until I asked the late Mr. (Henry) Jenner, and he said "Why, of course! Merry Kurse is *Mary's Cross*" . . .'

This extraordinary story takes us back to perhaps 1780-90, but it looks like a garbled memory, even then, of a much earlier custom. Whatever it represents—and if Henry Jenner was right, this is another piece of evidence for the cult of the Virgin Mary in Camborne—it can be seen that the supposed connection with Meriasek is less sure than Canon Doble's statement implied.

Was there a Camborne plain-an-gwarry?

Although a good many Cornish parishes, particularly in the west of the county, are known to have possessed plain-an-gwarrys[34], no instance of this class has ever positively been identified in Camborne. In his 1700 notes, Lhuyd includes this statement: 'Entrechmenents' (*sic*) 'here are calld Plains—Hent's one call'd Plain an gwari where they use to act, but no one alive remembers it.' There is no wholly convincing reason, beyond mere contiguity, to take this as referring to Camborne, where the term 'Plain an gwarry' is not otherwise recorded as a local place-name, and it probably refers to Redruth.

The town of Redruth did once possess a playing-place, now gone[35], somewhere in the district still called Plain-an-Gwarry. Michell has recorded references to it in 1739 and 1742[36], and William Borlase (who saw part of it) wrote in 1755[37]: 'At a place called Penguare there is a spacious green plot at the northern end of which there is part of a Plan-an-guare, the remaining Mound is high but ruinous, and shews no signs of ever having gone more than half round so that one would think it is rather a Theater than an amphitheatre—This work is about half a mile N. of the town of Redruth and very likely is what Dr. Stukely mentions somewhere as the remains of an amphitheatre near that town.'

There is a persistent local belief that there *was* a plain-an-gwarry at Treswithian, leading to such statements as this: ' . . . Merry Pit behind the Three Choughs Inn. This was once a plain-an-guare, or amphitheatre, where plays were performed by travelling players. Only half the circle can now been seen with a narrow path cutting it in half.'[38] The depression is in fact an old marling-pit (hence 'Marly Pit, Merry Pit') and the tenement to the south of Treswithian, once commonly known as 'Pengwarras' and regarded as containing the element C.*guary*, 'play', cited in support of this idea, is an alternative form of 'Gwelgwarras', *recte* Gwealgwartha(s) (1790 *Gwealgwarthas*, 1620 *Gwealgwartha in Crane*, from C.*gwel gwartha*, 'top field, upper field')[39].

The only probable locality is a field on Race Farm, north of Treswithian, formerly called 'Ring Close', and now occupied by the main block and northward extension of the Milk Marketing Board buildings. This field-name survived locally until the present century. The late James Thomas wrote[40]; 'I found my first flints at Race, when the late Mr. Bennett was farming it. When I asked him the name of the field, he told me that it was called "Ring-close" and that his grandfather remembered a circular enclosure there which the people of Camborne used for holding their sports in.' In his notes of about 1913[41], Mr. Thomas recalled that a great number of metal buttons had been picked up by him in this field. Some of these are now in a wall-case in the museum above Camborne Public Library; the memory of Mr. Bennett's grandfather would presumably refer to about 1800, and these buttons are not inconsistent with this date, or indeed of the 18th and even the 17th centuries. Ring Close is certainly the only place in the parish which, on the strength of these traditions, sounds as if it might have been a plain-an-gwarry.

Some recent performances of the drama
It is interesting to note that both fragments and translations of the original have been publicly performed in Cornwall during the present century. In 1924 (June 12th), Canon Doble, then curate at Redruth, produced an English version with the Guild of St. Nicholas, a local company, at St. Andrew's, Redruth; the Bishop of Truro was present, and the Bishop of Vannes sent his blessing and a special message[42]. In 1950, substantially the episode transcribed earlier in this chapter was acted, in Cornish, during the Celtic Congress at Truro, on September 1st, produced by Miss Helena Charles[43]; and, more interestingly, was given

again (under Miss Charles' direction, and by amateur players from Camborne and Redruth) in the plain-an-gwarry at Perran Round, as part of the 1951 Cornwall Amateur Drama Festival[44]. In 1952, a similar group, the Cornish Players, performed another extract ('Sylvester ha'n Dhragon', lines 3896 to 4180) on August 30th and September 3rd at the Community Centre, Camborne, again produced by Miss Charles[45]. A most ambitious production, by Miss Constance Murray Andrews, was a two-hour performance, with a large cast, of an abridged English version of the entire drama, given at Camborne by the girls of the Basset Road Secondary Modern School, on the 1st and 2nd of July, 1953[46]. The most recent instance noticed by the writer was in June 1963 when, for the Feast of St. Meriasek, the Rev. Martin Jupe (curate of Camborne) produced a short English version, acted by the children of the Sunday School, in Camborne parish church[47].

NOTES

1. *Meriadoc* is the OC.form; *Meriasek,* pronounced eventually something like (mer-*yaj*-ek), is the MC. and ModC. version, showing the shift from OC. internal *d* before unstressed front vowels to the *j* sound, spelled *s, g,* or *j* in MC. (Jackson, *Language and History in Early Britain* (1953), 397). Jackson regards this change as starting *c.*1100; in the instances cited here, the retention of the *written* form 'Meriadoc' may ' . . . be due to the usual tendency to orthographic conservatism' (Jackson, *op. cit.* 398).
2. RHR Grandisson I, 42.
3. Henderson, cited in Doble 1934, 38 n.1 (no source given).
4. RHR Lacy I.87.
5. Will of Dr. Reginald Mertherderwa (*WA* II (1882) 130; see p.91 below).
6. RHR Lacy I.335.
7. Peter 1903, 79.
8. Translation by F. R. Hoare, *The Western Fathers* (Sheed and Ward 1954), 14.
9. Not, as is usually stated, discovered by Whitley Stokes; cf. Davies 1939, 7.
10. For the MS. itself, cf. Davies 1939, 6-8; the edition (Stokes 1872) is *Beunans Meriasek. The Life of St. Meriasek, Bishop and Confessor;* ed., with transl. and notes, by Whitley Stokes (Trubner & co., London, 1872).
11. Typescript and MS. at RIC Truro.
12. Extracts from the Cornish Texts with unified spelling, and with amended translation (prepared by R. Morton Nance and A.S.D. Smith); *No. 1, Bewnans Meriasek lines 759-1096* (Camborne 1949), *No. 3, Sylvester ha'n Dhragon (BM 3896-4180)* (Marazion n.d.), *No. 1 (2nd edn.), St. Meriasek in Cornwall* (FOCS, Marazion 1967).

13. Richard Carew, *Survey of Cornwall* (1603), fol. 71 v.
14. RPC I.78.
15. Peter 1903; Fowler 1961.
16. Peter 1903, 79-80.
17. Doble 1934, 30-31; Doble 1935.
18. Doble 1934, 44 ff.
19. Doble 1934, 11-13.
20. Polsue-Lake IV, suppl. papers, 72.
21. Stokes 1872, 182-183.
22. Thomas 1950, 13-14.
23. Jenner 1928, 29 ff.
24. Notes and (partial) text in Doble 1926.
25. Doble 1934, 42-44; Doble 1935, 233.
26. E.g., Castilly in Luxulyan, shown by excavation to be a neolithic henge converted into a plain-an-gwarry in the 13th or 14th century; *CA* 3 (1964) 3-14.
27. Cf. E. B. Vivian in Camborniana 1897, 29-36; Thurstan Basset is said to appear on the Battle Abbey roll, Ralph Basset was Henry I's Justiciary, etc., and Francis Basset chose the family title 'De Dunstanville' when created a baron by Pitt in 1796.
28. The two words are of course cognate; cf. also French *pré*, ultimately English 'prairie'.
29. Doble 1934, 42 n.1.
30. E.g., Geoffrey of Monmouth's *Hist. Reg. Brit.*, V, 12; and the Mabinogion tale *The Dream of Macsen Wledig*.
31. Doble 1934, 42-44.
32. Doble 1934, 41 n.2; see also *OC* I.1 (1925), 17.
33. Stephens 1925.
34. Summary by Nance, *JRIC* XXIV.3 (1935), 190.
35. Mr. Michael Tangye tells the writer that he believes a small portion may still survive, unrecognised, in a bank in a garden there.
36. Michell 1948, *s.a.*
37. MS. Borlase 41, 180.
38. *CRP*, 13 Sept. 1960, pp.8-9.
39. This corrupt form is unfortunately perpetuated in 'Pengwarras Road', Camborne, part of the inter-war Council Estate.
40. *OC* I.4 (1926), 14.
41. MS. James Thomas.
42. Doble 1934, 6 n.1.
43. See notice by the writer, *Cornishman* 7 September 1950.
44. *CR* 9 (1951), 51-53.
45. Probably noticed in *Cornishman*, 4 September or 11 September 1952.
46. *Cornishman* 9 July 1953.
47. *Cornishman* 14 June 1963.

III

EARLY CHRISTIANITY IN CORNWALL

During the later centuries of the Roman period, the Christian faith became firmly, if sparsely, established over parts of the British Isles, notably in south-east England, south Wales, the south-west peninsula of Dorset, Somerset, Devon and Cornwall, and an undefined region of North Britain focussed on the military frontier zone of Hadrian's Wall[1]. This was an organised church, which was supervised by a number of bishops exercising pastoral oversight from (as far as our evidence goes) Roman towns in Britain. Remains of Christian art, of burials and coffins, mosaics with Christian symbols, and even what are probably one or two small churches, can be identified. A century later—by, say, A.D. 475— the focus of Christianity can be seen to have shifted, and the most important Christian areas are now south-west Scotland, north-west and south Wales, and parts of Cornwall and Devon[2]. The nature of our evidence for fifth-century Christianity, whether it takes the form of inscribed memorial tomb-stones, a variety of imported pottery types, or even what can safely be deduced as to church organisation and practice, all suggests that this Church in Atlantic Britain was by now in close contact with the surviving metropolitan (city-based) Church in Gaul, with Iberia (north-west Spain and Portugal), and with the Mediterranean, notably the northern shores and the Levant. The central problem is thus to ascertain whether Christianity, extinguished in southern and eastern England by a period of civil upheaval and by the Germanic pagan settlements, had been reintroduced to western Britain by sea from the Continent, or had been taken there as an aspect of a wholesale refugee movement westward from the eastern half of England. The older viewpoint, that it *was* primarily due to such a refugee movement, is tending to be replaced by the belief that Continental re-introductions played by far the greatest part, and that the degree of survival from Roman times was a minor one, affecting only a few localities.

One such locality, rather interestingly, may be west Cornwall. During Roman times, the peninsula was left comparatively to itself, and the very term 'Romano-British Cornwall' is something of a misnomer[3]. Continuous external contact from the estuarine ports of Cornwall is perfectly likely, and if one had to choose from within the county those places most likely to have possessed Christian communities in the late Roman era, these natural harbours would suggest themselves. In west Cornwall, some limited evidence for this can be found in the parish of Lelant and Phillack, around the Hayle estuary, on the northern end of the isthmus dividing the Land's End promontory from the rest of Cornwall; and this evidence has recently been summarised in detail in a short guide to Phillack parish church[4].

The earliest definitely-known area of post-Roman Christianity in Cornwall is the coastal belt running east from the Camel estuary to the present frontier with Devon. In this region there are traces of a number of monastic settlements—Tintagel, *Landocco* (St. Kew), *Lanwethinoc* (Padstow); and probably also *Langorroc* (Crantock) and *Lanpiran* (Perran sands) west of the Camel—of which the earliest is undoubtedly Tintagel, founded, on the evidence of pottery imports, in the last quarter of the 5th century. The distribution of memorial stones inscribed both in Roman ('Latin') capitals and in the stroke-writing known as *ogam*, the linguistic affinities of the personal names so inscribed, and to a very much less reliable extent the quasi-historical traditions embodied in saints' Lives, and parochial dedications, all combine to show that this monastic phase mainly of the 6th century, was part of a wider movement embracing the south Welsh coastal plain and south-east and central Ireland, emanating (*via* south Gaul and perhaps Spain) from what is now Greece, Turkey, Syria and the Holy Land.

Archaeological research in the last two decades points to a second wave of external influences affecting west Cornwall a little later, probably not before the period A.D.550-600. This assumed the form of a substantial settlement along the north coast of west Cornwall, from the Isles of Scilly to the Gannel mouth by Newquay. Traditional, if rather late, accounts ascribe this 'invasion' to the converted Irish (omitting the likelihood that the post-Roman Irish colonies in south-west Wales, in addition to natives of Ireland proper, could have been involved); and a large number of 'saints', patrons of parishes and chapels in west Cornwall, have for centuries been associated with it. Within limits, the results of archaeological work do broadly confirm this tradition. Cornwall is unusual in post-Roman Britain in that ordinary domestic pottery—jars, dishes, cooking-vessels—continued to be made throughout the Roman centuries, either in the home or at village-industry level. In most other areas, the advent of inexpensive mass-produced Roman wheel-made wares rendered this activity inappropriate and killed off local pot-making habits, leaving a distinct vacuum in the 5th century which, archaeologists like to assume, was partially filled by containers of wood or leather. Moreover, hand-made pottery continued to be produced and used in Cornwall throughout the first millenium A.D., and the typological sequence—which allows any given collection of such pottery or potsherds to be (relatively) dated—has now been worked out on the basis of some thirty separate sites. On a number of these, mostly peasant homesteads, the local pottery of the 5th and 6th centuries, which maintains with slight divergences the pottery styles and shapes of the Roman centuries, is replaced by quite a different kind of pottery—different shapes, different techniques of potting, even different colours—at a stage which can be assumed to be about the latter part of the 6th century (Fig. 8). This intrusive style is called 'grass-marked ware'. The cooking-pots were placed to dry on stones or planks covered with chopped dried vegetation before firing, and the negative, fired-out, impression of this material can be seen subsequently on the underside of these pots. It is by no means easy to match this

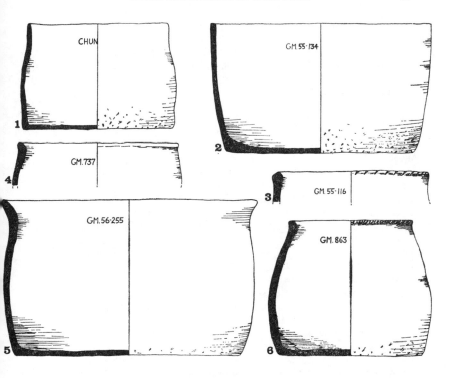

Fig. 8
Grass-marked pottery from west Cornwall (scale: one-fifth). (1) from Chun Castle; (2-6) from Gwithian, site I. (1, 2, 3), late 6th or 7th cents, A.D., (4), possibly 7th cent., (5, 6), 8th or 9th cents. (See CA 3 (1964), p.56 and fig. 15).

elsewhere outside west Cornwall. However, the closest parallels, and they are very close indeed, occur in the domestic hand-made pottery of the north-east region of Ireland at much the same time, a style known as 'souterrain ware'[5]. Now the appearance in any given region of an exotic, intrusive, and (perhaps, most important) domestic hand-made pottery style is usually, and reasonably, taken to be an index of actual intrusive settlements; settlements involving not merely adventurous bachelors, who are not given to pot-making and who marry the local women if they marry anybody, but whole families. A (Christian) Irish colonisation, perhaps of purely local intensity, in west Cornwall and Scilly in the later 6th century is thus an acceptable working hypothesis.

The appropriate Christian sites and remains of this episode were not full monasteries, as in the slightly earlier introductions in the north-east of Cornwall, nor were they full-scale parish churches of the kind found in

the Middle Ages. A good deal is known of the remains of Irish Christianity at this time, not only from Ireland, but also from other Irish settlements in north-west Wales, the Isle of Man, and the western and northern
coastal fringes of Scotland. We should therefore expect to find similar
Irish-inspired manifestations in Cornwall, especially west Cornwall, and
we do find them.

The burial of the Christian dead in the immediate post-Roman period
(the fifth century) was often by our modern standards rather casual;
isolated burials out in the countryside, by some trackway, or within a
deserted homestead, are found, and presumably only those families who
could afford it went to the trouble and expense of an appropriately-
inscribed stone pillar. The 5th-century tombstone of *Cunaide* at Carnsew,
Hayle[6], within an abandoned cliff-fortlet, is a typical example, and there
may have been another within the bounds of Camborne (p.162). In areas
more closely associated with surviving traditions of late Roman
Christianity, and by the sixth century in most of western Britain, burials
tended to be confined to distinct consecrated cemeteries. These cemeteries,
enclosed in some kind of surrounding bank and ditch, normally oval or
circular in plan, constitute the primary Christian sites of post-Roman
western Britain. The origin of this habit may in part be Roman, since
walled cemeteries (by Roman civil law, sited outside settlements and
normally found by a road-side) of the 3rd and 4th centuries A.D. are
known in this country. It may also in part be native, since, though we
know surprisingly little about the nature of either Iron Age or native,
pagan, Romano-British cemeteries in Britain, there are numerous examples
of post-Roman Christian cemeteries which appear deliberately to have
been sited upon, and thus in a sense to continue, pre-Christian burial
grounds.

As such cemeteries would normally constitute the only fixed visible
outward sign of Christianity in the countryside of the sixth century (apart
from such hypothetical things as standing wooden crosses, which cannot
now be detected and may anyhow represent a rather later aspect of the
faith), we find that the physical development of rural Christianity was
based on these cemeteries. Sufficient examples have now been excavated
to show the outlines of what transpired. In a manner very broadly analo-
gous to the work of mission-fields in the nineteenth century, individual
clerics came out, or were sent out, from the larger monasteries—which
had by the sixth century taken over the role of bishops' seats, and had
replaced the episcopal diocese with the monastic *paruchia* (an untrans-
latable word meaning, roughly, 'sphere of influence')—to minister to local
Christian communities. Many of these clerics or monks, and it must be
remembered that women also took part in this work, were independent
of monasteries, despite their early training or upbringing within such
establishments, and have been guided by inner convictions, the advice of
Christian friends, or their own contacts with God. Insofar as these people
became attached for any length of time to any one locality, they became
attached to these cemeteries, which were the main fixed points of local
Christian life.

By the late 6th century, if not before, additional features can be detected. The tombs of such holy men and women were frequently marked with memorial pillars of a superior kind, distinguished by simple incised crosses in addition to any inscription, and the grave itself could be denoted by some above-ground element like a tiny enclosure of stone slabs, a recumbent grave-stone, or a box-like platform of boulders. Subsequent worship at such sites now had a visible focus, the grave of a *sanctus* or 'saint', which also served as an open-air altar. Burials as close as possible to such a tomb or shrine would be made, so that those buried there could share in any prayers made at the saint's tomb, and moreover could be assured of participation in the final Resurrection. Often the dwelling-place, during life, of such a saint, within or on the edge of the original cemetery, might be (if not inhabited by his or her successor) maintained as an associated shrine or place of special holiness. It is possible that, by the later 6th century and certainly in the 7th century, small rectangular wooden buildings—strictly, *chapels* if they contained a fixed altar for the celebration of Mass, *oratories* if they were designed only to accommodate one saying prayers and had no such altar—had been erected. The tomb of the original (or of any early) saint is almost always right by such a structure, normally by the external south-east corner; and subsequent burials for which there is no longer any room next to the saint's own grave are ranged as close to the chapel or oratory as possible.

By the end of the 7th century and during the 8th, in most parts of western Britain (and this includes both Cornwall and Scilly), small but stoutly-built chapels of stone appear. Excavated examples show that the usual custom was to site these on top of the earlier wooden chapels, which had been pulled down, and as the stone chapels tend to be rather larger than their timber predecessors, the chapel walls are now frequently discovered to be sitting directly over those burials which, a generation or so before, had been deposited alongside the walls of the wooden structures. The tradition of the inscribed memorial stone pillar continued for some time; but a related tradition grew up; that of the erection of pillars inscribed with decorative crosses, not as individual memorials but as reminders of the Faith, symbols of aspects of the Gospel, and in commemoration of re-dedications, re-buildings, or merely events of importance, grew up. Frequently these are encountered just within the entrance to what was an original cemetery enclosure.

The end-point of this fascinating sequence is, over much of Cornwall, the parish church of the 20th century, and in many places it is probable that the sequence is an unbroken one. To cite only some examples which will be familiar to Cornish readers, the present churches of Sancreed, St. Buryan, Ludgvan, Phillack, Breage, and Mawnan, almost certainly went through all or most of the phases described above. In most of these places, and in many others, the outline (prior to the necessary enlargements of the period 1750-1850) of the old churchyard is essentially the outline of the original post-Roman enclosed cemetery, its circumference wall re-built on numerous occasions (but on the same circumference) to contain the rising ground-level within, raised by displacement through

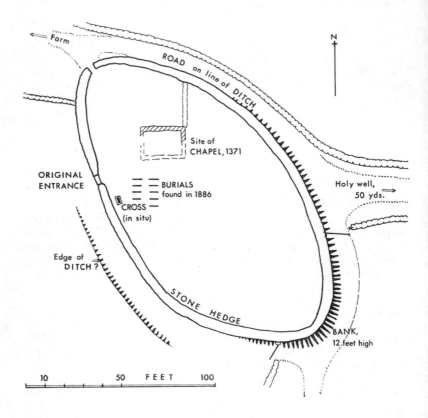

Fig. 9
Plan of the 'lan' at Merther-Uny, Wendron.

centuries of successive interments. In a very few places, among which Merther-Uny in Wendron is an outstanding example (fig. 9), a site of this nature was *not* selected in an 11th or 12th century to serve as a parish church, and therefore still physically reproduces to some extent its pre-Norman appearance.

Throughout the areas of Britain where Celtic languages are, or have been, spoken, the terminology of this primary Christian site-sequence refers to its various components. The oldest-known term in use on the British mainland for the enclosed cemetery was *lanon, meaning 'flat, cleared, or open space (cf. Latin *planum*, and our "plain"); enclosure'. This has given both the Welsh *llan* and the Cornish *lan*, and the survival of this place-name element as the prefix to so many parish names (e.g., in Cornwall, Lansallos, Lanlivery, Lelant or Lanant, and in the now-lost names of a good many more like *Langostentyn*, St. Constantine; *Lanuthinoch*, St. Erth; *Lannowen*, Cubert) is therefore quite explicable as a reflection of this origin. In Ireland and the Irish-settled areas of the north-west, for some reason, the Latin word *cella*, 'cell', was borrowed, presumably referring either to the living-place of the saint or even to some original timber oratory, and this has given Irish *cill*, Manx *keeill*, and the 'Kil-' prefix so common in Scottish place-names. In the British colonies in Armorica (Brittany), the actual *tomb* of the saint may later have been singled out, if this be the origin of the Breton *loc'h* (presumed to be from the late Latin *locus* (*depositionis*), 'place (of a grave), grave'). In Scotland and Ireland, there is also a word *teampull*, from the Latin *templum*, 'church' perhaps with reference to the first stone structure, not however known to occur in Cornwall. A very interesting final alternative is the Cornish *merther*, Welsh *merthyr* (cf. 'Merthyr Tydfil'), which is from the Latin *martyrium* and the Greek *martyrion*, and has the specialised meaning of 'a place where the actual physical relics of a saint (originally, of a *martyr*, one who has suffered for Christ) are preserved'.

In the Cornish *lan-* names, the second element is very rarely descriptive (e.g. Lanvean, *lan vyghan*, 'little lan') but, as with most Irish and Scottish Kil- or *cill* names, is a proper personal appellation. There are a handful of British instances where one can be almost certain that the name in question was that of the original 'saint' who ministered at such a site, since in these instances the same name occurs on what is presumably the earliest memorial inscription within the enclosure (e.g. the enclosed cemetery at Kilfountain, co. Kerry, Ireland, where the first Christian inscription reads *SCI* (for *SANCTI*) *FINTEN*). In some of the Cornish examples, the personal name in question is independently known to be that of a saint; for example, Lelant, Lanant, contains a name *Anta* which is found in Chapel Anjer Rock, probably the site of a medieval light-house chapel, and since it is female, probably also the unspecified name of the 'very holy virgin' encountered by St. Ia and her companions when they arrived in St. Ives Bay[7]. The fact that Lelant church is dedicated in honour of the much more popular local male saint, St. Euny, whose shrine it allegedly contained in 1478[8], does not alter this original ascription. The lan of St. Anta's original patronage may have been a little east of the present graveyard[9]. In other instances, it has long been noticed (by both Doble and the late Charles Henderson) that the personal name following the *Lan-* prefix is not always that of the patron saint. The explanation may be that there was an early shift of dedication (in pre-medieval times, and therefore nowhere recorded) from an obscure local saint to a better-known figure, or even to an universal saint like one of the Apostles, following the obtaining of a suitable relic; or that the personal name following *Lan-* belonged, not to any saint, but to a local chieftain or landlord who either continued to own the site, or who had presented it to the Church. In both Ireland and Scotland it is not uncommon to find that outlying sites which have been founded, or administered, by a brother sent out from a large monastery will bear the name of the founder or principal *sanctus* of the parent monastery as the second element. Thus many of the places called *Kilcolm* in Scotland probably embody as their second element *Colum* or Columba (521-597), indicating an origin in the missionary activities of the monastery of Iona. The virtual absence of this class of name in Cornwall reinforces the impression one obtains from the admittedly much later surviving Lives of Cornish saints, namely that the Cornish lans were in most cases built up by independent evangelists and may belong to the initial phases of the monastic era (the 6th century) rather than to the seventh.

Monasteries are also, in a sense, 'primary Christian sites', and those in Cornwall frequently bear *Lan* as the first element of their names. Physically, the full monastery was very much larger than any *lan*, and contained numerous buildings including one or more chapels, the principal one of which could be an *ecclesia* or real church capable of accommodating many people; and monasteries were distinguished by rather more massive enclosures (earthen banks and ditches, stone walls, ramparts across promontory-necks) to which the Latin term *vallum* was applied. There were no monasteries in the parish of Camborne—indeed, few in west Cornwall at all, and those few were small ones—and this aspect need not be further explored.

Certain enclosed cemeteries seem never to have progressed beyond the stage of simple burial-grounds, perhaps not even possessing a saint's tomb or any memorial pillars, and the term 'undeveloped cemetery' (in contrast to the 'developed' *lan-* or *cill-* type) can be applied to these. The relative neglect of these places may have resulted from population shifts— during the 4th to 7th centuries, the whole mode of popular settlement and land-usage in Cornwall seems to have been undergoing fairly radical change—or it may have been due to eclipse by more popular sites, especially those at whose shrines miraculous cures or visions could be reported. There are examples, usually revealed by the plough, of such undeveloped cemeteries over most of the county, but it cannot be expected that place-names will still be attached to them. The world *lan* can itself be misleading. One can be tolerably sure that any churchyard founded after the 11th century will *not* possess a *lan* name; but there are examples of pre-Norman churches and chapels in oval enclosures for which no *lan* name is recorded. In these instances, the name has probably been forgotten; or it has been replaced by another one, perhaps following a change of dedication; or the site was a specialised chapel with no attendant burial-ground; or the original name was compounded with some element like *merther*. Finally, in Cornwall as in Wales, the word *lan* had a secular meaning, 'enclosure, yard', and one finds compounds like C.*corlan*, 'sheep-fold', or field-names such as 'Lanwaffer' (*lan wartha*, 'the higher enclosure'), which need have no ecclesiastical significance at all.

Under the heading 'Secondary Christian sites' one could group a bewildering variety of phenomena which, in general, are of later origin than the primary series discussed above. The most striking instances are the specialised chapel-sites, which may be, and frequently are, contained in some kind of enclosing bank or wall, but whose function does not include anything to do with a burial-ground. The cult of the holy well, a cult which most students of the period would probably agree has pronounced pagan roots, but which—hallowed, after all, by the action of Moses in the desert (*Exodus* xvii.6; *Numbers* xx.11)—became a prominent facet of insular Christianity, was elaborated in the later pre-Norman centuries through the construction of special *well-chapels*; usually ascribed to the saint through whose action water first sprang miraculously from the ground (cf.p.27 above), some of these were proper chapels of considerable size. The earliest Cornish example is perhaps the well-chapel of St. Constantine at St. Merryn [10], which may go back to the 9th or even to the 8th century; most are later. Many of the patronal saints of Cornwall traditionally landed, from Ireland or Wales, at some given spot, where the first prayer was said, and the first Communion offered; *landing-place chapels*, to which a burial-ground might be added later (as at St. Gothian's, Gwithian [11]) or might not be (as at Chapel Jane, near Gurnard's Head, Zennor [12]), could follow this. In isolated places or on high rocks, *hermitage chapels* included a cell for an anchorite, whose functions might embrace prayers for a specific soul or the maintenance of a beacon-light, and *light-house chapels*, associated wholly with this second function, are also known [13]. When we enter the full Middle Ages, we find that something like one-third to one-half of the pre-Norman *lan* chapels or 'developed cemeteries' in Cornwall were selected, possibly through earlier associations with 10th- and 11th-century vills or estates in a quasi-parochial status, to serve as full parish churches with rights of burial, resident priests, and allotted tithes. Others less conveniently placed but often of great antiquity or popular esteem continued as so-called 'free chapels', relying for their upkeep upon the generosity of pilgrims and visitors, to whom however indulgences might be promised in return for concrete support (labour, money, or other gifts).

Lastly, with the rise of the local armigerous families, in reality no more than resident landlord-farmers taking their names from their tenements, and with the construction of more elaborate manor-houses, we find the rising demand for domestic oratories, which required an episcopal licence before they could be used for the celebration of Mass. The bulk of these were no more than rooms—solars or first-floor chambers —fitted up as oratories, and as such of very little interest to the ecclesiologist. In some cases, however, a manor-house might adjoin (and might have done since the 7th century) a pre-Norman chapel with a disused burial-ground or *lan*, and there are quite a few instances of such chapels being appropriated and re-furbished, in some style, as domestic chapels [14]. Throughout the whole of Cornwall and Scilly, if one assumes (as one is now entitled to do on the evidence) that each parish possesses traces of, on the average, three to four chapel sites of all types, pre-Norman and post-Norman, the sum total for the county should be the staggering figure of seven hundred or so; and indeed Canon Adams has already given this estimate in print[15].

The interest of the chapels in Camborne parish, a group rather larger than the average, is that they offer a very fair sample of the material discussed above in a comparatively restricted compass. The evidence concerning some of them warrants a much wider interest than hitherto, mainly from the lack of adequate research, it has attracted.

NOTES

1. The following bibliography covers the most recent views of this subject: J. M. C. Toynbee, 'Christianity in Roman Britain', *JBAA* XVI (1953), 1-24; W. H. C. Frend, 'Religion in Roman Britain in the Fourth Century', *JBAA* XVIII (1955), 1-18 (with map); D. A. Binchy, 'Patrick and his Biographers: Ancient and Modern', *Studia Hibernica* (Dublin), 2 (1962), 7-173; P. A. Wilson, 'Romano-British-Welsh Christianity: Continuity or Discontinuity?' *Welsh Hist. Rev.* vol. 3 (1966) 5-21.
2. General surveys; N. K. Chadwick, *Celtic Britain* (Thames and Hudson 1963), C. Thomas, 'Celtic Britain and the Anglo-Saxons', chap. 12 of *The Dark Ages*, ed. D. Talbot Rice (Thames and Hudson 1965).
3. Most recent summary, 'The character and origins of Roman Dumnonia', in *Rural Settlement in Roman Britain*, ed. C. Thomas (C.B.A., London, 1966), 74-98.
4. Thomas 1963a.
5. *PWCFC* II.2 (1958), 63-72, with map; *CA* 3 (1964), 37-62.
6. Macalister, *CIIC* I, no. 479; *OC* V.3 (1953), 125, and V.3 (1953), 173.
7. Doble 1926, 12.
8. According to William of Worcester ('Sanctus Uny . . . jacet in ecclesiae parochiali Sancti Uny prope villam Lallant').
9. Cf. the 19th century discoveries here, described by Cyril Noall in *CA* 3 (1964), 34-36.
10. Account by Penrose Williams, in *Proceedings of the Society of Antiquaries of London*, 2nd ser., XXIV (1911-12), 96-102.
11. Thomas 1964, with plans.
12. Forthcoming report, *CA* 6 (1967), by P. Pool and V. Russell.
13. Adams 1957, where this whole field is described.
14. Adams 1957, 59-62.
15. Adams 1957, 48.

IV

EARLY CHAPELS IN CAMBORNE

Local tradition

'The names of seven chapels are associated with our ancient parish' wrote the late James Thomas [1], and a similar statement frequently occurs in local guide books and newspaper articles. Earlier, Arthur Adams when vicar of Tuckingmill had referred to 'the seven chapels once existing in the parish' [2], and the authority for this tradition has long been believed to reside in the eighteenth-century writings of Dr. William Borlase. But all that Borlase actually stated in his *Parochial Memoranda* (see Appendix B) was that he had seen the remains of a chapel at Troon, and that there had formerly been chapels dedicated to St. James, St. Ye and St. Derwe, and St. Margaret and St. Anne. The chapel at Troon had been visited in the course of field-work, and the references to the others had been given to Borlase by his friend and fellow-antiquary Jeremiah Milles (1718-1784), Precentor and later Dean of Exeter, from the then unpublished Registers of the medieval bishops of Exeter. Taken at face value, Borlase refers only to *four* chapels, and there is no reason to suppose that he thought there were more than these. Others apparently followed him, and this source may have been known to Charles Sandoe Gilbert when the latter wrote [3] 'There were formerly four chapels in this parish, all of which we may suppose were destroyed at, or soon after, the reformation of Henry VIII'.

The 'seven chapels' belief is a widespread one; it is found in connection with such prominent centres of insular Christianity as Clonmacnoise, Glendalough, and Iona, and others less well-known, frequently without any real foundation and as frequently including chapels and churches of widely divergent dates to make up the requisite total. This belief has early, even Biblical, roots [4], and occurs elsewhere in Cornwall, notably at Crantock, where the 6th (?) century monastic foundation of *Langorroc* or *Langarrow*, centred on the present Crantock church, was alleged to have had 'seven churches . . . remarkable for their beauty and their size' [5].

Borlase's list is erroneous on several counts. He follows a clerical confusion in the episcopal registers, in conflating the separate chapels of 'St. Ye and St. Derwe'—incidentally these are latinised feminine genitive singular forms, and should read *Ia* (or *Ya*) and *Derwa*—but even so, this still leaves him with only four, as the chapel of St. Ia is the one which he saw at Troon. 'St. Margaret and St. Anne' should read 'St. Mary and St. Anne', and 'Margaret' probably arose from a misreading of the Latin *Mariae et* ('Mary and').

A more reliable catalogue is that given in a series of field-notes in a small manuscript note-book, now in the Bodleian Library (MS. Rawlinson D.997), which must almost certainly be attributed to the Welsh antiquary Edward Lhuyd (?1650-1709). Lhuyd is known to have visited Cornwall in

1700, and his notes concern both place-names and ecclesiastical antiquities. Under Camborne, he lists seven chapels (six together, the seventh as an additional entry), and his informant in this case was probably Charles Basset, rector from 1684 to 1709. The text of these notes is given in Appendix A. The list is a perfectly reliable one and all seven chapels can with some plausibility be identified. There remains, therefore, the distinct possibility that the 'seven chapels' tradition, cited by Arthur Adams, a curate of antiquarian tastes, in 1890, had always existed in the parish, and had by-passed the purely literary total of four chapels given by Borlase, C. S. Gilbert, and one or two later authors. The sites themselves may now be considered. Fig. 10 shows their respective locations within the parish.

St. Derwa's Chapel, Menadarva

The present farmhouse of Menadarva, situated in a sheltered and wooded part of the Red River valley, and beautifully maintained, still exhibits many traces of the large stone house built by a branch of the Arundell family in the 16th century. Menadarva passed to the Bassets of Tehidy in the 18th century, and though not a manor, has always been known as a barton.

The original holding here, farming a large south-facing area on the side of the valley beyond the house, gave its name to the family of Merther-derwa, who attained some prominence. Dr. Reginald Mertherderwa, who was in holy orders, became the Principal of Bull Hall, Oxford, subsequently merged in Corpus Christi College[6]. In 1509, Nicholas de Merther-derwa is mentioned in a Valuation of the lands of the hundred of Penwith, but the property eventually passed through an heiress to the Bevills of Gwarnack and thence by another marriage to the Arundells[7].

The older place-name of *Mertherderwa* is mentioned in 1285, and again as late as 1530, after which it becomes *Menedarva* (1600), *Menadarva* (1790), as at present. There is a slight puzzle here; the more likely corruption would have been 'Meradarva' with erosion of the internal -*th* (cf. the common 'gwarra' for *gwartha*, 'upper') and it is conceivable that an alternative word is involved. Possibilities are *men an Derwa* ('stone of D.') and even, relying on a form *Menethderva* Mill of 1622 reported by Henderson, *meneth (an) Derwa*, 'hill of D.', particularly since this word usually becomes *mena*, *mener* in late Cornish names[8].

The older name implies the site of a chapel of pre-Norman date which contained the shrine and relics of St. Derwa, a chapel moreover suffic-iently well-known to give its name to a secular holding. The first mention of such a chapel occurs in Bishop Lacy's *Registrum Commune* for 12th August 1429 (Lacy I.223), recording a licence for divine service by suitable priests *in capella sanctarum Ye et Derwe virginum* in the parish of Cam-borne. This must contain a clerical error—*capella* for *capellis*—since two chapels are involved and a licence concerning two chapels must have been intended.

In his will, dated 11th February 1447[9], Reginald Mertherderwa be-queathed to *capelle sancte Derwe* a pair of green silk vestments, a new

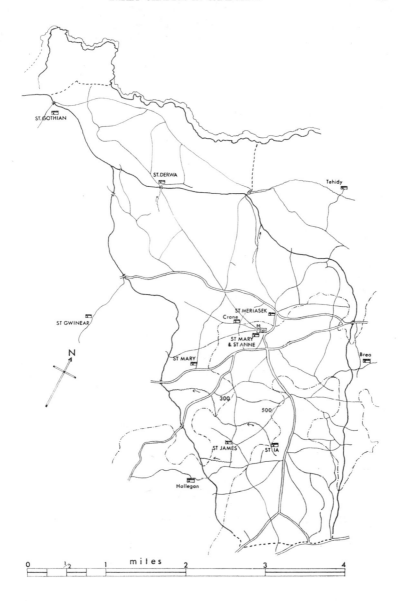

Fig. 10
Camborne parish, showing locations of the chapels listed in chap. IV, and the nearest chapels in contiguous parishes. Names in capitals are 'free' chapels; the others are domestic oratories.

missal, and a super-altar. He was also concerned with the maintenance of a customary church-way from the northern part of the parish to Camborne parish church, making provision for a series of churchway crosses along it (p.91) and for the bridge near his old home, probably the only permanent crossing of the Red River, over which this churchway still runs. 'I leave to the repair of the Bridge of Derwa 13s. 4d. provided that the parishioners repair it within a year. If they do not they shall have nothing' he wrote.

His bequest implies a substantial chapel and indeed, as will be shown, this chapel possessed a fine font which cannot be dated much later than A.D. 1100 (p.113). In view of the distance from Camborne church town (see fig. 10), it looks as if the chapel at Menadarva had for some centuries, and in some respects (though not those of burial, apparently), been serving as a chapel of ease for persons living in the northern third of the parish[10].

There is not much doubt that it stood somewhere by the present house. Two fields named Higher and Lower Chapel Close, on the immediate north-east side of the house (TA nos. 88 and 90), may indicate its whereabouts, though no remains of any kind are visible. A farm-building on the west side of the yard has, in the past, been pointed out as 'the old chapel', apparently because it incorporates 16th-century window surrounds that must have come from some demolished part of the older house, but it lies nearly north-south and the worked stones are clearly inserted. 'There was an old chapel in a fairly recognisable condition at Menadarva a few years ago' F. J. Stephens wrote in 1925[11]; as he lived not far away, it must be assumed he was referring to some actual ruin which he had seen, but unfortunately he never expanded this tantalising statement. A still earlier reference is a poem, entitled 'Reflections on sublunary enjoyment; an elegy written Aug. 13th, 1806, near the ruins of Menadarva', by Miss Blanche Harris of St. Agnes (Stephens, St. Agnes, n.d.: single sheet), which can hardly have described the dwelling-house and must have dealt with some picturesque Gothick ruins viewed by moonlight— the remains of the chapel? It has proved impossible to trace a copy of this poem[12]. Lhuyd includes in his list of chapels '5, at Manadarva', which suggests that the site was still recognisable in 1700.

St. Derwa's chapel was most probably of pre-Conquest origin, holding the saint's shrine, and possibly stood within a *lan* now no longer detectable. If so, this chapel was rebuilt in the late 11th or early 12th century (the date of the surviving font from it) by the Mertherderwa family, either as a chapel of ease or as a private oratory. The saint herself will be mentioned again below (p.69).

St. Meriasek's Well-Chapel, Camborne

The various passages in *BM*, considered in chapter II, do not actually state that the saint built a chapel beside the well which he founded; the references to his *oratry* (oratory) in lines 639 and 654 concern the supposed fore-runner of the parish church. However, a holy well of such fame as Meriasek's is likely to have attracted a building over it, and this seems to be implied by Nicholas Roscarrock, writing about 1600[13], when he says 'There is a chapel in the parish of Camburn in Cornwall dedicated to a sainct called Marazaack in Cornishe . . . there is a well wch also bereth that name'. In his notes, a century later (Appendix A), Edward Lhuyd gives his chapel no. 4 as being 'at Rhoszwern'. This is Rosewarne, Lhuyd's *sz* standing for the voiced *s* (as English 'rose') common in Late Cornish but absent in his native Welsh. The area of Rosewarne, presumably a pre-Conquest holding, lay north and north-east of the churchtown, and by medieval times had been divided between Higher Rosewarne (*Rosowhorn warthas*, 1400) and Lower Rosewarne (*Rosewarne wollas*, 1591), of which only the latter's much altered 14th/15th-century hall house survives. What had probably started as open grazing on Lower Rosewarne, with a small farm-house added to it, was enclosed soon after 1800 by William Harris, who pulled down the farm and built a Georgian mansion. The position of St. Meriasek's well is known, even if it has subsequently disappeared (p.125), and in Lhuyd's time it would have been on the tenement of Rosewarne. His chapel 'at Rhoszwern' must therefore be the well-chapel mentioned earlier by Roscarrock, since there is no trace of any other chapel having stood on this tenement at any time.

The chapel need not have been, and in all probability was not, a very impressive structure. Most Cornish well-chapels are quite small— compare those described in the Misses (M. and L.) Quiller-Couch's *Ancient and Holy Wells of Cornwall* (1894)—and the best-known instances are either medieval in themselves, or medieval replacements of supposedly earlier ones. There is no valid reason to suppose that St. Meriasek's well-chapel was pre-Norman; it may not have been constructed before the 14th or 15th century, for all we know. The complete absence of any remains, the failure of the text of *BM* to refer specifically to this chapel, and the predominance of the well itself in all recorded tradition, are features which taken together point to some comparatively humble building.

The Chapel of St. Mary of Camborne
Dr. William Borlase's reference (Appendix B) to the chapel of 'St. Margaret and St. Anne' must, as Charles Henderson saw, be a mistake for 'St. Mary and St. Anne'. Borlase's source here was the appropriate epis-copal register at Exeter; for on 7th November 1435, Bishop Lacy gave forty days' indulgence to all persons visiting the free chapel of the Blessed Virgin *Mary* and St. Anne in the parish of Camborne, or contri-buting to its upkeep. In the three centuries intervening between these two references, there are other records. The will of John Carnell, rector of Haccombe (near Newton Abbot), dated 1445, includes a bequest of 6d. to 'the store of St. Mary of Camborne'[14]. The Cornish episode from *BM* analysed in the preceding chapter is itself good evidence that, *circa* 1500, a chapel of Mary of Camborne existed, and was moreover a shrine of some fame in the region. 'Where are you from, that you ask *that*?' the serving-man says to Meriasek, when the saint enquires whose the chapel might be. Edward Lhuyd's notes on the Camborne chapels tend to confirm what we have already suspected from the *BM* text, namely that

the Chapel of Mary stood close to the parish church; ' . . . one in ye churchyard *An*' he wrote. In no case does he state to whom any particular chapel was ascribed, but in this case the mysterious '*An*' may perhaps refer to the St. Anne (mother of the Virgin) who, in Lacy's 1435 Indulgence (Lacy I.316), is coupled with the Virgin in the dedication.

It is now impossible to locate the site. Total excavation of the churchyard, as impracticable as it would be exciting, might conceivably reveal it, but nothing less could do so. However, fragments may survive and the most likely fate of the building itself can be guessed. In 1670-71, Francis Basset conveyed[15] to the Rector and parish a small plot of land within the tenement of Camborne Veor, situate on the south side of the Glebe, for the construction of a new poor-house or Parish House (see p.158; the last vestiges of it were removed only in 1954). Canon Carah in his analysis of the Camborne Rate Book[16] wrote 'It is interesting to find there was a Chapel in the Alms House, and this to be of better work—There is a charge for "hewing of stones which are in the Chappell" 4s. 6d.' However, this proves to be an error. F. J. Stephens, in whose possession this particular Rate Book then was—it has since disappeared (p.160)—noted what must have been more or less a neighbouring entry in the same account[17]; 'Paid to them (the masons) for dressing and removing stones *from the old Chappel*' (author's italics).

This implies something quite different. There was in any case no vestige of any chapel in the Parish House at any later stage, no other record of such, and, one might add, little likelihood of there ever having been one there. But if, in 1670, a source of suitable worked granite for jambs, lintels, and coigns was being sought, a ruinous chapel in the churchyard, the property of the parish and not (as the other chapel remains all were) within privately-owned land, would form the obvious quarry. When one also reckons that this would be the nearest chapel to the Parish House site, standing only a quarter-mile distant and at the other end of an existing lane[18], there cannot be much doubt that 'the old Chappel' was St. Mary's.

It is also possible that various odds and ends were not required for the Parish House, and suffered a different fate. F. J. Stephens continued[19] 'Mr. James Thomas has pointed out some bits of ancient carved stone built into walls along Gas Lane' (now the east, or Union Street, end, of Gas Street—these walls were demolished about 1961) 'which may be of ecclesiastical origin.' The cottages which sprang up in this part of the town were mainly of early to mid-19th century date, and the stones, if really worked, are as likely to have come from the remains of St. Meriasek's chapel, or the ruins of Higher Rosewarne house, or several other potential sources, as from the churchyard; but it is interesting to note that what may be a stoup (p.116, and fig.25,b) is said to have been found in a wall of an old cottage in New Connexion Street, which opens north off the former Gas Lane. This, it is easier to believe, may well have come from the ruins of St. Mary's chapel.

Among the numerous worked stones now in a large pile in the walled yard behind the Rectory, and also built into the kerbs of the paths, in the churchyard at Camborne, there are some fragments which do not all look as if they were derived from the 1878 restoration of the church. One in particular, a small arched window-head, may have been over a long-side window in a medieval chapel, and there are other rather more fragmentary pieces which it is difficult to envisage as part of the pre-1878 south wall or south aisle of the parish church.

There is independent evidence for a former cult of the Blessed Virgin Mary at Camborne. There is considerable emphasis on the Virgin in *BM*, not merely in the Cornish episode, though that episode itself lays some stress on her devotion. Again, the curious tradition about the 'Merry Kurse' (Mary's cross?) reported by F. J. Stephens (p.37) points in this direction; and, as we shall see below, it appears that there was a *second* St. Mary's Chapel within the parish.

What is more difficult to decide is whether the supposed presence of a separate chapel in the churchyard indicates a pre-Norman origin for the churchyard site. In the first chapter, it was suggested that *Cambron* was originally a land-holding on the slope of Carn Camborne, and that the churchtown (to which the name was eventually transferred) grew up on the northern edge of this holding. In favour of the view of a Celtic origin one might argue that no particular geographical reason can be shown to underlie this choice of churchyard site, and that a pre-existing Celtic chapel does therefore offer as good a reason as any other. Independent or 'free' chapels in churchyards do seem, in Cornwall, to be fairly good pointers to pre-Norman origins; an example is the present parish church of St. Kew, in origin the 6th-century monastery of *Landocco*, where a chapel of St. Kew was still, ruinously, visible in the churchyard as late as 1745[20]. Against this view it could be stated that, physically, Camborne churchyard shows no signs of having been a *lan*; it may be doubted whether the earliest stone cross (no. 1, p.86) is older than the 12th century and there are no pre-Norman remains; the ascription to St. Meriasek could have been transferred from the saint's holy well when the church was built; and the ascription of a chapel to the Blessed Virgin Mary is not on the whole very likely in pre-Norman Cornwall[21]. (See, however, p.15, where it was suggested that the chapel of St. Mary may have been built as a late pre-Conquest chapel for the postulated vill of *Cambron*.)

The Chapel at Crane

The manor of Crane was one of a number of small manors within the parish of Camborne—Rosewarne, Crane, Penpons and Baripper, Treslothan, and probably Treswithian as well. It gave rise to a family of the same name, first mentioned in the 13th century, who continued to live at Crane until the seventeenth. Early forms of this place-name involve some curious spellings—*Kaervran* 1283, *Kaerwran* 1380, *Karan* 1417, *Crane* 1469 —which show that the actual place mentioned must have been a *ker*, a 'round' or fortified homestead-earthwork of a variety common in Cornwall originating before the Roman period. This *ker*, like a good many others could have been re-occupied in the early Middle Ages, and the alternative spelling *Carhain* 1313 (*ker hen*, 'the old fort') tends to confirm this. There is no trace whatsoever of any such earthwork at Crane, and the name must therefore have been transferred to Crane, through the agency of a shift of residence within the family's manor, from some earlier homestead. Mention of the manor as 'Crane and Gear' in both 1570 and 1683[22] indicates that the present farm called Gear, which does stand within a *ker* or earthwork of this kind, and which is barely half-a-mile south of Crane itself, was the older seat, possibly vacated in the 11th and 12th centuries (see fig. 3).

The old Crane manor house, or what was left of it, was demolished in 1960 (of this, more below). The writer has been unable to trace any grant of a licence for Divine Service to the Crane family, or any documentary record of a chapel in or beside their manorial seat; but both local tradition and substantial architectural evidence point to the former existence of some elaborate domestic oratory.

The late S. T. Russell, writing about 1875, noted that 'Tradition saith that Crane was once the site of a nunnery. The chapel belonging to the old nunnery was taken down by Mr. Mills, builder of this town, about 20 years since' (i.e. about 1855) 'and the stones taken to Roseworthy to build outhouses for Mr. Paul, who told me that there were a great number of carvings on the stones which were all turned inside the building'[23].

Mr. Paull was then farming Merry Meeting, Roseworthy hill. On a tour of inspection in 1949, the present writer noticed a stone (fig. 12, J) which has now disappeared, but which was then standing, upside-down and whitewashed, as a support for a water tank in the yard. It has triple-moulding, and appears to be a double spandrel for two pointed lights, cut out of the lintel of a square-headed opening. There was also a small section of an intricate granite cornice seen in the garden of a cottage a short distance away[24]. The fate of the rest of the worked stone is uncertain. Canon Carah, who had read S. T. Russell's notes, printed this report of the demolition of the supposed chapel (Carah 1927, 10). What is less generally known is that, a few years later, he was able to add to this[25]. 'A farmer in my parish' he wrote 'has been pulling down an old cottage which had been faced with stone; they were worked pieces. These turned out to be the very stones about which I had written which had been removed many years ago from the old manor house at Crane and taken to Merry Meeting farm.' The manuscript version of this particular contribution, in the writer's possession, is slightly fuller; it also fails to mention which farm was involved, but as it includes the name 'Mr. Paull' it was presumably Merry Meeting.

The problem of the exact whereabouts of any supposed chapel at Crane depends to a large extent upon what can be made of the architectural history of this house-complex. In fig. 11, its more recent stages are shown in a series of ground plans at uniform scale. 'C' is based on the 1906 O.S. 25-in. plan, with considerable modification. In 1959, part of the structure marked 'Old Part' collapsed through sheer age, and in 1960 the Camborne-Redruth U.D.C. commenced to demolish the rest of the complex. The writer was able to persuade the Council to delay this work until as much as possible had been recorded. Preliminary measured plans, had, for-

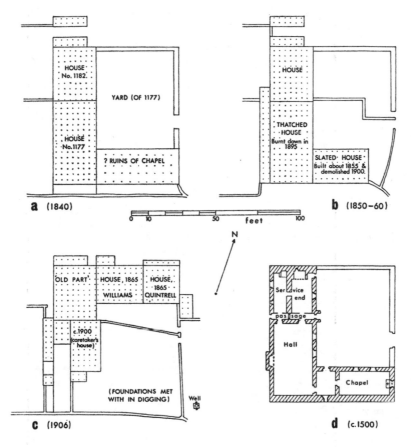

Fig. 11
Crane Manor, showing reconstructions of its various phases.

tunately, been made of some of the site in 1958, and it was now possible to supplement these with a series of photographs, and a set of architectural drawings made under expert direction[26].

In 1959, the general lay-out was very much as in 'C'. The late Mr. Ernest Williams was then living in the portion marked 'Old Part'. Mr. Williams, with whom the writer had many long and detailed talks about the structural history of Crane, was the son of the Mr. Williams who, as also marked on 'C', lived in the next door block added about 1865.

'B' in fig. 11 is taken from a Basset estate map (by courtesy of Tehidy Minerals Ltd., Camborne), one of a series made about 1855-1860. It takes us back a stage to an L-shaped complex, whose shorter arm was a cottage with a *slate* roof. This, notable for such an unusual covering, was occupied by a Mr. Odgers, and Mr. Ernest Williams could recall its demolition about 1900. The southern part of the longer arm of the L was a thatched house of antique appearance, burnt down in 1895 (also witnessed by Mr. Williams) and, its ruins having been cleared, the present two-storey modern dwelling occupied by the groundsman of the Camborne Recreation Ground, was erected in its stead, accompanied by numerous odd sheds and glass-houses.

In fig. 11, 'A', blown-up from the Tithe Apportionment Map of 1840, a rather similar L-shaped lay-out appears. The two small cottages of 'C' have not yet appeared on the north side of the yard, and the short arm of the 'L' is rather longer than it was when the slate-roofed Odgers cottage was put up. It is worth noting that, in the Tithe Survey, this arm is marked as unoccupied (it has no number, and is not bracketed to any numbered plot); for, traditionally, this is where the supposed chapel stood. Apparently, then, such ruins as still existed were cleared about 1855-60 to make way for the Odgers cottage, and the stones were disposed of by Mr. Mills, the builder, who took them down to the Paulls at Merry Meeting.

Fig. 11 'D', is a tentative restored plan based on this interpretation, and on what was found in the 1960 demolition. The portions of the old medieval house which were in some measure retained until 1960 were the 'Old Part' as shown in 'C', which proved to be the service-rooms of the medieval house, and the north-east part of the medieval courtyard garth-wall. The latter, a wall nearly three feet thick, consisting of huge granite blocks laid horizontally along the courses, had been incorporated into the north-side walls of the two cottages (Williams and Quintrell) shown in 'C'.

The ground-floor plan of the 'Old Part', only very slightly adapted by Mr. Williams and his predecessors here, still included the medieval kitchen (right) and a smaller room (left), each with a deeply-recessed hearth. The hearth in the kitchen also held an alcove with an inner recess (fig. 12, K) for the storage of salt.

Crane Manor forms a good instance of the so-called 'hall and cross-passage' plan, found in small Cornish manor-houses of the 15th, and probably 14th, centuries. The cross-passage itself survived until 1960, providing as it did Mr. Ernest Williams' front and back doorways. Where it passed through the thick longitudinal wall which divided the kitchen from the room on its left, there was a fine four-centred archway of granite, which has often been photographed and also visited by the curious in the past. It was rescued, together with certain other pieces, by the writer and his brother. The form of the arch and the moulding suggest that this is no earlier than about 1450, if that early, but if (as inspection during the demolition made tolerably certain) it was still *in situ*, it affords a general date for the main building.

The hall, the major component of the manor-house, would have been where the 'thatched cottage' is shown in fig. 11, 'B', and the walls of this cottage no doubt rested on the line of the hall foundations. The closest local parallel to Crane is perhaps Truthall, Sithney parish[27], a 15th century home of the Nance family, whose lay-out resembles that of Crane quite well. The arrangement of the parallel service-rooms, from which food cooked in open hearths would be brought across the cross-passage into the hall, is not wholly conventional; but it is also found in the now-ruined house called Drannack Vean in Gwinear, actually the old manor-house of Drannack. Here the service-room end, converted into a small farm-house about 1800, and now a hay-store, shows an exactly similar arrangement of two parallel and unequal rooms, each with its own substantial hearth. The L-shaped plan, forming part of a private court-yard, is echoed by Methrose, in Luxulyan, mid-Cornwall[28], where the hall is much smaller than is envisaged at Crane, and where there is no evidence that the shorter arm was other than purely domestic in function. In drawing out fig. 11, 'D', the writer has assumed that the length indicated on the Tithe Map, if in any way accurate and not just schematic, is rather extensive for a domestic oratory, and it is thus possible that a gap, store, or ante-chapel existed at the west end.

It is likely that the Crane family, when they first settled at Crane (and gave the house their name?), resided in a much more humble sort of manor-house. The type is shown by the 12th-14th century two-room affair at Crane Godrevy, none the less a manor and home of the Godrevy family until the 17th century[29]. The building reconstructed in fig. 11, 'D', goes with the very possession of an adjoined domestic oratory as putative evidence of the family's increased wealth and prestige in the later 15th century, and presumably a licence was sought during this period. Most of the fragments recovered during and after the demolition were of 15th or 16th century date, like the window-head shown in fig. 12, L (this was unearthed many years ago in the caretaker's garden and promptly re-buried, though not before Canon Carah had arrived and sketched it!) But when the central and north walls of the 'Old Part', walls built between (say) 1450 and 1550, were pulled down, they were seen to contain numerous dressed granite blocks set across the line of the wall, and parts of small round-headed lights built in as filling. These are good evidence for there having been an older house on the same spot, hauled down to permit the construction of a more sumptuous manor.

The chapel at Crane was not mentioned by William Borlase. It is, how-ever, very probably that listed by Edward Lhuyd in 1700 (Appendix A) as his no. 6, 'at Tredzothan'. Lhuyd wrote *dz* for the Cornish *j*, or Cornish intervocalic *s* pronounced as *j*, and this must be for 'Trejothan', which, under the forms Jothan, Juthan, or Jethan, is still the local vernacular for *Treswithian*, recalling the older spellings *Treswithen* (1884), *Treswethen* (1677), and the medieval *Trevaswethen* (1302). There is no record of any chapel at Treswithian, but as the manor-house at Crane lies very close to the pathway which formerly separated Crane from Treswithian, one can see how this confusion could have arisen.

On the other hand, this need not have been an early chapel at all. It may have been an innovation of the late 14th or early 15th century, added when the house itself was reconstructed. It is unlikely (insofar as one can now ascertain any form of plan) to have been much larger internally than

14 feet by 30 feet, and would have been a domestic chapel for the Crane family. Canon Adams has commented[30] on this odd Cornish habit of erecting, even at late dates, a separate building for a domestic oratory, instead of simply converting an inner chamber. He has suggested that it reflects an earlier manorial practice, that of appropriating disused or defunct Celtic (pre-Conquest) chapels standing close to manor-houses, and rebuilding them as private ones. The instance of Menadarva, where this very probably happened about 1100 or before, comes to mind (p.54). Here, at Crane, we may be seeing the final pre-Reformation reflection of this habit.

The Chapel of St. Mary at Penpons

The old east-west highway across the centre of the parish enters it by crossing the Conor stream at Baripper. This odd name devolves from an original (Norman French) *beau repaire*—so *Beau Repere* 1397, *Beaurepper* 1430, *Berepper* 1530—and the traditional explanation that this referred to a pilgrims' hostel, on the site of the present St. Michael's Mount Inn, is doubtless correct. This would be the last stage on the way to the Mount. The present road bridge is carried on vast granite slabs and may be a replacement of a medieval one. An earlier name is preserved in the adjacent tenement on the west, or Gwinear, side of the crossing—Pons-ferrans (*Ponsferas* 1659; possibly broken down from *pons for' vras*, 'bridge of the great road'?)[31]. There is another ancient-looking granite bridge of the clapper type a short way down-stream (pl.IX), already mentioned on p.18.

The original Penpons was clearly that part of the village now called 'Higher Penpons', a short way off the old highway about a half-mile from Baripper. This can be shown, not only from such sources as Martyn's Map of Cornwall (fig. 5) and the earlier one by Joel Gascoyne (fig. 4), but also from the relative age of the buildings in 'Higher Penpons' and in Penpons village proper. The name means 'Bridge End' and, apart from the hostelry and any accessory structures at Baripper, this would have been the first hamlet encountered as one entered the parish.

In August 1427, Bishop Lacy ordained a number of local youths, including Philip Godryvy from Crane Godrevy in Gwithian, at *Beau-ripper*, and Lacy's suffragan conducted a similar ordination at the same place in 1433[32]. Whether this took place in the hostelry or merely in the vicinity is not known; but there is a reference to an Inquisition held in the 'Chapel of Blessed Marie of Penpons' in 1421[33], and this forms the most likely setting. Where was this chapel? Canon Adams has suggested[34] that it may have originated as a hermit's chapel by the ford at Baripper; but this seems a little dubious. 'Penpons' is specified, and if this is read literally, the chapel was not by the river, ford, or bridge, at all.

The former Manor of Penpons and Baripper passed to the St. Aubyn family of Clowance in Crowan, and was an extensive one (a little over 500 acres) only dispersed by sale in the last forty years. Henderson quotes references to this Manor in 1473. In 1445, Richard Penpons and Amisia his wife were granted a licence to celebrate Divine Service. No place is specified, beyond any suitable place in the diocese (Lacy II.348; 10th November 1445), but at this date Richard Penpons was presumably living at the house of that name. (He may have been the same 'Richard Penpons' who was admitted as a clerk by Bishop Stafford in 1409.) It is an obvious assumption, and perhaps not an unfair one, that he had some family or tenurial connection with the chapel of St. Mary of Penpons and that this stood at or hard by his home—indeed, may have been regarded by the Penpons family as their domestic oratory.

There is no documentary evidence as to the site of the manor-house of Penpons. Carah drew attention [35] to the large number of worked granite stones in and around Penpons, some of which he duly rescued and set up in the vicarage garden. He concluded 'Somewhere and sometime there can be little doubt that a fine old house stood at Penpons ... there remain signs which cannot well be put aside. Evidently the old house fell, and was used as a quarry for later builders, for sharp eyes can detect several of these old stones built into the cottages in the neighbourhood.'

The writer and his brother (N. D. Thomas), after a careful examination of the village in 1961, felt that the most likely site of the manor-house was the large cottage in Higher Penpons, almost opposite Richard Trevithick's thatched homestead, now called 'Ivy Cottage'. Fig. 12 shows, in sketch form and at uniform scale, a number of the worked stones to which Canon Carah referred, and several which he seems to have missed. The most noteworthy is the fragmentary but handsome door-frame (fig. 12, D— see also pl.II) which, now blocked and partly removed, surrounds the downstairs front left window of Ivy Cottage. Other aspects of this interesting house, inspection of which was most kindly permitted by its owners, confirm the impression that it constitutes the remnants of a rectangular or L-shaped building of the fifteenth century. The three-light mullion and fireplace surround, in fig. 12, were recovered by Canon Carah about 1921 when 'an old thatched cottage was demolished at Higher Penpons' (Carah 1925, 43) and may well have come from the manor-house; Carah built them into a sort of summer-house in the vicarage garden, where they still are.

St. Mary's Chapel may therefore have been near where Ivy Cottage stands, and in any event is more likely to have stood in Higher Penpons than anywhere else yet suggested. It is conceivable that some trace of it may, one day, come to light. As with the other Chapel of Mary, the one in the churchyard, a really early origin seems improbable; and if not wholly manorial in foundation, this may have been a reflection of the local cult of Mary close to a famous pilgrims' hostel. The tantalising thing is that ruins may have been visible as late as 1700, since Edward Lhuyd includes in his list ' . . . 3 At Penpons', and he must have been shown some putative ruin. His ascription also confirms the most probable whereabouts of this chapel; i.e., at the 'Penpons' shown on Gascoyne's contemporary map (fig. 4).

St. James' Chapel at Treslothan

This also occurs in Lhuyd's list: '. . . 2. At Treslothan' and the information as to its exact site is a little more positive. A licence was granted on 21st August 1427 to 'sir John Petyt, chaplain, for divine service celebrated by himself and others in the chapel of St. James at Cambron' (Lacy I.204). The family of Petyt or Petit had their main seat from about A.D. 1200 at Ardevora in Philleigh, but at one period also owned the Manor of Treslothan; the licence in this case probably refers to the John Petit who died in 1429. One-half of Treslothan was bought in 1619 by Alexander Pendarves from the Prideaux family; the other moiety was obtained through an Arundell marriage, the Arundells having doubtless inherited the Petit interest through an intricate series of marriages and descents which can be traced in numerous Cornish pedigrees.

About 1839, the Pendarves family decided to construct a Chapel of Ease at Treslothan to serve what was then a rather isolated part of Camborne. This became, of course, the present Treslothan Church (p.168 below). 'The rector . . . has generously given £100 to provide a curate for a Chapel of Ease which has just been completed in Pendarves Park' wrote Dr. Richard Lanyon the following year[36]. 'Borlase, in his History of the County, states that six chapels once existed in Camborne, but we have no further knowledge of them, unless we except a legend, or conjecture, that the remains of one were removed a year since, to make room for the erection of the handsome Gothic chapel just alluded to . . .' This is the statement of a resident of Camborne, drawing upon local knowledge, but it receives some confirmation from the remarks of T. C. Paris, writing the text for the first (1850) edition of John Murray's famous *Hand-Book for Travellers in Devon and Cornwall*. Paris states (*ibid.*, 121) that '. . . the handsome chapel, erected in 1842 . . . contains an old font, and occupies the site of an ancient chapel, among the ruins of which the workmen discovered an inscribed and curiously sculptured tablet of granite.' (This 'tablet' was the altar mensa to be described below, p.103). It is possible that the reference [37] in Hitchins and Drew's *The History of Cornwall, etc.* to '. . . the manor of Treslothan, upon which estate there are some remains of ancient chapel' alludes to the same ruins.

It must be suspected that the Chapel of Ease was built quite deliberately upon the remains of the older shrine. The Pendarves family were for many generations staunch supporters of the established church in Camborne, and presumably desired to perpetuate a once-consecrated chapel. Treslothan church is a most illogical site, on the periphery of Pendarves

Fig. 12 (opposite)

Carved or worked granite pieces from Crane and Penpons manor houses.
A, B, F; in Penpons village, C, a back window, and D, the original front
doorway, now a window, at Ivy Cottage, Penpons. E, G, probably from
next to Ivy Cottage, now in the garden of the former vicarage at Penpons.
H, the cross-passage arched door-frame from Crane Manor, now removed,
and K, detail of 'salt alcove' found behind a fireplace; J, window spandrel,
removed to Merry Meeting, now lost; L, a buried window-head, both also
from Crane.

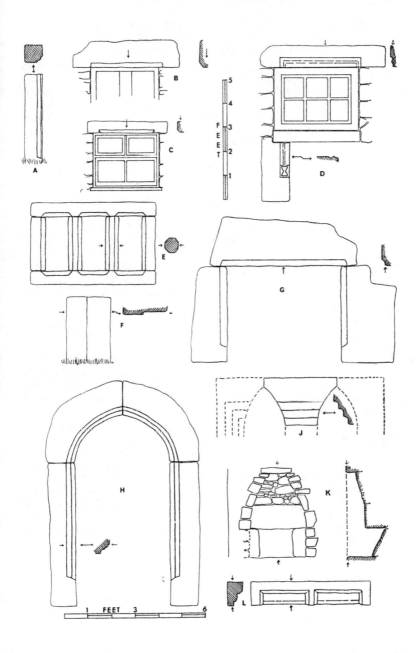

estate, and when built, must have stood in the middle of field-paths and the recently-planted woodlands. The small village of Treslothan, a delightful example of a Victorian model hamlet, grew up (or was, more accurately, constructed in uniform style) around the church; prior to this, there had been nothing but a couple of cob cottages, now entirely gone, several hundred yards away by a stile. Did anyone realise that the 'ruins' belonged to a chapel of St. James? The present Vicar of Treslothan (Rev. P. L. Eustice) draws the writer's attention to the fact that, although the church is dedicated in honour of St. John, it was actually consecrated (on 25th July, 1842) on the Feast of St. *James*.

The original date of St. James' chapel is probably given us by the granite altar slab discussed more fully in chapter VII. This belongs to the eleventh century, perhaps the earlier eleventh century. Taken in conjunction with the name inscribed on it, a local rendering of an English name which may be *Aegfrid*, this looks very like an instance of an estate chapel of the late pre-Conquest era, constructed at the instigation of an English land-holder. The tenement name 'Treslothan' goes back to such forms as 1283 *Tresulwythen*, implying *tre-* plus a personal (Cornish) name like **Sulu-ueten*. This tenement was, one assumes, in English hands in the eleventh century, and as a manor, in the demesne of someone of Norman origin (like the Petit family) by the twelfth. Where was 'Treslothan'? No farm of this name exists, and the name now refers to the 1842 village. The most likely explanation is that the original Treslothan occupied, in part, the area of the later Pendarves park—prior to its enclosure about 1815-20, this had been called 'Treslothan Moor'— and that the original homestead was replaced by the Georgian mansion of Pendarves House (demolished, 1954-55). The family of Pendarves appear to have given their name to their holding and not, as usual, *vice versa*. Indeed, there remains some uncertainty as to the origin of this family. According to William Hals, who has been accused of inventing what he could not discover, the family migrated from Tresona (or Tresawna) in St. Enoder in the 16th century. A family of Tresawna undoubtedly existed (e.g., in Probus, in the 18th century) but no connection is known. The Pendarves family, in the Heralds' Visitations, are not uniformly associated with Camborne—in the late 16th and early 17th century, many of them were in the neigh-bouring parish of Crowan—and genealogists will be aware that they afford an interesting example of the evolution of surnames. Richard Carew, in 1603, wrote that '*Iohn*, the sonne of *Thomas*, dwelling at *Pendaruis*, is called *Iohn Thomas Pendarvis. Rich*. his yonger brother is named, *Richard Thomas Pendaruis*, &c'[38] and he cites this as an illustration of a custom whereby the Cornish 'intitle one another with his owne & his fathers christen name, and conclude with the place of his dwelling'. Whether or not Carew actually had the Pendarves family in mind, it should be noted that Alexander Pendarves who died in 1624 described himself in his will as 'Alexander Thomas *alias* Pendarves', Thomas being his father's name.

Though it is possible that *Pendarves* is a lost Camborne place-name, it seems more likely that it was acquired, as a surname, from some holding of that name in another parish. (There is, for example, a 'Pendarves', a farm, in the parish of Veryan.) Alternating with the use of patronymics, it was transferred by a family who moved into Camborne to their family seat, the name 'Treslothan' being retained for the larger manor and for the lands lying south and west of the park. By the mid-19th century, the Pendarves land-holding in the parish was getting on for two thousand acres. That this place-name division had taken place at least as early as *circa* 1700 is clear from Joel Gascoyne's map (fig. 4), which shows *Pendarvis* (the house) a short way from *Treluthen* (Treslothan).

The construction of Treslothan Church destroyed (as might be expected) all traces of any earlier remains. Save for the altar slab (p.103) and the little font (p.115), both putatively of the 11th century, nothing remains of St. James' Chapel. The outline of a light-coloured rectangle, indicating perhaps buried foundations, is visible just west of the church on an aerial photograph[39]. This may just possibly be an indication of where the buildings, if any, of 'Treslothan', prior to the 1842 village, should be sought.

St. Ia's Chapel at Troon

This chapel, all trace of which had been lost for over two hundred years, was recently located and excavated by the writer. To avoid the irruption of archaeology into a historical narrative, an account of this excavation has been written as a separate chapter (chapter V), and only the historical background will be given here.

The licence granted by Bishop Edmund Lacy in 1429 (Lacy I.223) has already been mentioned, since it confusingly refers to two separate chapels—St. Derwa's at Menadarva (p.52), and another described as of St. *Ya*. *Ya* is clearly intended as a disyllabic name, pronounced 'ee-a'. As the late Charles Henderson noted[40], this must be the virgin saint better known as the patron of St. Ives, whose name is conventionally written as 'Ia' or 'Eia'. Her name occurs four times as St. Ives—*Porth-ia*, the harbour and churchtown, also used as the Cornish name of St. Ives as a whole; *Dinas-ia* or St. Ives Island; *Ayr* (*Arthia*, 1659), the upper part of the town; and *Venton-ia*, the old town well by Porthmeor beach. This in itself is unusual and suggests a strong local cult. Henderson suggested Nanj*ivey* as a fifth example—this is unlikely—and also noted that Wendron parish church was called *Eglos-iga* in the middle ages. Unfortunately this is equally unlikely to contain the name '*Ia*'; the -*g*- in *iga* probably stands for the sound of *j*, a sound assumed in Middle and Late Cornish by the letter *s* between vowels, and actually written as *g*, *j*, or even (as Edward Lhuyd preferred), *dz*. The personal name at Wendron, if it is a personal name, would be **Isa* (pronounced 'eeja') and one thinks of the personal name (*Ida*, **Isa*), presumably of a female saint, in the parochial dedications of St. Issey and of Mevagissey[41].

The reference in Lacy's Register apart, the earliest mention of this chapel is Edward Lhuyd's in 1700 (see Appendix A). Lhuyd gives this, as an afterthought, on the verso of his page 1, opposite the other Camborne notes, as 'another chappel at Trewn call'd Ia. The well is called fenten Ia in the parish of Cambron'. Together with the chapels numbered 1 to 6 in the body of his notes, this makes the total of seven discussed above (p.52).

The oldest description is Dr. William Borlase's. Borlase was engaged in field-work in the area in 1750, when he visited Troon and was apparently directed to the site. His account is given in full as Appendix B. He describes what he saw; a holy well, a standing cross, and the walls of a chapel, all in close proximity to each other, the well being called *Fenton-Er*. In his little field note-book, he drew the cross (see fig. 19 below) and scribbled by the sketch 'a Well noted for Physical water just by calld Fenton Neer— or Eer.'

This makes it certain that the holy well was really *Fenton-Ia*, St. Ia's spring, and the chapel hard by it must be the Chapel of St. Ya mentioned in Lacy's Register.

Apart from the examples of the cult of St. Ia in and around St. Ives (*Dinas-ia*, etc., cited earlier), this is the only example outside St. Ives which can be accepted as an ascription to this particular saint. What is known of Ia, and what is the possible significance—as to context and date —of a dedication like this?

St. Ia belongs to a group of saints whose names are preserved in the dedications of parish churches, chapels, and holy wells, centred on a restricted area of west Cornwall (the eastern half of Penwith hundred). These saints are largely interconnected through being mentioned in contemporary sources, as brothers, sisters, or companions of each other. The sources are without exception late (i.e., medieval) and consist of the following; the Life of St. Gwinear, attributed to Anselm (about 1300)[42]; some notes made by William of Worcester on a visit to the Westcountry in 1478, either at first-hand or from an informant in Tavistock[43]; fragments from four Lives (of St. Breaca, St. Gwinear, St. Elwin, and St. Ia) recorded about 1540 by John Leland, on his antiquarian tour of Cornwall[44]; and scattered entries in registers and martyrologies.

One or two of these saints cannot now be located or further identified (e.g., Maruanus the monk, Helena) but the others are commemorated in various ways. It is easiest to show this in a simple diagram, indicating *family* relationship (i.e. brother-sister,) by brackets to the left, and contextual relationship (mentioned in the same Life or contiguous entries, or said to have travelled together) by being in the same column (see p.69). Medieval Cornishmen had no doubt whatsoever as to the historicity of this band—several of them were widely believed to be buried in their appropriate patronal churches—nor as to their country of origin. They were regarded as Irish, three of the Lives seen by Leland linking them with St. Barricius, one of the companions of St. Patrick. St. Breaca was said to have been born in parts of Leinster and Ulster (*in partibus Lagoniae et Ultoniae*), St. Sinninus or Sithney, in the plagiarized Breton Life of St. Sezni given by Albert le Grand, was born in *Ultonia* as well; Gwinear, Piala, and Ia all came from noble Irish families. Moreover, all this band landed on the north coast of Cornwall, in St. Ives bay, whence they proceeded to evangelise the district; and independently in Anselm's Life of

A	B	C	D	E	F
		⌠UNY			IVA
		⟨ HERYGH b.			
HYA v.	YA v.	⌊ HYA v.			
⌠FINGAR m.			WYNIERUS		
⎰PIALA v.					
with		GYERMOCUS b.		GERMMOCHUS k.	
a		BRANCA v.		BREACA	
large				SINNINUS a.	
party				MARUANUS mk.	
				ELWEN	ELWINE
				CREWENNA	and
				HELENA	many
	DERWA v.				others
ANTA v. ?					

Table of saints traditionally hailing from Ireland

a, Abbot; *b*, Bishop; *k*, King; *m*, Martyr; *mk*, Monk; *v*, Virgin.
Sources: (A) Anselm's Life of Fingar or Guigner. c. 1300. (B), Lacy's Register, 1429. (C), William of Worcester's notes, 1478. (D), another Life of Guigner. (E), Life of Breaca. (F), Life of Iva (Ia). Brackets: brothers and sisters. (D), (E), (F) are reported by Leland, c. 1540.

Gwinear, and the Life of Breaca as noted by Leland, the tyrant Teudar whom we have already encountered in the *Bewnans Meriasek* play (p.28) slew some of them.

While firmly emphasising again that these sources are comparatively, very late—the Lives seen by Leland are unlikely to have been any earlier than Anselm's Life of Gwinear and may well have been later still—and that a degree of literary plagiarism or borrowing probably existed, the overall impression one none the less gets is that this is a distorted medieval reflection of some actual historical phase. It was pointed out earlier that archaeological evidence, in the shape of the appearance of an intrusive pottery technique, does support the idea of Irish settlement in precisely this area (p.42) from the later sixth century A.D. A sketch map (fig. 13) shows that the area is a fairly compact one. The map locates churches, chapels, and holy wells involving the persons who are mentioned above including both St. Anta of Lelant, who seems to be obliquely hinted at in the life of Gwinear, and St. Gothian of Gwithian, traditionally Cornwall's proto-martyr, who may have been among those slain almost upon landing, as again the Life of Gwinear and the Life of Breaca suggest.

If, in the first place, these persons represent the founders of the various *lans* which later become parish churches, and which in a number of cases appear to have held their enshrined remains until the Reformation[45], the various chapels and holy-wells must reflect extensions of their cults,

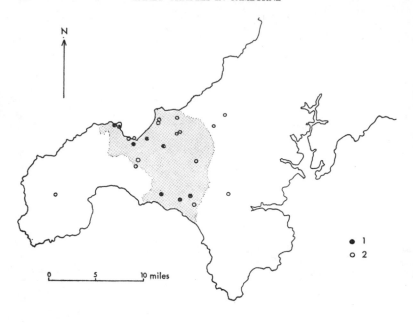

Fig. 13
Distribution of parish churches, chapels, and wells ascribed to 'Irish' saints (see p.69). (1), churches which claimed their patrons' actual remains; (2), all other sites. Stippled area: parishes with 'Irish' patrons.

based either on the possession of relics or upon alleged traditional assoc-iations. In the case of St. Ia's chapel at Troon, the important facet is not the chapel, whose name (though given in Lacy's 1429 entry) was clearly forgotten by Borlase's day, but the holy well, Fenton-Ia, whose name equally clearly survived. This must have been the crucial spot, and pre-sumably pre-Norman inhabitants of Camborne or Troon believed that the holy Virgin Ia had visited the place, and like Gwinear and Meriasek, had caused water to flow from the rocks. We may discount the miracle, but we would be unjustified in discounting completely the possibility of an association between some post-Roman *sanctus*, Irish or not, and a natural spring, or the possibility of a genuine historical tradition surviving until the point in time—the 10th century?—when this association was com-memorated by the building of a well-chapel. If the rock-pile on the opposite side of the stream really was the *Carrek Veryasek* of the miracle play, beneath which Meriasek hid himself to evade Teudar's henchmen[46], this place must have held very special attractions in the locality.

The evidence derived from the excavation of this chapel is given at length in the next chapter, and need only be touched upon here. A primi-tive well-chapel was probably built in the 10th century. In the 12th, it was entirely re-built on different lines, and in the 13th, considerably enlarged, probably to serve as a chapel of ease for the Troon district. The last two phases involved slate roofs, and such features as painted designs on internal lime-washing. The main accessories were the great Leuiut altar slab, first designed as a frontal and re-used in the second phase as an altar mensa (see chapter VII), and a cross which stood close to the chapel and was sketched *in situ* by Borlase (fig. 19); both these objects are now at Camborne parish church, and serve to indicate a 10th-century starting point. The well itself, now disappeared, may have been ascribed to St. Ia some centuries before this, as was mentioned above. The chapel stood in a little enclosure, like a lan, but no burials were located and there is no direct evidence that they took place there. Arthur Langdon, from a source which he does not cite, believed that the chapel was finally destroyed about 1780, by which time the *Leuiut* slab had been taken to Camborne churchyard, and the cross may have been moved at this period. All trace of the chapel, which had become covered with soil to a depth of some feet, was lost, and almost all tradition about it, until the writer and his brother, following Dr. Borlase's notes, re-discovered it in 1962.

The 'Newton' confusion and the fragments from Brea

St. Ia's chapel stands on the *east* bank of the un-named stream which flows from Troon down the Reens valley to Pendarves, and though Dr. Borlase (fig. 19) describes the cross beside it as being on Troon or Chitoden Moor, it is actually not on Chytodden (the *west* bank of the stream) at all, but on the former tenement of Newton, now called Troon Farm (Mr. Jenkins). Newton was so called in 1420 and represents an early intake of the croft lying west of Troon; the present 'Newton Road' from Troon to Beacon commemorates it. Unfortunately there is another 'Newton', over a mile to the east, which contains Newton Moor, an area of marshy croft on the Camborne-Illogan boundary, through which the Red River flows on its way from Bolenowe Moors to Tuckingmill. This Newton, which in a sense is closer to Troon than to any other centre of population, has a customary well (now enclosed) of some age and local fame, and higher up, at Bolenowe, there is a 'Vincent's Well' (p.120) which, like Fenton-Ia, has alleged medicinal properties.

This offers ripe ground for confusion, and confusion there certainly has been. Though both Arthur Adams and A. G. Langdon (in 1890, 1897, and 1906) seem to have realised that the *Leuiut* altar slab, and thus the (St. Ia's) chapel, belonged to the Newton at Troon (p.102) and not the other, eastern Newton, others were less percipient. The late James Thomas, a local postman-antiquary, started the story (subsequently repeated about once every five years in local guides and newspaper articles) that St. *James'* chapel had stood on *Newton* Moor—by attaching the un-located 'St. James' (actually Treslothan) to the un-named chapel at 'Newton' (actually St. Ia's) and re-locating this hybrid at the wrong Newton. Even Charles Henderson wavered between Vincent's Well near Newton Moor, and the supposed holy well at Newton (Troon), as the true identification of Borlase's 'Fenton-Er', and such local guides as *The Story of Camborne Parish*

Church (by Douglas E. Morton, Rector: 1936) stated (*ibidem*, p.10) that the ancient chapels of Camborne included '. . . St. James (which stood on Newton Moor in 1473)'.

What has long been regarded as confirmation of this mis-identification was provided in a letter written by James Thomas in 1921, in a correspondence about the *Leuiut* stone[47]:

'About ten years ago, whilst taking down an old cottage at Bray village, a little more than a mile from Newton, workmen found in the walls of the cottage granite arches and pillars, window mullions, and a stoup. The late Mr. T. C. Peter secured the arches and pillars and took them to Redruth, but the stoup and a part of the mullion of the window is with me, and I trust that the time is not far distant when the discovery of the font will be made.'

The rest of the letter makes it clear that these remains were regarded as coming from a former chapel (converted into a cottage, like Chapel Idne at Sennen Cove?), which was to be identified with the chapel at Newton (rightly, Newton by Troon, and *not* Newton (Moor) within a mile of Bray or Brea village) from which the Leuiut slab had originated. Only in recent years has any light been thrown on this most interesting letter. The stoup (fig. 25, A, and see p.116) is now in the museum at Camborne; the 'part of the mullion' and the 'arches' cannot be traced, but Mr. Michael Tangye has now located what seem to be the two pillars in a garden in Redruth, within a short distance of the house where Thurstan C. Peter lived.

Now all these fragments may very well have come from some early medieval chapel at Brea, converted in post-Reformation times into a cottage, but this is well inside the parish of Illogan, and can have nothing to do with Camborne, still less with either St. James' chapel at Treslothan, or with St. Ia's at Newton, Troon. On 24th June 1449, an indulgence was issued to all persons frequenting, and contributing to the upkeep of, the chapels of St. John the Baptist, St. John the Evangelist, and St. Constantine, in the parish of Illogan[48]. These sound like free chapels in a large and sparsely-populated parish, and the potential sites of free chapels (whose dedications have not survived) are known within Illogan from Nance, Nancekuke, and, on the evidence given here, Brea. The Brea remains ought to be those of one of the three mentioned in 1449[49]. It is to be hoped, however, that the foregoing account finally disposes of any lingering belief in a chapel on 'Newton Moor', in 1473 or at any other time.

NOTES

1. Undated cutting from *WDM*, 1921.
2. *PZNHAS* (*n.s.*) III (1888-92), 206.
3. Gilbert 1817, III, 694.
4. *Revelation* chap. I, v. 4 ('John to the seven churches which are in Asia').
5. Hunt, 1871, 199.
6. By an odd coincidence, the writer of this book (as an undergraduate of this College) had rooms for two years on the site of Bull Hall; probably the first Camborne man to do so for centuries.
7. The pedigree, from William Mertherderwa (d.1306), occurs in Vivian's *Visitations of Cornwall* (1887), 31, from Brit. Mus. Harleian MS. 4031.

8. C.*meneghy*, 'sanctuary' (from *managh*, pl. *menegh*, 'monk'), has a penultimate stress and usually gives 'Manhay' or 'Mennaye' in place-names; it seems unlikely here.
9. English version, *WA II* (1889), 130; Latin transcript, from original in *Registr. Cancellarii Oxon.*, 1447/8 Feb. 11, fol. 60, *penes* Henderson MSS, RIC.
10. It may have been licensed as such, but before the commencement of the surviving Registers of the Bishops of Exeter (1257).
11. Stephens 1925.
12. Not at British Museum, RIC, or Penzance Library; uncertain where the compilers of *Bib. Cornub.* saw it.
13. Cited in Doble 1934, 40.
14. Henderson, *JRIC* (*n.s.*) II.3 (1955), 69.
15. Deed of conveyance *penes* RIC, Truro (Henderson colln.).
16. Carah 1927, 8.
17. Stephens 1925.
18. The lane called *Bounder Vean* (see fig. 26), running from the east side of the churchyard, through the back of Basset Road and Lowenac Gardens to Pendarves Road.
19. Stephens 1925.
20. CCG, 120.
21. Though of course in Anglian Northumbria one does find this as early as Bede's time (late 7th and 8th centuries A.D.), e.g. at Bridlington and Jervaulx.
22. Henderson MSS., RIC (*Topography of Penwith*).
23. MS. Russell; cf. Carah 1927, 10.
24. Formerly occupied by a Mr. Gardiner; now entirely demolished.
25. In the *Cornish Almanack*, Camborne Printing Co., Camborne, 1932 issue, 112.
26. By Mr. Martin Weaver, of the G.L.C. Historic Buildings service, to whom the writer is most grateful for his help.
27. E. M. Jope, 'Cornish Houses, 1400-1700', in *Studies in Building History* (ed. Jope), Odhams Press Ltd. (1961), 199, fig. 10.3.
28. Jope, *op. cit.*, 201.
29. Thomas 1958, 28-30 and fig. 14.
30. Adams 1957, 31-32.
31. Henderson and Coates, *Old Cornish Bridges* (Exeter, 1928), 35, 103.
32. RHR Lacy, s.a.
33. RHR Lacy I. 46.
34. In *JRIC* (*n.s.*) II.3 (1955), 70 n.51.
35. Carah 1925, 43; 1927, 10.
36. Lanyon 1841, 111.
37. Drew 1824, II.144.
38. *Survey of Cornwall*, 1st edn. (1603), 55. In the previous century, David Pendarves of Crowan had been described as 'David John Rawe, alias Pendarves, Gent'. (*per* T. R. Harris).
39. 3G TUD UK 209 pt.1, run A-11, pair 5704-5 of 15 May 1946.
40. Henderson 1935, 83.
41. CCG 160.
42. Doble 1926.
43. Given in Polsue-Lake. IV supplement, 98.
44. *Ibidem.*, 72-3.
45. E.g., St. Uny at Lelant, St. Ia at St. Ives, St. Sithney at Sithney.
46. As will be seen in fig. 14, the chapel enclosure, and the ruins which may represent a priest's cell, practically touch Reens Rock.
47. Undated cutting, *WDM*, late in 1921.
48. Cited by Henderson, *JRIC* (*n.s.*) III.2 (1958), 227.
49. Mr. Tangye kindly informs the writer further (September, 1966), that he has located a 'Church Field' at Brea on Doidge's 1737 Map of Tehidy (CRO, Truro); this may prove to be the original chapel site to which these remains refer.

V

THE EXCAVATION OF ST. IA'S CHAPEL

The site of this chapel, whose rediscovery was briefly recorded a few years ago[1], is a sheltered position in the little wooded valley which commences just below the playing field at Troon, and runs westward about a mile to Pendarves park. The valley, or rather the Troon end of it, is known as 'The Reens' (C. *ryn*, 'slope'), and a small stream runs its whole length, feeding the ornamental lake at Pendarves. The present abundant cover of deciduous trees and shrubs dates only from the nineteenth century; prior to this, the valley was quite open, with occasional small plots on its flanks, and further down there were not only various tin-stream stamps, but also a now-forgotten farm (Chingwith).

At the point where the chapel lay (SW 65833815) only three fields away from the centre of Troon, there is a junction between the granite and a softer metamorphosed rock. Water action has cut down the latter, producing a step—this junction runs transversely across the valley—forming the 'cascade' which excited Borlase's attention (Appendix B) and throwing the massive carn of Reens Rock, actually the weathered front of the granite, into prominence. It is easy to see how a water-course, coming from the north across the old Newton tenement along this geological weakness, would have opened into the valley at this point, and this must be the basis of the natural spring called Fenton-Ia by Lhuyd and Borlase. The total disappearance of this spring is probably due to its diversion before the water reaches the valley, either by mining operations (Tolcarne or Wheal Grenville) or by a storm-water sewer from Troon which comes into the valley a short distance up the stream.

The remains encountered in 1962 were not very encouraging. Under a heavy cover of brambles, nettles, and young trees, all that could be seen was a roughly rectangular setting of tumbled stones. Only an outline plan could then be made[2]. It was assumed that these stones represented the basal courses of any chapel—as it happens, an erroneous assumption. At the west end of the remains there was a vertical drop of some feet into a narrow gully, which ran directly from the external west wall some twenty or thirty feet down to the stream-bed; and under the ferns it was possible to see that the vertical drop was due to a revetment wall of large stones set across the gully at this point, a wall on which the west end of the supposed chapel was resting.

The excavation

During the period from May to September 1966, excavation took place (averaging two or three whole or half-days a week) in connection with an extra-mural class at Truro, and was almost entirely undertaken by members of that class and by members of the Cornwall Archaeological Society

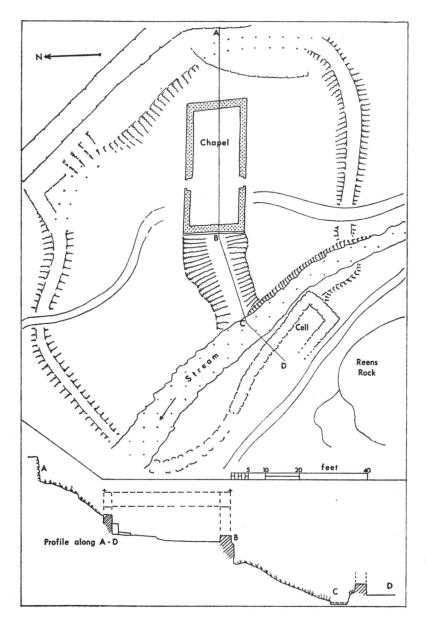

Fig. 14
Site-plan of St. Ia's Chapel, Troon, 1966, showing traces of a surrounding
'lan' and the Phase 3 (?) cell.

—to all of whom, as also to the tenant of the Reens, Mr. Williams (Chytodden), and the adjoining proprietor (Mr. Jenkins, Troon Farm, who kindly permitted access), the writer offers his most sincere thanks.

The site was cleared of all undergrowth, and after a preliminary cutting had been made, it transpired that far from being the foundation course the stones visible along the lines of the walls were really at a fairly high level, and that the east end of the chapel still stood to a height of some five feet. An extraordinary amount of soil had been washed down into the valley at this point, doubtless a by-product of cultivation of the Newton fields (which lie on a slight slope), and this, together with the partial collapse of the walls, had filled the whole interior of the chapel with three to four feet of compact debris.

In the end, it proved impossible with the available time and labour to excavate so large a site totally, but all the walls were exposed inside and out, over half the interior—ten feet at the east end and six at the west— was taken to the lowest level, the exterior surrounds adequately explored, and ample evidence so obtained to establish the sequence satisfactorily. Three major phases are represented.

Phase 1: the earliest well-chapel

The site rests on the side of the valley, and is consequently on a slight slope (see profile, fig. 14). At a depth of six to seven feet below the present level of the west end, dry-stone walls of a crude and massive build were encountered, resting immediately on 'rab', the moist and usually ferruginous gravel layer which represents the weathered surface of the bedrock and which, all over Cornwall, indicates the undisturbed bottom of any digging. These heavy walls were encountered all round the west end of the site, and define a roughly rectangular area (see fig. 15, top); the south wall is about five feet thick, and the west wall is probably thicker still, the north wall being a little slighter than the south. There was no sign of any remaining east wall, but the rise of the ground eastward implies that one may not have been necessary. Without destroying all the later walls above them, which would have been undesirable, it was not feasible to examine these lowest walls in all parts, but it seems probable that they have crude stone faces and a packed earth and rubble core.

Fig. 15, top, shows what was found, with tentative lines of reconstruction. The configurations of the ground surface suggest that the water constituting the Fenton-Ia 'holy well' would have issued forth approximately in the centre of a rectangular enclosure, internally 9 feet N-S and perhaps 6 feet (?) E-W, externally of the order of 19 feet by 14.

It is difficult to see these foundations as a conventional well-chapel, though the north-south axis—here dictated by the nature of the ground— does not of itself rule out a chapel as such[3]. The most likely explanation is that this rectangular setting represents the *lower* portion (not entirely visible, and therefore not particularly neatly built) of a two-stage structure, the lower foundations containing the actual well, the waters of which must have flowed through or under the west wall and down the gully into the stream. The upper story, carried on a wooden floor, with slighter stone

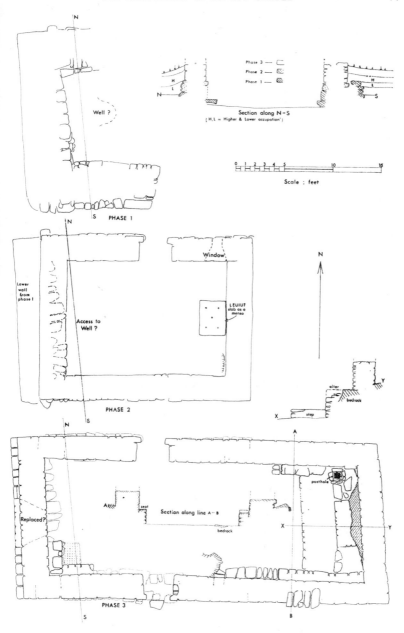

Fig. 15
St. Ia's Chapel, Troon; the three main phases, from the 1966 excavations.

walls of (say) 2 feet 6 inches width, or even a wholly timber superstructure, would have constituted the actual chapel, with access to the well through the floor, and—though this must be conjectural—an entrance on the north side and an altar on the south, resting on the inner half of the underlying south wall foundation. This should be compared with the plan of what is probably the oldest surviving pre-Norman well-chapel in Cornwall, St. Constantine's in St. Merryn parish[4]. In a much grander vein and admittedly much later (the 15th century), the two-stage well-chapel of St. Winifred's at Holywell, Flint, may serve as an instance of this pattern[5]. There were no small finds attributable to this phase.

Phase 2: the early chapel

In the second phase, any such superstructure was removed, and the foundation walls levelled off at a height which, on the west side, was internally three feet. Large stones—these have been lightly indicated in fig. 15, centre—were then laid across the top of this wall to carry the lowest course of a new, slighter, west wall; and on the south side much the same happened, except that the new wall was perched on the inner part of the early south wall. This relationship is shown in the profile, fig. 15, top right.

It is probable that the space forming the interior of the Phase I substructure, the actual area round the holy well, was maintained in some fashion. This area was found in the course of the excavation to have been filled with massive rocks and loose soil, but the filling seems on balance more likely to be a feature of the final phase 3.

The resultant Phase 2 building was a neat, well-built one, internally of the order of 11 ft. 9 inches N-S and 16 ft. 6 ins. E-W. The walls, though not regularly coursed, were made of both granite and metamorphosed rock, set to a fair face externally and internally in packed earth or stream-bed clay with numerous little spalls. The doorway is on the north side, and is defined by two large granite slabs, which form the lower parts of the jambs, the eastern one being slightly recessed to take the door-frame, and the outer faces of both dressed flat by irregular hammering or tooling. The upper part of the doorway was probably built with smaller stones brought to a straight edge, and was subsequently covered with a fine mortar or plaster, which was itself competently finished to give a neat, sharp right-angle. Similar hard white plaster, but with the angle chamfered, was found outside at a low level some feet to the east, suggesting that a small (square-headed?) window existed in the north wall near the north-west corner. Fig. 16, top, shows a reconstruction (north aspect) based on this evidence.

The slates used for the roof, large quantities of which were found, were small, mostly of a grey-green shade with iron staining and rarely with dendritic manganese. This suggests a source in the Godrevy area at Gwithian, a few miles away, where exactly similar slate can still be hacked out of the low cliffs. Pottery ridge-tiles or 'crests' were used for the ridge, and these (cf. fig. 17, A.B.) indicate that the roof may have been fairly low—a pitch of 33 to 35 degrees, locally called 'third pitch'—and perhaps carried on simple collar-beam framing.

A large number of sherds occurred, in the doorway and outside it, and also on the south side, in the lower of the two stratified 'occupation' deposits which were found both north and south of the chapel complex. The bulk of these belonged to small, coarse, occasionally hand-made cooking-pots of a variety recently defined by the writer, and called by him 'Sandy Lane style', after the type-site of that name a few miles away in the parish of Gwithian[6]. They offer good dating evidence, and will be discussed below.

Phase 3: the later chapel

In this phase—the evidence suggests within a comparatively short interval after phase 2—the chapel was considerably enlarged. The east wall was removed, and the side walls continued eastward a further fourteen to fifteen feet. In so doing, a snag was encountered. The old east wall had rested, at its southern end, on bedrock—indeed, in the old south-east inner corner, a protruding knob of bedrock had previously been cut down —and the new eastern extension, running back into the side of the valley, soon encountered the bedrock at a higher level. This fact was turned to some advantage, as a ridge of bedrock was used as the base of the new east wall, and its protrusion into the chapel was cut flat, like a ledge, at the height corresponding to the level on which the mensa of the altar would now rest.

At the west end, the wall was extended 2 feet at the south-west corner and 3 feet at the north-west. But this extension was an elaborate one. The whole gully was widened to about 17 feet, and a revetment wall built right across it, resting on the rab. It seems probable that this revetment was really a re-facing, or tidying-up, of the old outer face of the lower storey of the phase 1 well-surround, and was thus not obliged to take, suddenly, what would otherwise have been an enormous downhill thrust. The revetment was carried up to a height of four feet, and at this level, a course of carefully chosen and (to some extent) shaped stones was laid, forming a rough but effective plinth or apron-course, stepping the new west wall back some nine inches. The plinth does not exhibit the same regularity the whole way across, and an irregular area in the central six feet, which seems to have been replaced, strongly suggests that a recess or doorway, perhaps a true arch, perhaps square-headed, was included here, to frame the outflow of the water, and to permit access (to an uncertain depth) to the holy well.

Above the plinth, which represents the floor-level of this Phase 3 enlargement, the walls rose in a superior fashion. Much of the phase 2 wall seems to have been stripped to the lowest two or three courses, and the whole chapel then re-built, this time using not merely whatever stone happened to be available, but to a predominant extent horizontally-laid blocks and slabs of granite, with a deliberate aim of regular horizontal courses. On the north side, one such massive slab, five feet long and a foot high, must have been the original lintel of the north door, and the grey-green phase 2 roofing slates were now widely employed as spalls.

The old north doorway was not blocked, though its upper part must have been re-built; but a new doorway was made approximately opposite it on the south side (see fig. 16, centre; reconstruction of the south elevation). This south doorway is slightly splayed, is checked just inside the jambs to take the wooden door-frame, and has a doorstep outside; though the basal level of the doorway is the phase 2 chapel foundation running through beneath it. A window was made near the east end of the south wall, to light the altar—this may be a slightly later addition—and its sill was carried on four slabs set across the wall and protruding outwards a little. Fragments of worked granite found inside the chapel here show that it was a simple two-light window with chamfered jambs and mullion, the glass being set in a diamond-pattern lead framing (pieces of this framing were also recovered).

The east end is rather complex. Originally, a masonry block was built up from the floor, in front of the bedrock ledge, to complete the altar; and two side benches, about a foot wide and nineteen inches high, ran from the inner corners some eight or nine feet westward (see fig. 15, lower, profile along A-B). Later—not necessarily very much later—the easternmost six feet became a raised chancel, with a low step built across the east end and the ground east of it raised with stone and rammed gravel (see fig. 15, profile along X-Y). A little platform, some six inches high, was then added on the south side of the altar. On the north side, there is a similar partial platform, abutting on to a large post-socket. This socket, which contained clear traces of having held a squared upright (? timber) about 6 ins. across, may itself have necessitated the removal of the eastern end of the north-side bench.

In the south-west inner corner, where the basal flat course of the phase 2 chapel was apparently also at the new floor level, another small side bench was constructed, with a little L-shaped extension on the south wall, and the front faces of these benches were plastered, the plaster being carried down to an area on the floor (stippled in fig. 15, lower). The west end had in this phase been filled up with large granite slabs and soil to the general internal floor level and there is no sign of any internal access to the holy well. Indeed, the postulated *external* access (above) through some kind of arch cannot have been a success; it either collapsed or was removed, and its place in both the revetment and the plinth above taken by some notably inferior stonework[7].

Other features of the phase 3 chapel include ridge-tiles of a slightly different pattern (fig. 17, C,D,E), including an unique example with a small free-standing cross modelled on it, which may have come from the centre of the roof; some vague evidence that the north doorway may have possessed a small external porch, with a little transverse slate- and ridge-tile roof and guttering (a cast-iron gutter bracket with internal lead-sulphide deposit was found here); a higher roof than in the phase 2 chapel, the ridge-tiles indicating a pitch more like 45 degrees, with the use of a very large quantity of slates (over three thousand would have been needed) of a blue-grey kind, which may be local[8] but is not the phase 2 Godrevy slate; the employment of a different kind of white plaster, now using shell-sand instead of crushed limestone as the calcareous element[9];

and the use of white lime-wash. This lime-wash was particularly noticeable, from collapsed areas of it found on the floor, on the internal east wall, and the inner south-west corner. In both places, the lime-wash had been painted, using a restricted palette of very dark grey, blue-grey, orange, a deep red, a salmon-pink, and a dull yellow ('mustard'); some areas of painting had subsequently been re-washed in white, and this outer wash had to be removed painstakingly with a scalpel. The designs cannot, from such small fragments, be reconstructed with any certainty, but seem to have been floral or geometric rather than anything as exciting as figure scenes[10].

Inside and outside—predominantly outside, and on the south—the upper of the two 'occupation' levels produced many hundreds of sherds, most of them common types of wheel-made cooking-pots, chronologically later than the phase 2 'Sandy Lane' vessels.

Dating

In the absence of direct evidence, it is not easy to determine when the phase 1 structure was built, The very crudity of its construction removes the normal clues to be derived from masonry and lay-out. However, one can make an informed guess by association. The cross, seen and drawn here *in situ* by Borlase, probably on the north side of the whole complex, can rather loosely be assigned to the 10th century (p.90); and this is also the period to which one can place the original face of the *Leuiut* slab (p.106), which seems on all the evidence to have come from this particular site, with the proviso that either the slab is a little earlier than the cross, or that they have a common date in the generation *circa* 950 A.D. An altar-frontal must imply an altar and thus a chapel, so the superstructure is unlikely to have been any later than this; the sub-structure may be earlier, but on balance seems most likely to be linked with the enclosure bank (see below) which again is not likely to be any later than the standing cross that must have marked its principal entrance (as, for example, at Merther Uny, showing in fig. 9).

The phase 2 chapel presents rather more in the way of clues. The associated pottery is both abundant and diagnostic. The 'Sandy Lane' series consists of three consecutive styles, which represent in west Cornwall the transition, in terms of perhaps the commonest kind of kitchen vessel, from the old post-Roman 'grass-marked' cooking-pot (shown in fig. 8) to the medieval English type with everted rim and sagging base[11]. Phase 2 here lacks the Style 1 of Sandy Lane, and the earliest pots are all Style 2, combining both the final grass-marked base and the incipient everted rim, a class which may be dated to the period A.D. 1100-1150[12]. This date is borne out by the coarse hand-made ridge tile (fig. 17, A) with its high hand-moulded peaks, which should be 12th century[13], and, like the fact that the north doorway is checked back internally for the door-frame, really rules out an 11th-century date. The Sandy Lane pottery, and probably also the use of fine white plaster to outline the north doorway and the supposed north window, an architectural device of Saxon origin, prohibit anything as late as the 13th century. Finally there is the question of the re-use of the Leuiut slab as a *mensa*, with its five consecration crosses bunched together toward the centre, an abnormal placing which does occur elsewhere in Cornwall on two mensae (Tintagel and Tywardreath, see p.109) that should be regarded as twelfth-century in date. If, as seems most probable, this re-use of the slab coincides with the initiation of the phase 2 chapel as a place of worship, then all the evidence taken together points to the period A.D. 1100-1150—perhaps, more closely, 1125-1150— as the date for this chapel's construction.

Phase 3 also offers a number of indications. It is post-1150 and pre-Reformation, and from its irregular ground plan and comparative coarseness of masonry, should belong to an early stage of these intervening centuries. The plinth, clearly an imitation from some larger model like a church, suggests the early part of the 13th century; the same century is also indicated by the roof-tiles (fig. 17, C, D) which are devolved versions of fig. 17, A, but obviously not far away, and still unglazed with hand-moulded peaks. The pottery includes small necked jugs in a thin red ware, a type known elsewhere in the area[14] and probably the second half of the 13th century, but also wheel-made cooking-pots of Sandy Lane style 3 type, which seem to have been current about 1150-1250. Finally there is the question of the phase 3 altar (see fig. 15, lower). Its exact size is preserved by the masonry base and the *Leuiut* slab cannot have been used, either as frontal or mensa. What must be fragments of the mensa—a slab of white, fine-grained granite about 3 inches thick, with neat diagonal dressing—were found, and these include a large corner piece which is plain on both surfaces. An unconsecrated mensa of these dimensions, 30 by 56 inches, falls within a class which in Cornwall belongs to the first half of the 13th century (p.110). Phase 3 is therefore, on the evidence outlined above, to be ascribed to the period A.D. 1200—1250. None of the pottery in the upper occupation layer appears to be later than c.1400, which covers the period suggested by the insertion of the two-light mullion in the south wall (? after, rather than before, 1300) and the replacement of the opening in the west wall.

Function
    The three phases distinguished above need not all have seen their successive structures performing the same role. The earliest well-chapel was, presumably, a chapel and not merely a well-covering, if only because of the supposed use of the *Leuiut* slab in this phase as an altar frontal. The total absence of any domestic remains, like pottery, of the period *circa* 950-1100—and Cornwall is one of the few areas outside the Saxon regions where the pottery sequence for this period is known[15]—rules out any idea of a resident priest. If this were a chapel, then it was a shrine visited only on such occasions as feasts. The cross, and the enclosure bank shown in fig. 14, imply that the site had been set aside, however, as ecclesiastical property.
    In phase 2, we see what may be a chapel in regular use, a chapel which possessed (like the Madron well-chapel of much the same date[16]) an internal holy well, but which, judging from the pottery, was staffed by

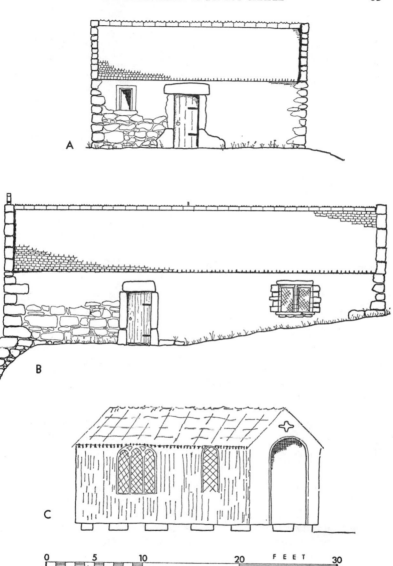

Fig. 16
(A), St. Ia's Chapel, phase 2, the north elevation reconstructed; (B), the
same, phase 3, south elevation reconstructed; (C) the only known medieval
depiction of a medieval Cornish chapel, from Dr. Borlase's 1740 drawing of
a lost wall-painting in Ludgvan Church (see JRIC IV (1872), p.50, illus.).

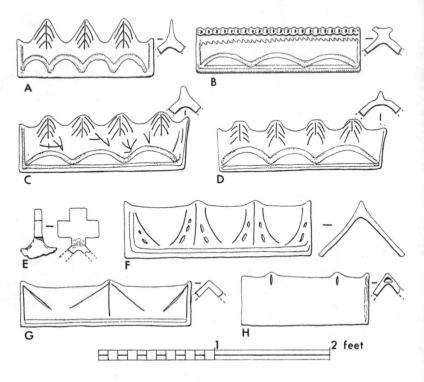

Fig. 17
'Crests' or ridge-tiles from Cornwall. (*A*), *St. Ia's Chapel, phase 2 (12th cent.); (B), (C), (D), (E), the same, phase 3, 13th or 14th centuries; (F), Crane Manor, 15th or 16th centuries; (G), roof of Gwithian church tower, 17th century (?); (H), from a site at Gwithian, 17th or 18th centuries.*

one or more clerics, had its own consecrated altar, and may have had living-cells within the enclosure; though no trace of the latter could be found. As at St. Derwa's chapel, Menadarva, where the font is of the same period as Phase 2 (p.114), this may be an instance of an outlying chapel within the parish which has been rebuilt or refurbished to serve as a chapel of ease.

In the final phase, this is even clearer. It has become necessary to enlarge the whole structure, doubtless to accommodate an increase of worshippers; the rebuilding could have been carried out by local labour, but the ridge-tiles and slates must have been purchased, possibly from a distance; the interior of the chapel boasts wall-painting, common enough in Cornish churches but excessively rare in mere chapels[17]; and there is some evidence for a little cell (shown in fig. 14) on the other bank of the stream, where preliminary clearance revealed stray sherds of 13th-century type. This all bespeaks regular, and regulated, use as a chapel of ease; and one suspects that the Petit or Petyt family, as lords of Treslothan, may have borne the cost of the reconstruction, and may indeed have obtained an episcopal licence for a chapel of ease from Exeter[18]. The joint licence for Divine Service here and at Menadarva issued in 1429 by Bishop Lacy was not, like the licence of 1427 for St. James' chapel, Treslothan, issued specifically to 'John Petyt', and may be no more than a confirmation of the position of two ancient free chapels at opposite ends of the parish.

Nothing is really known of the later history and desertion of the site. The removal of the *Leuiut* stone, and the large cross, are elsewhere discussed (pp.80,101). Borlase in 1750 cannot have seen much beyond ruins, even if the well was still flowing down the gully from under the west wall, and Langdon's date of *circa* 1780 for some final demolition may be correct, if it refers to stone-robbing; but the volume of soil and stones covering the site does suggest that use of this chapel, as a chapel, is not likely to have survived the Reformation.

NOTES

1. *CA* 2 (1963), 77.
2. *Ibidem*, fig. 23 (by Mr. P. J. Fowler and the writer).
3. Cf. St. Constantine's well-chapel, lying due N-S.
4. Report, with plans, by Penrose Williams, *Proceedings of the Society of Antiquaries of London*, 2nd ser., XXIV (1911-12), 96.
5. *Roy. Comm. Anc. Monts., Wales & Monm.; Flint* (1912), no. 126.
6. *CA* 3 (1964), 48, 56, figs. 17, 18. This is now known from some half-dozen sites in west Cornwall.
7. Some of this again collapsed in 1964, and was re-built by the writer, using the same stones and in the same style.
8. E. M. Jope and G. C. Dunning, 'The use of blue slate for roofing in medieval England,' *Ant. J.* XXXIV (1954), 209-217. One feels that some local west Cornish quarry is here inherently more probable as a source than the north coastal (Delabole) area.
9. Analyses by Miss E. M. Rule and the writer; there are four kinds of plaster, two of phase 2, two of phase 3.
10. Summary of wall-paintings in Cornish churches: *JRIC.* XV (1902), 141 ff.
11. Cf. note 6 above.
12. *CA* 3 (1964), 50; cf. also Dunning on the St. Helen's, Scilly, equivalents (*Arch. J.* CXXXI (1964), fig. 5, nos. 1-6, and p.59—from 'c.1100 in round figures' to 'the end of the 12th century').
13. Dunning, *op. cit.* note 12, fig. 8, shows a similar one from St. Helen's. The dating of the numerous regional series of these ridge-tiles is still insecure, partly because it is unusual (as here) to recover anything like complete specimens.
14. Cf. *CA* 3 (1964), 50, 58, fig. 19.
15. Final bar-lug pottery until *c.*1000 or later; Sandy Lane style 1, a type with straight, 'pre-everted', rim, may originate far back in the grass-marked series but is most widely current in the 11th century.
16. Its altar is of 12th-century type: see p.108 below.
17. An example is the elaborate fourteenth-century two-storey domestic chapel at Earth Barton, near Saltash: Jope in *Studies in Building History* (ed. E. M. Jope), 1961, 202.
18. The surviving Registers (as printed, see RHR) commence only from 1257 and would thus be too late for the postulated date.

VI

EARLY CROSSES

The parish of Camborne contains a wide selection of the stone crosses which characterised both the early Christian and the medieval periods in the Cornish countryside. In the account which follows, each cross (or, where the cross has been lost, cross site) is allotted a number, and these numbers are repeated both in the captions to the relevant illustrations, and on the location map (fig. 18). This map shows the earliest recorded position of each cross, regardless of its present whereabouts. The chapter concludes with a short discussion of the various functions which these, and similar, crosses are generally considered to have performed.

1 The Churchyard Cross (pl. IV)

Only the head of this now remains; it is of worn, rather coarse, granite, 1 ft. 7 ins. high and 1 ft. 7½ ins. wide. It is built into the exterior face of the east wall of the south chancel of the parish church. Its thickness is consequently unknown, but a rough pencil-sketch made about 1860 or so by J. T. Blight[1], if one can base an estimate on this, suggests no great thickness—perhaps five inches. Langdon[2] regarded the end of the upper arm as having been deliberately worked concave; if so, a unique feature, as he pointed out. Thurstan Peter thought this 'concavity' was the result of injury and wear, not of design[3], and a careful examination shows that this is more probable.

In 1890, Arthur Adams, who was then Vicar of Tuckingmill, and a former curate of Camborne, told a party of antiquarian visitors[4]:

'There was . . . a granite cross head, once lying outside the church, now built into the eastern wall of the new south aisle. I remember the amusement of the architect' (Piers St. Aubyn) 'at the proposal of the builder to re-cut this, and thus, as he said, to turn it into a new cross.'

The base of this cross is quite flat and regular, which implies that it was either tenoned into or mortared on to the flat top of a simple shaft. It is most probable that the whole cross stood somewhere on the south side of the church, the side where the principal entrance seems to have been prior to about 1800 (see p.154). The base in which this cross stood is almost certainly that which now holds cross no. 2 (below). The now-obscured reverse face was in all likelihood a repetition of the visible front, an expanded-armed 'Greek' cross in low relief. There is a very similar cross, complete, in the churchyard at Gwinear[5]. If the cross was, as seems most likely, a *churchyard cross* (p.98), it should date from the time when the original parish church was built (in the 12th century?).

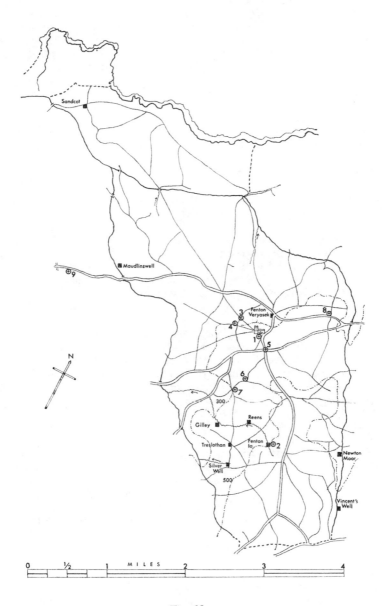

Fig. 18
Camborne parish, showing original locations of early crosses (numbered as in chap. VI), and holy wells (black squares, named as in chap. IX).

2   St. Ia's Cross (pl. III and fig. 19)

This handsome granite cross now stands outside the main south porch of Camborne parish church, in a cross-base which does not belong to it— it seems to be that of cross no. 1 above—and which is not *in situ*[6], as the photograph in pl. III makes clear. The base must have been in the church-yard, however[7], and is itself not without some interest. There is an iron staple let into one corner of it, with a couple of links of hand-forged iron chain still attached. T. C. Peter was told[8] that at one time the parish stocks had been chained to this. In his old age, Arthur Adams was able to recall rather more detail of this tradition. 'There are no stocks at Camborne now (1925)' he wrote, 'but there is still in the churchyard an iron ring attached to a cross-base, now carrying an old cross from Crane. This ring used to secure the old stocks, and when I was curate of Camborne nearly 50 years ago, I was told by an old inhabitant that any man found drunk on Saturday night was placed in the stocks on Sunday morning and left there until after morning service, that he might be seen by people going to morning church[9]'.

The cross itself has a complex and mysterious history. The record commences with Dr. Borlase's visit to Fenton-Ia chapel and holy well at Troon, about 1750. The cross then stood '. . . a few paces distant' (from the holy well) and '. . . about 3 yds.' from the wall of the chapel (Appendix B). 'The Cross is very singular' Borlase wrote, and he drew it, together with its dimensions (total height 7 ft. 7 ins.), showing what was probably the southern face (fig. 19).

After 1750, the cross disappears from view, and is next encountered in July of 1896 (just too late for inclusion in A. G. Langdon's survey). It was then discovered by a Mr. Joseph Holman, a member of the old Camborne Students' Association, serving as a side-member of a well-head at Crane— just outside the line of the medieval yard-wall (fig. 11, D)—and with the iron supports of the windlass fixed into it. A short illustrated account in the magazine *Black and White*, for 1896, states that 'A few days since a blacksmith engaged in examining the ironwork on a well noticed some marks on one of the stones. On clearing it away he found the stone was one of those old crosses so frequent in Cornwall . . . etc.' The cross was exhumed, taken to the churchyard, and set up in the convenient cross-base there. As pl. III shows, part of the head had been trimmed or broken, and the base of the cross is also mutilated (this does not now show).

The late Charles Henderson was the first person to realise[10] that this cross found at Crane was identical with that sketched by Borlase in 1750 at Troon. Why, and precisely when, this large and heavy object was removed from Troon to Crane, and on whose initiative; whether it ever stood upright at Crane, and if so how it came by such an ignominious fate, are questions to which there seem no obvious answers.

Some seven feet of the cross now show above the base. The reverse side has a head like that on the front, but the shaft is much worn and of little interest, bearing no more detail than two parallel lines or grooves four inches apart running down the centre (judging by pl. III, this face was

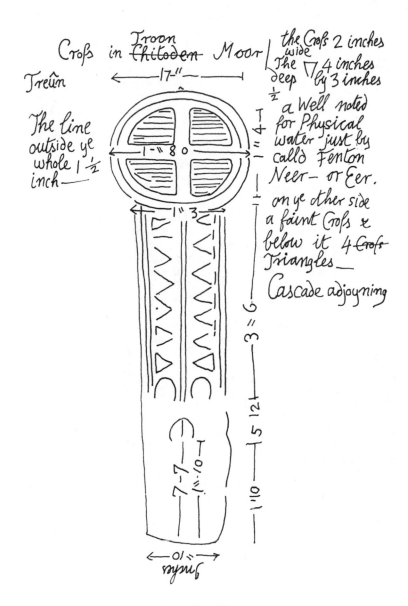

Fig. 19
William Borlase's sketch of the 'large Crane Cross' (no. 2) in situ besides St. Ia's Chapel, Troon, in 1750.

uppermost when the cross was unearthed in 1896). The front of the cross is of some complexity, as Borlase's sketch (fig. 19) shows. The following précis is taken from Thurstan C. Peter's account[11], written soon after the cross had been found again:

'Wheel cross at top; projections at neck. Bold ridge runs down one side of shaft and no doubt there was once a ridge down the other side also. Down the centre of the shaft, a straight incised groove. To the right of the groove, a bold zigzag, two interlaced circles, and below them some plaited design. To the left of the groove, what appears to me to be an incised figure (probably *not* Christ), standing on a shield, bottoms of legs of figure extending to just opposite lowest of holes' (i.e. made for the iron well-hand) 'shown in the illustration. The shield has below it two interlaced circles, similar to those above, and beneath them again more interlaced pattern. Above the figure, something I am quite unable to make out.'

Anyone inspecting the actual cross will be far from able to agree that all this is now visible, or indeed may ever have been. One can however make out the ornament as drawn by Borlase.

The cross belongs to a small and localised class, combining simple equal-armed crosses in sunken fields on the circular heads with decorated shafts bearing so-called 'sunk chevron' ornament (T. C. Peter's 'zigzag') and a variety of curvilinear motifs. The others are (page numbers as in Langdon 1896); Clowance no 3, formerly at a cross-roads by the southeast tip of Camborne parish (329), Helston no. 3, formerly by Trelill Holy Well in Wendron (331), and the rather superior Scorrier no. 2 (333) which once stood at a road junction at SW 72653395. This last bears, like the Crane cross, projections at the neck, a feature probably derived from a specialised treatment of the lower arm of a wheel-headed cross with a figure of Christ (e.g. Sancreed no. 4, 364, or Lanherne (formerly at Gwinear), 358). In west Cornwall this first appears in the mid-10th century. The Scorrier no. 2 cross and the Crane cross should be about this period, and the Clowance no. 3 and Helston no. 3 instances, which are more devolved, in the later part of the 10th century. In the case of the original siting at Fenton-Ia, this is very much the date for the chapel's foundation given by the *Leuiut* altar frontal (p.106). The last three crosses mentioned all originally stood within a few miles of each other and were probably the work of a single (Wendron?) craftsman.

3 The Institute Cross (*pl. IV*)

This stands today in the yard of the Literary Institute, Chapel Street, Camborne (visible from the pavement), in a base which appears to have belonged to cross no. 8, and which will be mentioned again below.

The cross formerly stood in the lane once known as 'Crane Drive', at a point where the old churchway path from Menadarva, Kehelland, and Treswithian crossed this lane and continued a short distance across the Glebe to the parish church (see map, fig. 18). Langdon wrote of it[12] 'Original site, not known', but in the next year, Thurstan Peter was able to say[13]:

'I have, as a result of an appeal through the *Cornish Post*' (the now-defunct Camborne newspaper) 'for information, obtained over-whelming evidence that the Institute Cross was formerly on the hedge of a field, once used for cricket, and on the west side of the road formerly the drive to Crane Manor House, opposite the stile leading to the parish church, and that it was removed from there about 30 years ago' (i.e., about 1870) 'and after lying in the yard of the Institute for some time, was at length erected in its present unsatisfactory position.'

The Camborne (Literary and Scientific) Institute is on record[14] as having possessed, in 1879, a library of 1,100 volumes and a museum containing some 400 'valuable and old specimens representing many different kinds of minerals and curiosities.' The removal of the cross from Crane Drive to the Institute's yard was thus doubtless undertaken for laudable, if perhaps misguided, antiquarian reasons (it should of course have been placed in the churchyard). The exact spot where the cross stood before removal, in the hedge of what today is called 'Crane Road', is given by the point of intersection of the old Crane Drive and the churchway path on the 1840 Tithe Map. The relevant field-names here were Higher and Lower Cross Close (nos. 1172, 1173). The churchway links the parish church to Menadarva (fig. 10) and reminds us that in 1447, Dr. Reginald Mertherderwa's will contained the following provision:

Volo quod sumptibus meis et expensis ordinentur et de novo exigantur nove cruces de lapidibus quales habentur in illis partibus in Cornubia incipiendo a Kayr Rescasek usque ad ecclesiam de Camborn et ponentur in locis ubi solebant corpora defunctorum portantorum ad sepulturam deponi pro orationibus fundendis ibidem et allevacione portancium . . .

'I wish that new crosses of stone, of the sort which they have in those parts of Cornwall, be ordered . . . and be newly set up, beginning at *Kayr Rescasek* and going as far as Camborne church; and that they be placed in those places where it has been the custom for the bodies of the dead, being carried to burial, to be set down, for the reciting of prayers and for the relief of the bearers.'

Apart from the considerable interest of this passage as showing the antiquity of this funeral custom, it is superficially very tempting to take this as a warrant for regarding the Institute cross as the last of this series. The cross, after all, stood on the churchway in question; the present writer has elsewhere shown quite conclusively that *Kayr Rescasek* is an earthwork in a field called *Gerrier* on Menadarva tenement[15]. There are objections. Firstly, we have no proof that this provision was ever carried out. Secondly, crosses of the mid-15th century would have been Gothic crosses of the lantern-headed kind[16]. The Institute Cross is patently both different and earlier. It seems more likely that crosses *had* once existed along this churchway—the phrases '*new* crosses' and '*newly* set up' seem to imply a pre-existing series—and if so, the Institute Cross would pre-sumably be one such. In that case, it could scarcely antedate the parish church, and would be 12th or 13th century. Again, its original stance was on the limit or boundary of the Glebe, a piece of land probably given to

the church by the lords of Tehidy at much the same date; and the cross
may thus be no more than a boundary cross for the church estate.

The cross is now only 2 ft. 7 ins. high, the circular head being 1 ft.
11 ins. across. One face bears a Latin cross within a bold beaded border,
the cross on a sunken field; the other has a crude and late figure of Christ
in a similar border. The so-called 'ears' or projections below the head
refer to a widening of the shaft, which is broken off just below this point,
and which apparently originally contained further ornament.

There is an interesting postscript. In 1924, Joseph Vivian (then in his
eighties, and living at St. Maradox Villa, Camborne) wrote a long letter
containing many of his early memories to Canon Carah. He stated in this
(see Appendix F):

'There was formerly . . . at Crane . . . a roadside cross, and a Mrs.
Dennis of Troon, who was born at Kehelland and used with her companions to go to school in the churchtown told me (some forty years
ago) that when they passed this cross they used to curtsey to it.'

4   The Small Crane Cross (pl. III)

This can now be found immediately inside the south door of Camborne
church, to the left as one enters, affixed to the floor. It is a plain rectangular
slab of rough granite, 2 ft. 2 ins. high and about 1 ft. 4 ins. wide. On one
face there is a plain Latin cross carved in relief (pl. III). An initial
attempt to carve another (similar?) cross on the other side seems to have
been abandoned, perhaps in despair at the texture of the stone.

It was found in 1896, also in the well-head at Crane, and immediately
below cross no. 2 above. Nothing else is known of its history. Presumably
at some stage it stood in a visible position at Crane, or may even have been
intended as an external feature of the chapel there (p. 62). Langdon[17]
shows some similar little crosses; but it must be stressed that, beyond a
general impression that these are medieval, and fall quite late in the
overall Cornish series, it is not really possible to date anything so simple
with any confidence.

5   The Camborne Cross (fig. 20)

The point where the main north-south trackway from Troon to Camborne church (down Camborne hill, over the level crossing at the station,
and down Cross Street) intersects one of the main east-west highways
across the parish (Trevenson Street and South Terrace) has long been
called 'Camborne Cross', a name not yet forgotten. This name refers, not
to the actual crossing of the roadways, but to the former presence of an
actual cross. In the 1840 Tithe Map, this is marked by three fields—no.
1717, Lower Cross Close, nos. 1724 and 1746, together called Higher
Cross Close—once part of the farmlands of Camborne Vean tenement.
Lower Cross Close is approximately where Messrs. Holman Bros.' works
now stands opposite the railway station.

The cross is said to have been taken down (it probably stood on the
hedge by the roadside) in the mid-19th century, when these fields were
developed for housing. It was removed, for safety, to the garden of
Trevu, Camborne, by Dr. George Smith. In 1935 his descendant Mr.

W. D. Tyack presented the cross to the town, and it stands today on a
modern base inside the north-east hedge of the Recreation Ground at
Camborne. A plaque commemorating this gift may be seen beside it.
This cross is now 2 ft. 7 ins high, the width of the head being 1 ft. 6 ins.
and of the shaft 1 ft. 3 ins. It is made of medium-coarse granite. One face
bears a Latin cross and the other an equal-limbed (Greek) cross with
slightly expanded arms and a central hollow[18]. This face resembles the
visible face of cross no. 1, and a similar date—the 12th or 13th century—
is probable.

6   The Kitty's Lane Cross   (fig. 20)

The cross now stands in Mr. W. D. Tyacks' garden at 4 Beacon Terrace,
Camborne, having been brought there some years ago from the garden at
Trevu (cf. no. 5). Langdon stated[19] that a Mr. W. Roberts, gardener at
Trevu, had told him that he found the cross in 1883. It was then said to
have been in a hedge of 'the old Roman road (sic) from Penzance to
London which runs at the back of these grounds'; i.e., the lane running
east from Baripper to Ramsgate, Little Pendarves, Killivose, and up the
hill to Beacon. In a footnote, Langdon adds that the same informant
told him that '. . . a small bronze image of the Madonna and Child was
found behind it.'

This, if true, would have been an association of no little interest.
Thurstan Peter probed this point, but found that the figure was not
bronze, but earthenware; that it was not discovered near this cross at all,
but with another one elsewhere; and that to take it for a Madonna and
Child '. . . requires a great deal of imagination'[20].

There seems little doubt that the original stance was the T-junction
where Kitty's Lane, now re-named Killivose Road, joins the 'old Roman
road' of Mr. W. Roberts. The field in the south-west angle of this junction,
part of Mr. John Eva's farm of Killivose, appears as 'Growsey' (no. 1625)
on the Tithe Map, a name formed from C. *an grows*, 'the cross' (*crows*).
Canon Carah also investigated this point[21] and concluded that 'the cross
had been dug out of a hedge in Kitty's Lane in 1883.'

The cross itself is 2 ft. 2 ins. high, the head being 1 ft. 6 ins. across. It is
made of a fine granite. One face bears a not quite equal-limbed cross in
low relief within a raised border. The other face bears the figure of Christ,
executed not in relief but in broad incised outline, a most unusual feature.

7   The Treslothan Cross   (pl. IV and fig 20)

About 1885 or so, S. T. Russell noted[22] in his scrap-book:
> 'At the cross-roads at Killavose in a wall there was to be seen until
> within the last ten years a small cross, something like a child with its
> arms extended. This I understand is taken to Pendarves.'

In 1880, a Mr. Nicholas Hare of Liskeard had published a sketch of
this cross in a magazine called *Illustrations*[23], showing it to be standing
on the top of a wall, built in so that only the head and a few inches of the
shaft were visible. It apparently fell down a few years later, and was removed to Pendarves and set up on the terrace in front of the mansion in

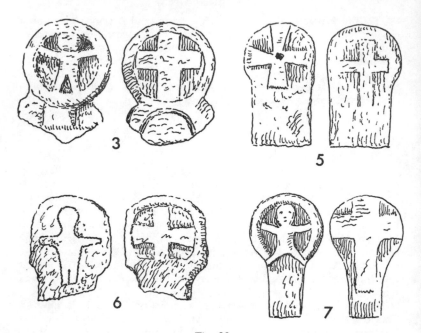

Fig. 20
Some early crosses from Camborne, after A. G. Langdon (1896), numbered
as in chap. VI; scale, one-twentyfourth actual size.

1888. In 1896, A. G. Langdon got into a muddle about this, largely
because of Hare's 1880 sketch and article. He apparently thought there
were *two* near-identical crosses, one being that shown by Hare, which he
called 'Treslothan cross' and which he regarded as having completely
disappeared, and the other being his 'Pendarves no. 1'. Of this, Langdon
wrote[24] that 'Mr. Pendarves informed me that this cross was found in a
ditch on his estate' and that it had been removed to Pendarves House for
its safety.

The confusion was not helped by the fact that Hare's sketch seems to
have been in some respects inaccurate. Thurstan Peter again came to the
rescue[25]:

'Many whom I have questioned on the subject remember a cross on
the wall at Killivose, many others not only remember its being there
but have no hesitation in recognising the one at Pendarves as the
same or at any rate exactly like it. Mr. Pendarves . . . replied to me
"I think the cross in the grounds here is the one you mention as it
comes from Killivose where it was lying in a ditch. I had it built into
a wall there, but it fell down, so I brought it here" (i.e., Pendarves
House). "I do not know where it originally stood." '

PLATE II

Blocked doorway of (?) Penpons Manor, now Ivy Cottage, Higher Penpons (p. 63). The relevant stones have been lightly outlined. (Photo: N. D. Thomas).

PLATE III

Above, left: cross no. 2, as discovered in 1896 (*Black and White*). Right: on its removal to Camborne churchyard. Below, left: as finally set up. Right: cross no. 4, found with it. (Photos: J. C. Burrow)

PLATE IV

Above, left: Treslothan cross (no. 7). Right: cross no. 1, in church wall. Below, left: Institute cross, back (no. 3). Right: present base of cross no. 2, showing chain for fastening parish stocks. (Photos: N. D. Thomas, and (below, left) Bennetts, Camborne)

PLATE V

Connor Downs cross, no. 9 (? 'Meane Cadoarth') in situ, *circa* 1890. (Photo: J. C. Burrow)

PLATE VI

Above: *Leuiut* slab, as set up in Camborne church about 1900 (Gibson, Penzance).
Below, left: former Camborne font, now in Treslothan church, and (right) font
in St. Ives parish church. (Photos: Capt. R. Arthur Thomas)

PLATE VII

Above: *Aegured* stone, now mounted as a side altar in Treslothan church.
Below: former Camborne font, now at Treslothan—detail of bowl. (Photos:
N. D. Thomas)

PLATE VIII
Above: Font from chapel at Menadarva, now in Tuckingmill church. Below:
stoup, in south wall of Camborne parish church. (Photos: N. D. Thomas)

The cross was moved yet again, about 1956, from Pendarves to Treslothan, and it now stands against the outer east end of Treslothan church. The base is a replacement. The cross is 2 ft. 7 ins. high, the head being 1 ft. 7 ins. wide, and the thin shaft to which the head tapers only 8½ ins. across. One face bears a Latin cross in relief, the lower limb being carried down on to the shaft. The other face has a figure of Christ in relief (pl. IV), within a raised border of an odd inverted-horseshoe shape. The whole monument is in very good condition, even the features of Christ's face being discernible. If, as Canon Carah seems to have gathered locally[26], the cross was 'dug up in the roadway to Treslothan church' before W. C. Pendarves had it fixed to the wall, this might account for its preservation, since it may have lain buried for several centuries. Stylistically it is probably rather late again—12th or 13th century, if no later—but there seems no warrant for Langdon's remark[27] that it is 'in so well preserved a condition that it bears the appearance of having been re-cut.'

8 The Roskear Cross

'At Tuckingmill, opposite the church, at the cross-roads, there used to be a cross, and a holed stone, which the people were wont to crawl through to cure crick in the back' wrote S. T. Russell, about 1885[28]. This cannot however have been the original position of this cross. The Tithe Map of 1840 marks the following fields at Roskear, a few hundred yards north of the cross-roads; nos. 1805 and 1882, Little Cross Close, and nos. 1879 and 1881, Cross Close. These represent divided fields taken in from Roskear Croft in the 18th century and must owe their names to the proximity of an actual stone cross. This suggests that the cross originally stood at the road intersection by the old Roskear Fuse Works, in a roadside position on the so-called 'Eastern Lane', the northernmost of the two original east-west highways across the parish (see fig. 18).

When Canon Carah was writing in the 1920's, both the cross and the 'holed stone' reported by Mr. Russell had gone. The cross-base remained in the little open triangle, centred around a large tree, in front of Roskear Cinema. When in 1924 the Committee of the Camborne Literary Institute wished to set up the cross from Crane Drive (no. 3 above) in their front yard, they decided to use this base; or so Mr Berriman, then the Chairman, told Canon Carah[29]. The base was accordingly 'lent' to them by Camborne Urban District Council and the cross was set up in it.

What, then, of the cross itself? The late Mr. William Blewett of Cross Street, Camborne, who possessed much local antiquarian knowledge, told the writer that early in the present century the cross was removed from Roskear and set up in the garden belonging to Mr. Charles Everitt, the steward of the Basset estate; and several other people seem to remember that this was so. When Tehidy and the Basset properties were sold about 1930, and the family removed to Henley Manor, Crewkerne, Somerset, Mr. Everitt went with them and apparently took the Roskear cross along with him. The Clerk to Crewkerne U.D.C. (K. Watson, Esq.) kindly informed the writer (in litt., 27.12.1962) that 'it is understood that three race-horses belonging to a Mr. Basset were buried at Henley Manor and a Cross was used to mark the burial place. It does not seem that this Cross is still at Henley Manor.' Unhappily this sheds little more light, as the Bassets themselves took *another* cross—from Illogan parish—with them, and it cannot now be ascertained whether this cross, or the Roskear cross removed by Mr. Everitt, was employed for this equine resting-place [30]. One cannot but deplore the whole affair; no one has any moral right to remove these medieval monuments out of the county and it may be questioned whether there is really any legal right to do so.

9 The Connor Downs Cross

Far from belonging to Camborne, this is really a Gwinear cross and was also a parish bound stone. It was brought to Camborne in the Rectorship of George Brereton Hooper (1900-1934) and set up on a plot of grass outside the west door of the church tower, where it may now be seen from the main road.

In 1755, William Borlase was riding toward Redruth. 'Near a mile before you come to Roseworthy' he wrote [31], 'there lies on its side a Cross of this shape'—and he gives a tiny but clear sketch of it in the margin of his note-book. '. . . It has some antient carving on the Western side—qu. if an inscription for one side I did not see.' A hundred years later, it had become a gate-post, on the southern side of the modern A.30, in the last big field just east of the Horsepool cross-roads at Connor Downs. J. C. Burrow's fine photograph (pl. V) shows it here, as does a sketch of about 1840(?) by H. A. Crozier of Penzance [32], a drawing published by J. T. Blight in 1856 [33], and Langdon in his survey [34].

Borlase probably saw this cross very close to its original stance, which must have been by this roadside. The Statement of Bounds between the parishes of Gwinear and Gwithian [35] refers to '. . . a Long Stone called Meane Cadoar' (1651) and an earlier (1613) version of the same Bounds calls it 'Meane Cadoarth'. The brothers Dexter, who seized on this as support for their thesis that Cornish crosses, far from being Christian and medieval, are really all prehistoric and pagan (sun-worship symbols, etc.), quote a form *Maen Carduan* of 1343 which they say refers to this [36].

The resemblance of the whole stone to a prehistoric menhir or standing stone has often been remarked, and it certainly looks very like one, trimmed to shape and squared off. James Thomas collected locally [37], and the present writer has also more recently collected, a fragmentary folk-tale to the effect that the number of dots on the ornamented panels of the cross shaft represent the number of people killed in some far-off battle which took place at Reskajeage, a farm in Camborne which lies a couple of miles to the north. The chief protagonist in this battle was 'General Jig', a kind of local bogey-man used to frighten former generations of Camborne children. Now 'General Jig', as the writer pointed out a few years ago [38], may just possibly be an actual survival of the personal name contained in the place-name Reskajeage, which seems to be *Cadiek (e.g., 1252 Roskediec, 'Cadiek's spur or upland'). This must mean something like 'warlike' or 'warrior' (it is an adjectival by-form from OC. cad-, cat- 'battle'), and about the only thing one can say about the Maen Cadoar, Cadoarth,

Carduan name for the long stone is that it *might* start with the same element. (*Maen*='stone'.) So some complex, but largely lost, folk-tale may really have linked, in some way, Reskajeage, 'General Jig' or Cadiek, and Maen Cadoar.

The cross is 6 ft. high, the base of the shaft being 1 ft. 6 ins. square, the top of the shaft 10 ins. square, the head only 11 ins. across. Both faces show saltire crosses formed by sinking little hollows between the arms. There are small roll projections on either side of the neck. Both front and back and one (if not both) of the sides of the shaft have crude ornament in the form of panels filled with irregular rows of dots or hollows.

Despite the fact that this *is* almost certainly a converted prehistoric menhir, it possesses features—the form of the crosshead, the roll projections, and the panel-of-dots motif—which occur elsewhere in west Cornwall. Two very similar crosses, the one removed from near Truro to Eastbourne by Davies Gilbert in 1817, and the Penzance Market Cross, could have provided the model[39]. The date of these is approximately given by the Penzance cross, which bears a largely illegible inscription in the lower shaft panels[40] that is unlikely, from the style of lettering employed, to be any older than the later 10th century. 'Maen Cadoar' may then have been converted into a cross in the 11th or 12th centuries. It is unlikely to have been converted any earlier, since its ornament is clearly a bad copy of the Penzance cross and not *vice-versa*, and it is hard to believe that such work could have been done much later into the full medieval period.

10 The so-called Small Pendarves Cross

This is not a cross at all. It was dug up about 1887 in the walled kitchen garden at Pendarves; the writer last saw it about 1949, lying in the long grass in front of Pendarves House, and its present whereabouts is not known.

It was a circular piece of granite with deep grooves on one face, in the shape of a circle with a cross inside it[41]. This makes it clear that it was the lower stone of a cheese-press, and in the copy of Langdon (1896) with MS. additions at the RIC, Truro, someone (Langdon?) has noted against it 'Really a cheese press.' Langdon shows another one from the north Cornish parish of Michaelstow[42] and there others, for example at Hallegan in Crowan in the front garden.

11 Possible cross-site at Pengigan

On the line of an old track to the churchtown leading through Pengigan or Pengegon, there were two fields, the western one of which adjoins the tenement of Camborne Vean. On the Tithe Map, these are marked as no. 2274, Cross Close, and 2275, Church Close. The latter name merely denotes a customary church-path. The former name is not really near enough to the site of cross no. 5 (the Camborne cross) to have anything to do with it, and a lost cross may be involved here.

12 Possible cross-site at Carwynnen

A small field on a croft next to Plantation Chapel, Carwynnen, is marked 'Cross Field' (no. 3722) on the Tithe Apportionment Survey. No trace of any cross or cross-base can be found here, nor does it seem a very likely site for any such.

13   Alleged cross-shaft at Reskadinnick

The late F. J. Stephens, when living at Reskadinnick, discovered part of a granite pillar somewhere by the drive. The writer saw this many years ago—it is probably no longer identifiable—and felt fairly certain that it was a broken gate-post. Stephens suggested it might be the shaft of one of the crosses mentioned in Dr. Reginald Mertherderwa's will[43]. This depends on an older and erroneous reading of the place-name Kayr *Rescasek* as 'Beslasek' or 'Belasek', an improbable form which Stephens wanted to equate with 'Belle Lake' (cf. p.10 above), thus making the line of crosses run in a round-about way down the Red River valley and *via* Reskadinnick.

Functions of the various crosses

The existing crosses described above illustrate very well the functions of these, and similar, monuments; and it must be remembered that something like five hundred crosses, dating from the 9th to the 15th centuries A.D., can still be traced in Cornwall.

Churchyard or *dedicatory* crosses were, as was shown in chapter III above, set up within a *lan* or consecrated enclosure, the most usual position in Cornwall being just inside the entrance, and often on the right hand as one enters. In west Cornwall in particular, there seems to have been a vogue for erecting such crosses within the lans of chapels in the late 10th and 11th centuries, probably under English influence, and probably too inspired by a fine series of 10th-century crosses (like the Cardinham one; Langdon 1896, 356) centred on the great monastery of St. Petroc at Bodmin. Cross no. 2, the Fenton-Ia cross, exemplifies this, and may well date from the foundation of the chapel some time after 950 A.D. Continuation of this custom into the post-Conquest period of the late 11th and 12th centuries is shown by crosses in churchyards which are likely to be Norman in origin, like Camborne; and cross no. 1 probably stood, south or south-west of the tower, near what was the older principal entrance into the churchyard (cf. p.154 below).

Dr. Mertherderwa's will of 1447 describes very adequately the part played by what may be called *churchway* crosses. They mark the old customary routes to the parish church and burial ground, routes whose use would probably over-ride any considerations of private property, and there is a tendency to site them at cross-roads or intersections. They indicate stations where the bearers would be allowed to rest, and where prayers for the dead would be recited. Crosses nos. 3, 5, 6, 7, 8 and (if it existed) 10 fall into this category. There are reasons for supposing that churchway crosses did not come into general use before the late 11th century when, with the advent of the parochial system, burial in the parish churchyard would tend to replace burial in the nearest convenient *lan*. We saw above that the relevant crosses in Camborne should all really be regarded as of the 12th century, if not in some cases a little later. Crosses no. 7, 6 and 5, in that order, may indeed mark an ancient customary route from the Treslothan district, *via* Killivose, Kitty's Lane, and Camborne Cross, to the churchyard, and they should therefore be regarded as potentially of the same date, despite minor differences in design.

Crosses can also be *sanctuary* crosses, and act as local bound stones for an ecclesiastical property, or as the limits of a former sanctuary area (e.g., as St. Buryan). Here, cross no. 3 may have indicated an early boundary of the Glebe, as well as acting as a churchway cross on the trackway from Menadarva and Kehelland. Finally, crosses may be merely *ornamental*, designed as part of some structure, and cross no. 4, the little relief Latin cross from Crane, is a probable example of this.

Concordance of references to the Camborne crosses

The accompanying diagram may be of some assistance to the reader; it shows, listed under the numbers as above, the references to the various crosses in a number of standard works.

Cross no.	A	B	C	D	E	F	Original position
1	57	46-7	1	3	a	54	SW 64534003?
2	—	—	2	1	b	49	SW 65843816
*2a	—	422	2	5	—	49	SW 64494003
3	—	310-11	5	4	e	55	SW 64034011
4	—	—	3	2	d	59	SW 64093995
5	viii	101	6	6	f	57	SW 64833979
6	—	286-7	7	7	g	56	SW 64793909
7	—	136-8	8	8	—	55	SW 64723870
8	—	—	—	—	—	—	SW 65654103?
*8a	—	—	—	—	—	—	SW 65664077
9	27	306-7	4	—	c	—	SW 60573934

Notes: *2a; the present base of cross no. 2, originally probably the base of no. 1. *8a, the present base of cross no. 3, originally the base of no. 8.
A—Blight 1856. B—Langdon 1896. C—Carah 1925, pp.26-28. D—Henderson's list, *JRIC* (*n.s.*) *II*.3 (1955), pp.71-72. E—Baird & White, under *Camborne*. F—Peter, in Camborniana 1897, 49. (For expanded references, see *Bibliography*, p. 196). Blight, Langdon and Peter are illustrated. 'Original position' is the 8-figure National Grid reference to the earliest ascertainable position of each monument, regardless of any subsequent moves or of present positions (see fig. 18).

NOTES

1. Blight SB I, fol. 31.
2. Langdon 1896, 46.
3. Camborniana 1897, 55.
4. *PZNHAS* (*n.s.*) III (1888-92), 205.
5. Langdon 1896, 48.
6. As is claimed by, e.g., Baird and White.
7. Langdon (1897) 422, describes it as south-*west* of the tower; but it is now more like south-south-*east* of it.
8. Camborniana 1897, 59.
9. In the series *Notes & Queries: Antiquarian Lore of the West*, which appeared in *WMN* from about 1922 to 1927, ed. J. Hambley Rowe; no. 66.
10. Henderson 1935, 83.
11. Camborniana 1897, 58.
12. Langdon 1896, 310.
13. Camborniana 1897, 55.
14. *History of the Camborne Literary Institution* (8vo., 38 pp.), Camborne Printing Co., Camborne, 1929.
15. The churchway passes through Menadarva townplace and then (still a right of way) up over the fields; shortly before reaching the road past Callean to Gwealavellan and Reskajeage, it traverses the earthwork which gives its name (*an ger hyr*, 'long camp') to the field.
16. Langdon 1896, 423 ff.
17. Langdon 1896, 36-39.
18. Langdon 1896, 101.
19. Langdon 1896, 286.
20. Camborniana 1897, 58.
21. Carah 1925, 28.
22. MS Russell.
23. The writer has been quite unable to trace this journal.
24. Langdon 1896, 136-8.
25. Camborniana 1897, 56.
26. Carah 1925, 28.
27. Langdon 1896, 137.
28. MS Russell.
29. MS Carah 22, 24.
30. *JRIC* (*n.s.*) III.2 (1958), 227; Baird & White, under 'Illogan'.
31. MS Borlase 41, fol. 180, under 27 May 1755.
32. Blight SB II, fol. 34.
33. Blight 1856, 27.
34. Langdon 1896, 306-7.
35. At CRO, Truro.
36. T. F. G. & H. Dexter, *Cornish Crosses Christian and Pagan* (London, n.d.) 73-4, 119-121, 126-7, and 176.
37. *Per* Mr. W. E. Wallace, Penpons.
38. Thomas 1950, 8.
39. Langdon 1896, 303, 308.
40. Macalister, *CIIC* II, no. 1051.
41. Langdon 1896, 244.
42. Langdon 1896, 249.

VII

EARLY ALTAR STONES

The parish of Camborne possesses two remarkable stone slabs, parts of altars, which are of pre-Norman date and in many other ways are of unusual interest. It seems therefore justifiable to accord them a short chapter to themselves.

The Leuiut stone (fig. 21)

This now forms the mensa, or horizontal slab, of a reconstructed altar in the south chancel aisle of the parish church. Its history in recent centuries is fairly fully documented. In 1754 it was 'a little without the churchyard of Cambron', and was then drawn and published by Dr. William Borlase[1]. In 1789, when Gough noticed and illustrated it, it was still 'just without Camborn churchyard'[2], and both these references probably imply that it lay in the lane south of the pre-1800 churchyard or on the open space which bordered this lane on the south (see p. 154). In 1824, however, Samuel Drew recorded that '. . . the ancient monumental stone which formerly lay near the church-yard . . . was lately removed by order of Lord De Dunstanville' (patron of the living) 'and placed against the wall of Camborne church.'[3] It was still there, apparently by the south porch, in 1838[4], and a pencil sketch by either H. A. Crozier or J. T. Blight—probably the former—done about the 1850's seems to show it standing upright, so that the inscribed face is visible, just by the east side of the old south porch, grotesquely flanked by a large iron boot-scraper[5]. In 1879, the Rector (Canon Chappel) moved the slab into the church, and placed it 'under the communion table', presumably in the main chancel, though this is not actually specified[6]. By 1900, the slab had been again set upright to form a kind of frontal panel under a communion table, and it seems that the holes for iron clamps now visible in the shorter sides must relate to this episode (see pl. VI). Around 1920, it was finally elevated to its present position, sitting on a slab of slate, 20 ins. by 30 ins with bevelled edges, which in turn caps a cylindrical slate pillar. Said to be based on an early altar in a church in Provence[7], this simple and dignified mounting is to be applauded, even if it is liturgically incorrect.

Neither William Borlase nor any of the later writers cited above appears to have known anything of its origins. Despite this, a local tradition concerning the point has never been lost, and may be accepted as an accurate one. In 1890, Arthur Adams told a party of antiquarian visitors[8], 'I think I have heard that it was brought from a hamlet in the parish called Newton, where stood one of the seven chapels existing in this parish.' In 1897, he repeated this: 'I have heard that it was brought from the remains of a little chapel at Troon'[9]. By 1906, when the *Victoria County History* of Cornwall appeared, Arthur Langdon had gleaned more details, possibly from the Pendarves family. The slab was said by him[10] to have come 'from a little church at Newton, near Treslothan, demolished about 120 years since' (i.e. about 1780). In 1924, Canon Carah, who had apparently been told this independently by James Thomas, the local antiquary-cum-rural postman, sought news from Pendarves again, but it was too late. Mrs. Alice Pendarves wrote to him[11] 'The altar stone now in Camborne church was, we believe, found on one of our farms in Treslothan parish . . . and we don't know how it got to Camborne'.

Despite the lateness of this tradition, the 'hamlet called Newton', 'little chapel at Troon', 'Newton, near Treslothan', and 'one of our farms in Treslothan parish' could be, and indeed must be, the same place, and it was shown above that the chapel of St. Ia on the tenement of Newton, Troon, which is now in Treslothan parish, is the only possible context.

The slab is a large flat piece of a reddish granite with coarse felspars, a rock which it would be hard to locate with certainty but which is certainly not common in the parish and may come from outside it. Allowing for slight irregularities, and the odd fracture resulting from the frequent removals, it is a rectangle, 31 to $31\frac{1}{2}$ ins. by 42 to 43 ins., and 7 ins thick. It must weigh several hundredweight at least, and four large jacks were apparently required to get it into its present position[12]. As it now lies, the front edge is dressed square—a fact which will be discussed further below—and the back edge is rather more rough and irregular. The (viewer's) left edge is very slightly chamfered, expanding toward the upper surface, and the right edge is approximately square, like the back.

On the upper surface, within a broadly incised border of the design known as 'T-fret', there is an inscription, in a mixture of late majuscule script, which reads: LEUIUT IUSIT HEC ALTARE PRO ANIMA SUA ('L. ordered this altar for (the sake of) his soul'). A small Latin cross which apparently ends the word ANIMA must be seen as an *initial* cross, coming before the name LEUIUT and thus commencing the whole inscription. In the centre is a plain outline equal-limbed cross, the arms slightly and unevenly expanding towards their terminals.

The present underside of the stone has been neatly dressed flat, like the upper, and though Dr. Borlase did not examine it (query: too heavy to be moved as it lay on the ground?), others did so later at a date. 'On one side are the usual five plain crosses' noted Arthur Adams in 1890[13]. 'The under-surface of the slab is quite rough, and five crosses are cut in the usual positions', wrote Edmund H. Sedding, before 1909[14]. As these crosses are not now visible at all, it is clear that all five must occupy the central area of the slab within a space not greater than 20 by 30 ins., the area of the underlying slate slab[15].

The best representation of the inscribed surface is that given by Arthur Langdon in 1889, also to be seen at a reduced scale in a later work[16]. It is to be preferred to R. A. S. Macalister's drawing, which is not quite so accurate[17].

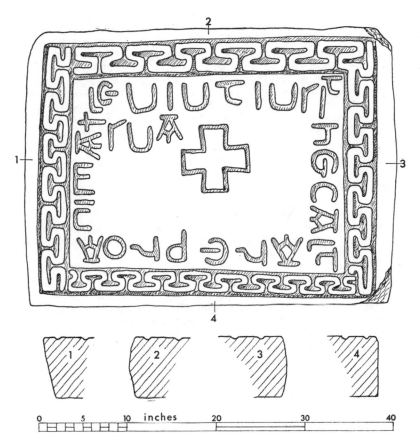

Fig. 21
The 'Leuiut' stone; measured plan, and profiles of the edges.

The Treslothan stone (fig. 22)

This similar but smaller relic is now mounted as an altar mensa in the east end of the south aisle of Treslothan church, used as a Lady Chapel, where it was set up in 1955. Prior to this, it had been used in the garden at Pendarves as the support for a circular bronze sundial, which was cemented to the upper, inscribed surface in a most regrettable manner.

As was discussed earlier (p.64), it appears that this was found in the ruins of St. James's Chapel at Treslothan, when the final demolition took place about 1840 to make way for the building of Treslothan church. This is the 'inscribed and curiously sculptured tablet of granite' which was found among the ruins, according to T. C. Paris writing ten years later[18].

The slab is of a medium-fine whiteish local granite, and has been rather badly chipped at the corners. It must have started as a rectangle, 27 to 28 ins. by 38 to 39 ins., and is about 9 ins. thick, decreasing slightly in thickness towards the smaller sides. The lower angles of these two sides are rounded off, and the present front edge has a chamfer, or more accurately a very shallow recess, commencing 4 ins. down from the upper surface. Within a border of T-fret, less angular and even than that to be seen on the Leuiut stone, there is a rectangle 12 ins. by 18 ins. containing a simple linear cross whose arms expand slightly where they join the rectangular frame. This work is broadly incised like that on the Leuiut stone. The rectangular frame is well off centre, and the resultant space, now on the viewer's right, contains an inscription which runs from front to back across the surface. The lettering is in minuscules of a very eccentric form. It appears to constitute a personal name, first read by the Rev. William Iago[19] as *Aegured*, a reading in which he was followed by Arthur Langdon[20]. Macalister preferred to see this as *Agured*. The present writer, from his own rubbings and inspection, favours the first form, though the uneven surfaces and shallowness of the lettering preclude certainty. The AE and UR are more or less ligatured or run together.

Discussion

Despite points of similarity—the use of granite, unusual thickness, borders of T-fret—it is hard to agree with Henderson[21] that the two slabs are 'not only the same date, but by the same craftsman'. It is probable, to start with, that they possessed different original functions, and in terms of date it also seems probable that the Treslothan slab is later than the Leuiut stone.

If we commence with the latter, we find that a variety of dates, mostly early in the post-Roman period, have been proposed for it. The really early dates can be ruled out at once. The formula 'pro anima sua' does not appear in Cornwall otherwise on anything earlier than the *Doniert* stone[22] at St. Cleer, which seems to be the remains of an inscribed panel on the base of a large cross and may plausibly be connected with a local king whose death is recorded in 871 A.D.[23]. The T-fret is similarly a late feature, seen across the Bristol Channel on a number of south Welsh crosses and cross-bases of the 10th and early 11th centuries[24], and in Cornwall 'key-patterns' of this general class are similarly associated with late monuments[25].

The lettering of the inscription includes the rare form of 'A' with crossed top, angular cross-bar, and a short line dependent from the angle of the cross-bar. This occurs also in the basal panel inscription[26] on the front of the Lanherne cross, formerly at St. Gwinear's Well, Roseworthy, the back of which bears in a matching basal panel the name 'Runhol'. Now the same person, obviously a master-mason, signs another cross at Sancreed[27] and on stylistic grounds can be regarded as the author of one or two others in Penwith hundred. On a variety of grounds, too detailed for discussion here, Runhol's activities are unlikely to be earlier than the middle of the tenth century and some such period as A.D. 940-960 may

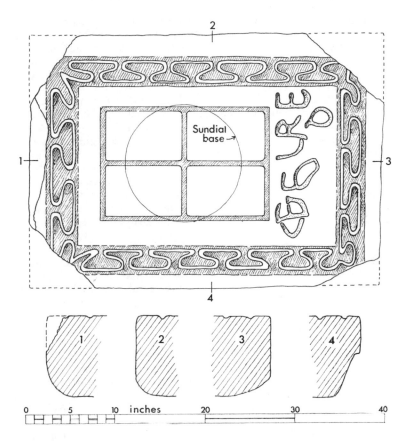

Fig. 22
The 'Aegured' stone; measured plan, and profiles of the edges.

be proposed for his own productions and for the more immediate imitations in the area[28].

Other letters of the inscription, notably the square *U*, the *M*, and the minuscule *h* and *t*, occur on the unreadable and mutilated inscription[29] on the front of the shaft of the Penzance Market cross, one of the small group with 'dot-ornamented panels' which, it was suggested above (p. 97), should be assigned to the tenth century as well.

If, then, the Leuiut stone be regarded as tenth-century in date, how early in the century could it be? There are certain features which, on so grand and visible a piece of work, must be seen as archaisms. The central cross in one sense is an example, the outline equal-limbed cross being current from the late 6th century in western Britain[30], so, too, the use of *iusit* with a single 's' (for *iussit*, 'he ordered'), the sign-post-like *r*, and the three examples of the semi-circular *e* with the centre bar standing away from the curve. These constitute grounds for suspecting that the stone really is a product of the 10th century, and not necessarily all that long, if at all, after A.D. 925-950.

The Treslothan stone is much more difficult to date. The inscription is shorter, is entirely in the most barbarous minuscules, and has no real parallels locally. The T-fret is not so well executed as on the Leuiut stone, even though on both stones the artist had some trouble in taking the design around the corners. The chamfer or recess or incipient hollow moulding on the front edge is again a feature normally associated with early Norman work and appears on altars of the late 11th century, though it may well represent an addition to the original slab. The most one can safely say is that, if the Leuiut stone is tenth century, the Treslothan slab is likely to be anything from fifty to a hundred years later.

Function

The Leuiut stone is clearly part of an altar. This fact is stated on it ('iusit hec *altare*'). It need not necessarily have been designed as the mensa or horizontal element, however, and there are good grounds for thinking that it started as a frontal. A long inscription of this kind would be rare, if not unique, on a mensa in the British Isles, and by the 10th century it is not likely that a mensa of this considerable size would lack the five consecration crosses.

The history of the separate altar frontal in pre-Norman Britain is most imperfectly known. In post-Roman Europe, the frontal commences as an embroidered textile, hanging down and concealing the front of such early altars, otherwise shaped like a domestic table with four pillar legs, as that shown on a mosaic in the bema of the apse at San Vitale, Ravenna[31]. This is mid-6th century. The central element is a simple equal-armed cross. A few dubious fragments apart, ornamental stone frontals commence with objects like the magnificent one now in San Martino, Cividale, commissioned by the Lombard king Ratchis about 734-7 in memory of his father, duke Pemmo[32]. The centre piece here is Christ in glory, flanked by seraphs with eye-studded wings[33], and shown in a mandorla surrounded by four angels. A partial frontal from Bregenz, Lake Constance, has a centre with a Latin cross flanked by stylised trees[34]. Most striking of all is the massive gold frontal of St. Ambrose's altar, Milan cathedral[35], which combines in the central panel an equal-armed cross and Christ in glory in an oval frame, has two flanking panels (with scenes) of equal width, and belongs to the second quarter of the 9th century.

These alternative frontal motifs—a simple cross, or Christ in glory—occur in pre-Norman Britain. Despite the oft-stated claim that the Leuiut slab, if it is a frontal, is unique, there are at least eight possible frontals of stone in Britain. Three are of the Christ variety, usually translated as Christ crucified rather than Christ in glory, and five of the central cross kind.

Six of these—one from Kingoldrum, Angus, east Scotland[36], the Phill-ack slab discussed below, and four from the Isle of Man[37]—are not wide enough to have covered the whole of the front of an altar, and must be seen as thin stone slabs which stood upright in a central position and were flanked by plain slabs on either side. There is however a complete frontal found at Flotta, Orkney, made of the local flagstone, and on stylistic grounds dated to some period in the late 8th century[38]. It is 65 ins. long and 32 ins. high, and has an incised equal-armed cross with interlace on the centre, inside a double rectangular frame. The undressed reverse has two vertical grooves, set 3 ins. in from the edges, to receive the front of the side-slabs of the altar block, and the lowest three or four inches of the slab are left rough, as if for insertion in a little trench in the ground in front of the altar (for stability).

The Leuiut stone falls well into this class. Its width (42 to 43 ins.) when set in position is near that of the masonry footing of the altar in the 10th century chapel of St. Gothian at Gwithian, which was said to be 46 ins. north to south[39]. It may well have been set slightly into the ground, and if so, a few inches have been dressed off it at a later date, accounting for the squared-off appearance of the present 'front edge' as contrasted with the back and right sides (see p.102 above). The Phillack slab, which was recently discussed by the present writer[40], may be a central frontal panel (this time, showing Christ crucified), and if so, shows that this custom was not unknown in Cornwall. The present height (31 ins.), which is what would be showing when the Leuiut stone was in position, compares with heights of 29 to 32 ins. for the other British stone frontal panels; allowing for footings, in the case of central panels, and in all cases for a stone mensa of some size above, this is acceptably near the customary height of 36 to 39 ins. above floor level for the mensa surface of early altars.

The five consecration crosses on the other side of the Leuiut stone show that, at some stage, it was converted into a mensa. In itself, this affords virtual proof that it did not originally constitute a mensa, and must have been a frontal. We can rule out the alternative sequence, since it is most unlikely that a consecrated mensa would be debased to the status of a frontal. In the context of St. Ia's Chapel, the slab may have been executed first as a frontal panel for the earliest well-chapel in the 10th century (p. 81), and then re-used as a mensa in the altar of the second phase (fig. 15, centre). Now there is a curious feature here; the consecration crosses on the *Leuiut* stone are not, as is usual, in the centre and at the four corners, but are all set towards a central area. The only other instances of this setting known to the writer both come from Cornwall (fig. 23), both on what are most probably 12th-century mensae. One is the slate mensa now to be seen in the little north chancel cell, used as a chapel, at the Norman church of Tintagel; this mensa measures 26 ins. by 52 ins., and the crosses occupy a central area of only 20 ins. by 25 ins. The other is at Tywardreath (the writer is indebted to Mr. C. J. Rickard for most kindly supplying measured drawings and rubbings of it). This mensa is about 32 ins. by 81 ins., and the crosses occupy an area of only 15 ins. by 20 ins. The 12th-century date of the Tintagel one arises mainly from its context; the Tywardreath slab, which has a hollow-moulded front edge, is a little earlier, possibly of the period around 1150, when the Priory at Tywardreath was becoming both wealthy and prominent, and an enlarged church was contemplated.

The Treslothan stone, on the other hand, does seem to be a mensa and not a frontal. Its considerable thickness, and the fact that if it were set upright, so that the rectangular frame would be above the inscribed name, it would be almost 40 ins. high, both tell against it being a central frontal panel, though of course this remains a possibility (with, say, 2 ins. sunk into the ground, and a very thin (slate?) mensa on top). The two things which tip the balance in favour of its being used as a mensa are firstly that the present front edge, presumably the original front edge, is recessed back from 4 ins. below the top, and secondly that its north-south length in this position, 38 to 39 ins., is in itself suggestive of a mensa. Without laying too much stress on this latter point, early medieval altars are susceptible of grouping according to both dimension and date. Thus during the late 12th and the early 13th centuries, five Cornish mensae have an average length of 52 ins., and it may be said here that the altar of the enlarged latest chapel at St. Ia's Chapel, which appears to have had an unconsecrated mensa and which is dated (p. 82) to the first half of the 13th century, really falls into the same class with dimensions (as far as can be ascertained, since the upper course of the block below the mensa is missing) of about 30 by 56 ins.; thus—

CHAPEL JANE, Zennor	32 × 51	Plain slab
CREED (13th cent).	36 × 55	Plain slab (?)
RAME (c.1259)	25 × 48	Imperfect, moulded edge
ST. MICHAEL PENKIVEL	24 × 54	Plain slab (in tower chapel)
TINTAGEL n.cell (later 12th?)	26 × 52	Five crosses

In the 12th century, mensae which survive seem to have been very much longer, and this may include such giants as that at St. Columb Major, which is about 8 feet overall, and the Tywardreath one, nearly 7 feet. The following will serve as examples:

ST. PIRAN'S, Cornwall[41]	27 × 63	(Two side cavities)
MADRON WELL-CHAPEL Cornwall	28 × 65	Plain, with relic recess
CALLINGTON, Cornwall	28 × 67½	Plain, with relic recess
ST. DAVID, Norwich	39 × 68½	Plain, with super-altar
CORSTORPHINE, Edinburgh	28 × 64	Five crosses
WHITHORN, Wigtownshire	27 × 61	Plain, with relic recess

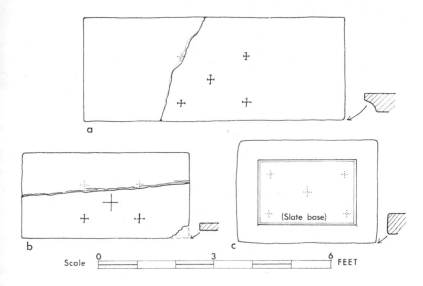

Fig. 23
The 'Leuiut' stone inverted as a mensa (c), with comparable examples of centralised crosses from Tywardreath (a) and Tintagel (b).

But we can also distinguish a few which seem to be of the later 11th and very early 12th centuries, early Norman mensae. As derivatives of the larger pre-Conquest portable altars, these do all bear the five consecration crosses, and the front edge is normally treated, either with a simple chamfer ('C') or some form of hollow moulding or recessing ('HM'). Thus—

PHILLACK, Cornwall[42]	20 × 34	HM	Five crosses
LESNEWTH, Cornwall	22 × 38	C	Five crosses
REJERRA, Newlyn E., Cornwall	$32\frac{1}{2} \times 32\frac{1}{2}$	HM	Two crosses visible
HOUGHAM, Kent[43]	31 × 36	HM	Five crosses

It is into this last category, with dimensions of 27-28 by 38-39, 'a hollow moulded' front edge, and perhaps the equivalent of five crosses, that the Treslothan slab most easily falls.

The eccentrically-placed rectangular cross frame may indeed represent the five consecration points, at the central intersection and the five corners, irregular though this would be. The eccentric placing finds an echo in the Hougham, Kent, altar mensa, though in the latter case there may have been some structural reason. The name (see below) is neither Cornish nor Norman, but English, and presumably, as on the *Leuiut* stone, that of the donor. It would be possible to explain this away any time up to the 1060's, and on the grounds outlined above, a mid-11th century date for this slab—and, by implication, for the chapel of St. James at Treslothan—should for the moment be borne in mind.

The later mensa at St. Ia's Chapel

It was stated briefly above that the *Leuiut* slab, either as a frontal or as a mensa, cannot have been employed in the latest enlarged chapel at St. Ia's, since it is of insufficient size. As at Chapel Jane, Zennor, which may also have been functioning in the 13th century as a free chapel, or local chapel of ease[44], it is likely that the mensa was a plain one, and that a small portable altar, consecrated by a bishop, was kept in some safe place by the cleric attached to the chapel. During actual celebrations of the Mass, this would be brought out and placed on the surface of the mensa. It is just possible that, as at both St. Madron's well-chapel ('Madron Baptistery') and some lost chapel at Callington, whose mensae were also considered in the second of the three dimensional tables discussed, the top of the mensa had a rectangular recess into which the portable altar could be fitted.

Fragments of what are most probably the plain 13th-century mensa were found at St. Ia's chapel, in the lowest levels of the debris filling the interior. The stone is a very fine white granite, and the fragments, diagonally tooled to a flat surface, include what is probably a corner—traces of white mortar adhere to it—and part of one side. The thickness is about 3 inches.

A note on the names Leuiut and Aegured

The first of these, as Henry Jenner pointed out[45], may lie behind the Cornish surname Blewitt or Blewett (*map Leuiut*, son of L.). In the form *leuiut* it occurs in the 12th century Cottonian Vocabulary[46], where it is glossed as *gubernator vel nauclerus* (governor, or ship's master). The Cornish *lewyth* has not actually been recorded, but the cognate Welsh word is *llywydd*, and the same root is seen in the Breton verb *leùiat*, 'gouverner ou diriger un navire'.

Aegured, if this is the correct reading, is not Cornish at all but Old English. It may represent some name like Aegfrið ('eternal peace, ever peace(ful)'), with the inscription—URED standing for the element *frið*, 'peace', pronounced something like *vredh* by the 11th century Cornish. The person in question was presumably a local thegn holding what later became the manor of Treslothan.

NOTES

1. Borlase 1754, 365, and pl. xxxii, vi.
2. Gough 1789, 14, and pl. 1, fig. 5.
3. Drew 1824, II, 142.
4. Penaluna 1838, I, 101.
5. Misc., fol. 46, no. 10.
6. *Archaeologia Cambrensis*, 5th ser., *VI* (1889), 356.
7. Carah 1925, 24; it also resembles the general class of 'Marseilles' altars of the 5th and 6th centuries.
8. *PZNHAS* (*n.s.*) III (1888-92), 206.
9. Camborniana 1897, 28.
10. VCH I, 415, and pl. iv, fig. 31.
11. MS. Carah 22, 7.
12. Personal communication from a participant, *c.* 1949.
13. Cf. note 8 *supra*.
14. *Norman Architecture in Cornwall* (1909), 163-4.
15. Dr. Radford points out to the writer that this concealment may have been intentional and, like the re-mounting in 'early Christian style', designed to emphasise the primitive Celtic, as opposed to 'Roman' (i.e., the five crosses), origins of Christianity in Britain. Some kind of ecclesiastical row was certainly going on in Camborne at this time, with accusations of Popish practices, etc.; see *WDM* for June 1921.
16. Cf. notes 6 and 10 *supra*.
17. *CIIC* II (1949), 177, pl. lxii (no. 1044).
18. *Murray's Handbook for Travellers in Cornwall & Devon*, 1st edn. (1850). T. C. Paris, editor, was the son of Dr. J. A. Paris ('A Physician, etc.') of Penzance, author of 'A Guide to the Mount's Bay and Land's End' (1816), one of the first of its kind.
19. *JRIC X* (1890-91), 262.
20. Cf. note 10 *supra*.
21. Henderson 1935, 83.
22. Langdon 1896, 377-9; Macalister, *CIIC* II, no. 1054.
23. *Annales Cambriae*, s.a. 875 ((*recte* 871), version *B: Dumnarth rex Cerneu id est Cornubiae mersus est.*
24. V. E. Nash-Williams, *The Early Christian Monuments of Wales* (1950), pl. lxviii, with refs. to monuments.
25. Cf. Langdon 1896, 412.
26. Langdon 1896, 358; Macalister, *CIIC* II, no. 1047.
27. Langdon 1896, 361; Macalister, *CIIC* II, no. 1058.
28. Langdon 1896, St. Buryan no. 2 (by *Runhol?*); Paul no. 2, St. Erth no. 3, immediate imitations; St. Erth no. 3, Breage, and Phillack no. 6, imitations a generation later.
29. Macalister, *CIIC* II, no. 1051 (with refs.). Is this possibly in *Cornish*, if not in Latin?
30. Probably commencing in Ireland and spreading first to north Britain, but by the 7th century also to the south-west.
31. F. van der Meer & Christine Mohrmann, *Atlas of the Early Christian World* (Nelson 1958), fig. 446.
32. *The Dark Ages*, ed. D. Talbot Rice (Thames & Hudson 1965), 166 illus.
33. Ezekiel chap. I, and chap. X, v.12.
34. *Zeitschrift f. Schweizer. Arch. u. Kunstgesch.* I (1939), taf. 95, 253-8.
35. Most recently in *Karl der Grosse; Werk und Wirkung* (Catalogue of the Charlemagne exhibition), Aachen (1965), 377-9; illus. in colour, D. A. Bullough, *The Age of Charlemagne* (Elek, 1965), pls. 48-49.

36. J. R. Allen and J. Anderson, *Early Christian Monuments of Scotland* (1903), pt. iii, 258 and fig. 268; in National Museum of Antiquities, Edinburgh (cat. IB 41) but not hitherto recognised as such.
37. Calf of Man, *Journal of the Manx Museum*, VI (1958), 75 and pl. 236; Ballaquinney, Marown, *PSAS* XLVI (1911-12), 61; Ballavarkish, Bride, *ibidem*. 69; Ronaldsway, *Ant.J.* XX (1940), 72 and pl. ix.2.
38. Allen and Anderson (see note 36 *supra*), 23.
39. *Arch. J.* II (1846), 230, with plan.
40. *Ant. J.* XLI (1961), 89, with illus.
41. Alleged original measurements of masonry base of altar.
42. Thomas 1963.
43. The writer is most grateful to Mr. Frank Conley, Vicar's Warden of Hougham, for checking the measurements of this. Cf. *Archaeologia Cantiana* XVI (1886), 269. An alleged 7th-century mensa in Valognes Museum, from Ham, possesses a single central cross; Rohault de Fleury, *La Messe*, vol. I (Paris, 1883), fig. xlv.
44. Forthcoming report, *CA* 6 (1967).
45. Letter, *WDM*, 29 June, 1921.
46. Graves 1962, 128. Dr. Graves' suggestion that the inscribed Leuiut contains OC. *leu*, 'rudder', and a termination *-iut* ('lord'), instead of the agentive *-it*, must be noted, but the other mis-spellings (*iusit, hec*) allow the idea that the recorded word *leuuit* was actually intended. See also Jackson, *BBCS* XIX (1960-62), 232-4.

VIII

FONTS, STOUPS, AND MORTARS

The three types of stone vessel normally encountered in connection with medieval churches or chapels are the *font*, which holds water for baptism, the *stoup*, which holds water for the worshippers to cross themselves with as they enter the building, and the *piscina*, which holds water to wash the communion vessels. The last two are normally built into the walls, the stoup near the main entrance, the piscina beside, or to the rear of, the altar; and both fonts and piscinae normally have drainage holes, in the latter communicating with the ground below and outside the east end.

Widely encountered in both Cornwall and Devon are two kinds of domestic stone vessel, the lower half of a (pot) quern, and the late medieval stone kitchen-mortar. The querns, in particular '. . . have been accepted as ecclesiastic antiquities, so to a greater extent have these small mortars, while a larger type is not infrequently claimed as a small font'[1]. This is hardly surprising when one realises that, for reasons which remain quite obscure, large collections of these mortars are often to be seen today at parish churches; for example, St. Enodoc, near Padstow, where a fine series fringe the path from the churchyard gate to the church door. This problem will be considered briefly below.

The Tuckingmill Font
This is not only the finest thing in this modern church (p.169); it is, as a font, one of the most notable early specimens in the county. Strangely, it has escaped mention by Sedding, Cox, Henderson, and more recent writers like Pevsner, and this is perhaps the first occasion on which detailed attention has been drawn to it (pl. VIII).

The bowl alone is original, with an external diameter of $25\frac{3}{4}$ ins. and an internal one of $20\frac{1}{4}$ ins. The overall external height of the bowl is a fraction under 11 ins. The material is a fine light stone of the granite group, perhaps from Gulval or Ludgvan, and the ornament is confined to the exterior. Below a deeply-cut running chevron or zig-zag, there is a double cable-moulding in herringbone style, and below that a series of dependent semi-circular arcs in flat relief, interlocked so that the right-hand half of any semi-circle overlies the next one. The lower spandrels bear single hemispherical roundels, the upper ones a series of opposed curves in decreasing relief. The general effect is both rich and restrained.

This font originally belonged to the chapel of St. Derwa at Menadarva. Canon Carah noted[2] that Arthur Adams had received from his predecessor at Tuckingmill, E. M. Pridemore (1850-53), a letter which stated that the font had been removed from Menadarva to Tehidy—this could have occurred any time after 1755, when the Bassets purchased this property—and had been set up as some kind of ornament in 'Miss Mary's Garden' there. When Tuckingmill church was built in 1844, largely through the Basset family's backing, the font was added to its furnishing.

On purely stylistic grounds, for example its partial relationship to the better-known 'Bodmin' series of mid-Cornish fonts, a date in the 12th century is likely; the few fonts in Cornwall which are at all likely to be 11th century are much cruder and less regular.

The First Camborne Font

This lovely font (pl. VI) is the earliest recorded font of Camborne parish church. It was apparently removed from the church in the 18th century— the damage done in earlier centuries, when the lid-staples were prised out and an angel's head knocked off, was probably never repaired—and was taken to Tehidy by the Bassets, as patrons of the living. It was doing duty there as a flower stand shortly before 1814, when the Lysons both saw and sketched it[3] ('the old font of Camborne now standing in the pleasure-ground at Tehidy'). It was still there a decade later, when Stockdale noticed it[4] ('Camborne; the church . . . its ancient font has been removed to the gardens at Tehiddy') and was last commented upon by Cyrus Redding, who gives a very bad drawing of it, in 1840 or a little before[5].

It was given to Treslothan church a year or so later at the request of the Pendarves family, and now stands there in the north-west angle of the nave. The carefully-mended bowl and the base are original, the pedestal being a fairly successful replacement. At the four corners of the bowl there are angels holding shields, which have illegible devices on them, and level with the tops of the shields there is a quadripartite band with lettering in relief. Below the rim is a continuous relief inscription, *Ecce Krisimi de Deo vero baptizabuntur spiritu sco* ('Behold, the Beloved of God shall in truth be baptised with his Holy Spirit').

The lettering on the quadripartite band below can be read but, as Cox and others following him have stated[6], their meaning 'has hitherto baffled solution'. Starting below *Ecce*, they read H.B.Q.A. / I.K.N.C. / C.S.B.E. / L.E.S.C. It is fairly safe to assume that this represents a baptismal formula, and though the full solution is admittedly elusive, the first three groups are not impossible. The writer, as a schoolboy, once painfully worked out the following, which he still regards as the most satisfactory attempt: *Hanc Baptismam Quam Ago / In Kristi Nomine, Conveniet / Communione Sanctorum Beatorumque, Et* ('This baptism which I make summons (thee) into the fellowship of the Saints and the Blessed, and . . .).

The base of the bowl exhibits a band of key-pattern, and the base of the whole font has four lion-like creatures chasing each other round anti-clockwise.

The stone used looks more like a grit or a sandstone than any of the fine granites and, considering the vicissitudes this monument has undergone, it is in very good condition. The date is presumably *circa* 1400 or so, a figure agreed by most writers. The nearest parallel is the slightly later font in St. Ives parish church, and the longer inscription *Ecce krisimi*, etc., is also found on fonts at St. Winnow and at St. Anthony-in-Meneage.

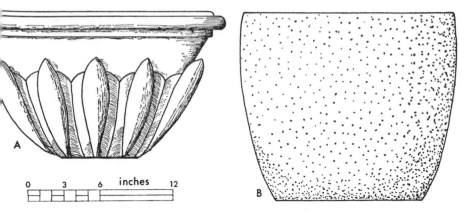

inches

Fig. 24
A, the second Camborne font (lost); B, the small font (?) at Treslothan.

The Second Camborne Font

This, which replaced the one just described in the parish church in the late 18th, or early 19th, century, was itself removed in the later 19th century restorations, and somehow got rescued by the late Canon Carah. It was for many years in the garden of 'Lis-Vean', his family house in the main street of Praze-an-Beeble, Crowan parish, where the writer sketched it in 1948 (fig. 24). It has subsequently disappeared altogether, and enquiries made by the writer in 1961 suggest that it was sold as a garden ornament without anyone realising what it was.

The font was a simple white marble piece with a beaded rim and flutings around the base. The overall height was 12 ins., the external rim diameter being 21 ins. There is a very similar font (presumably also 18th century) in the parish church of West Knoyle, by Mere, Wiltshire, which the writer saw in 1958.

The present (and third) Camborne font, and the font at Penpons church, are both modern, and do not merit further discussion.

A Possible Early Font

In the east end of the south aisle of Treslothan church, now (1966) acting as a support for the *Aegured* altar slab, is a granite object which looks very much like a small font of early type. Unfortunately it is cemented to the underside of the altar slab[7], perpetuating an arrangement which also held when the same slab stood as a sundial base in the garden at Pendarves prior to 1955. It seems most unlikely that it was cut to this shape for precisely this purpose. In profile, this piece of granite is a deep bowl-shaped object, with external diameters of (top) $17\frac{1}{2}$ ins., and (bottom) 12 ins., and an overall external height of about 15 ins. (fig. 24). Nothing is known of its previous history, nor indeed whether it is really hollowed out, but there must remain a strong suspicion that, like the altar slab, it was found in the ruins of St. James' chapel in 1840 and is the 11th-century font belonging to that chapel.

Stoup at Camborne Church

Inside the present south entrance of the church, on the left, is an attractive stoup which has been built into the wall. This was found in 1878-9, when the additional south aisle was constructed[8], and had presumably been built into the former south wall of the church in the 15th century. It has a protruding bowl in an angular frame with various horizontal mouldings, and appears to be of Polyphant stone. It must have belonged to the pre-15th century church (see p. 137).

Stoup from a Chapel at Brea (?)

This is shown in fig. 25, A. It is now in the museum at Camborne Public Library, labelled 'No. 2', and is a neat five-sided granite bowl, $6\frac{1}{2}$ ins. high, with rim diameters of from $8\frac{3}{4}$ to 10 ins., and an internal flat-based cavity 3 ins. deep. The five angles are emphasised by very rough ribs. The shallow cavity and the absence of any lower hole tells against this being a medieval pot-quern, and it may well be a stoup, as claimed. It is said to have been brought (by the late Mr. James Thomas?) from Brea, and to have come from the "old church on Newton Moor". This particular ascription is discussed on p.72, but it is possible that this did once belong to a chapel of ease at Brea in Illogan parish.

A Possible Stoup from Camborne

The object depicted in fig. 25, B, is a small irregularly nine-sided stone bowl, now in Camborne museum (labelled 'No. 1'), and made of some rough stone—the labels states 'trachyte'. It is from 7 to $7\frac{1}{2}$ ins. high, and has an internal cavity 4 ins. deep. A hole is pierced diagonally to the exterior; this hole, which is partially blocked with cement of some kind, is unevenly placed, and gives the impression of being an addition or secondary feature.

The label further states, without giving the date, that the object was 'found in an old cob wall in a cottage in New Connexion Street, Camborne, traditionally the site of an ancient church'. The latter part of this statement may be ignored, as this tradition is nowhere else mentioned or known, and the street itself only dates from the post-1800 period. But there is a possibility that, along with the other fragments of worked stone said to have been found in New Connexion Street and Gas Street (see p. 56), this comes from the former Chapel of St. Mary in the churchyard, that it was a stoup, and that the perforation refers to some later secular use. The internal cavity is of too small a diameter, and proportionately too deep, for this to be the lower half of a pot-quern.

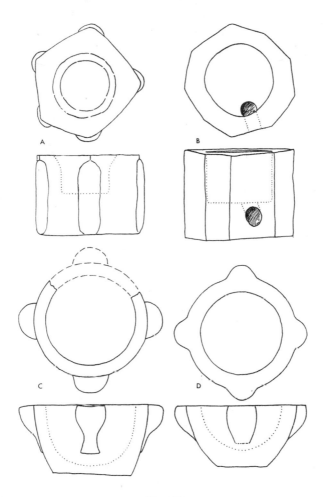

Fig. 25

A, stoup from Brea, Illogan; B, stoup found in New Connexion Street; C, mortar from Treslothan; D, mortar, probably from Camborne. Scale; one-eighth actual size.

Two early Stone Mortars

Despite their very common occurrence[9], there has been little discussion of medieval and post-medieval stone mortars; the only such that the writer is aware of are those by the late Mr. R. Hansford Worth (written in 1950, and reprinted with additions)[10], and, more recently, by Mr. G. C. Dunning[11].

Mortars of this class (fig. 25, C and D) may have been used for a variety of purposes. One such, the pounding or attrition of food-stuffs in the kitchen, has (like the word 'mortar') an ultimate origin in the Roman *mortarium*, which was normally a strong pottery vessel. The modern chemical or apothecary's mortar, made of extra-tough glass or a semi-precious stone, and very much smaller, represents a contemporary descendant. If mortars like the ones illustrated here did have any ecclesiastical significance—and this is by no means sure—the pounding of grain for eucharistic wafers, and the measuring of commodities like grain collected as tithes, have been suggested[12].

Fig. 25, C, has an interesting history. It is now in Treslothan church, on the floor by the font. It is a small bowl of white marble, about 6 ins. high and with an external rim diameter of $9\frac{1}{2}$ ins., has four small extruded hour-glass-shaped lugs or handles, an uneven base, and part of the rim missing. The writer understood from the Rev. Whalley (vicar of Treslothan, 1952-61), that it was found during the examination of the ruins of a structure along the lane behind the vicarage, in the last plot before the stile leading into Hound Field (or Hound Close). In the period before 1800, on the testimony of John Arthur[13], this ruin was a cottage serving as an early meeting-house for the area of Treslothan and the Stennack, within the Society at Troon; indeed the present writer's great-great-great-grandmother, Mary Thomas or 'Granny Polly', who figures in Mark Guy Pearse's *Daniel Quorm* stories, is said to have conducted prayer meetings here. Whether this mortar was used as an extempore font by these early Treslothan Methodists is not recorded, but this would constitute the explanation for its presence.

The other mortar, fig. 25, D, is slightly smaller but otherwise very similar. It is now in the museum at Camborne, labelled 'No. 3'. The label claims that this, or a similar, vessel, mounted on an oak stand, served as the font of Camborne church when the late Canon Chappel was appointed to the living (i.e., in 1858). This cannot be correct since, on the authority of Canon Carah, the second Camborne font was the one shown in fig. 24. The context of this mortar remains unknown.

Camborne museum, no. 4

This is a large four-sided stone bowl, not here illustrated, but mentioned to avoid any future confusion, which (so the label with it states) was removed from a church near Falmouth. The writer understands (from Mr. W. E. Wallace, Penpons) that it came from Budock parish, and that its removal some years ago is to be associated with the late Mr. James Thomas. It is certainly not a font, but may be a large mortar or a tithe measure.

Date of the mortars in fig. 25

Dunning has discussed[14] a series of mortars in Purbeck marble and burr-stone from the kitchen area of Northolt Manor, Middlesex, with comparanda from south-east England. He offers a provisional typology, which rests on the very strong assumption that they imitate cast bronze prototypes, and dates the Northolt ones to the period 1250-1350. The Camborne ones, which are made of an inferior white marble and represent a class found quite widely in Cornwall, show numerous points of devolution; they have rounded, instead of flat-based, interiors, lack rim-spouts, and while possessing four handles, have these as extruded lugs of clearly devolved pattern. It is difficult to think that they are older than the 15th century and they may well be of the 16th century. It must be stressed that this is little better than a guess, albeit a fair one, and that there is room for a great deal more work on the origin, function, and chronology of this type of thing.

NOTES

1. Worth, *op. cit.* n.10 below.
2. MS. Carah 22, 17.
3. Lysons 1814, 234.
4. F. W. L. Stockdale, *Excursions through Cornwall* (London 1824), 92.
5. Cyrus Redding, *An illustrated itinerary of the County of Cornwall* (London 1842), 103.
6. Cox 1912, 233; cf. Carah 1925, 33.
7. Arrangements are being made (autumn, 1966) to separate it again.
8. Creswell 1910, 11..
9. E.g., series at RIC, Truro, and by the Penzance Library, Morrab Gardens, Penzance, as well as at various churches.
10. R. Hansford Worth, *Dartmoor* (ed. G. M. Spooner and F. S. Russell), Plymouth (1953), 390.
11. 'Stone Mortars' (279-284, illus.), in J. G. Hurst's 'The Kitchen Area of Northholt Manor, Middlesex', *Med. Arch.* V (1961), 211.
12. E.g., by Worth, n.10 *supra*.
13. MS. Arthur.
14. *Op. cit.*, n.11 *supra*.

IX

HOLY WELLS

Over most of Cornwall, the word 'well' is used to describe both an artificially-dug vertical shaft, and a natural spring, whether flowing or static. The traditional 'holy wells' of Cornwall are seldom more than a foot or so deep, and can be nothing more than water issuing from the ground or from a rock. In Cornish, a single word normally suffices for both well and spring (OC. *funten*, MC. *fenten*, ModC. *fenton;* cf. OB. *funton*, ModB. *feunteun*),[1] derived from the Latin *fontana*, and apparently superseding some such purely Celtic word as that represented by OC. *pol*, 'pool, well'.[2] The strict term for a dug well, ModC. *pyth*, dialect 'peeth'[3], seems confined to domestic usage and does not occur in place-names, as far as is known.

The wells described in this chapter are all of some age, and have some claim to be regarded as 'holy' or 'lucky' in the broad sense, while at least three of them are, or were, thought to possess medicinal virtues. In no way can this be claimed as a complete catalogue of all such wells in the parish, and there must be many others unknown to the writer—indeed unknown to everyone except for the few people who live near them. The selection discussed below nevertheless forms a good representative group, such as may be found in most parishes in west Cornwall. These wells are shown on the map (fig. 18), and their eight-figure National Grid references are listed at the end of this chapter, as many of these wells have never been distinguished on the Ordnance Survey sheets.

1   Vincent's Well

This is a copious natural spring which forms one of the sources of the Red River. It can be found, with some difficulty, on the so-called Bolenowe Moors (actually a marsh with heavy scrub undergrowth), and is still esteemed in Bolenowe as being of great antiquity, and as possessing water of healing powers. An old and choked lane leads to it from the farmlands of the Forrest tenement of Illogan, and the well itself seems to be just on the Illogan side of the Camborne-Illogan bound. The spring issues out from under some horizontal granite slabs (pl. X).

Charles Henderson visited Vincent's Well in the 1930's, though he confused it with Fenton-Ia (no. 10 below). He wrote[4] 'It is famous throughout the district for its healing qualities especially with regard to the eyes. One old man asserted that doctors had frequently taken some of its waters away to London' (this claim was repeated to the writer at Bolenowe in 1962 by several ladies in the village) '. . . The spring is most difficult to find and approach. . . . It is a fine clear copious spring issuing from the ground, and there are no traces of any building covering it . . .'

Vincent's Well must be carefully distinguished from 'Vincent's Shute', the name of a spring and watercourse behind a house in Bolenowe village occupied (1962) by the Vincent family. In the case of Vincent's Well, the 'Vincent' part is probably, as in field-names, a corruption of the Cornish word *fenton*.

2 Newton Moor Well

A mile or so down the Red River valley from Vincent's Well there is a large patch of uncleared 'moor' resting on a bed of decomposed gravel. In the middle of Newton Moor, just south-east of the present Newton Farm, is this well; not very deep, but it has never been known to run dry, even in drought, and is enclosed in a high square granite structure, on top of which is a cast-iron Victorian pump. In front of the well is a paved area of square granite blocks. There is no reason to think that this well is regarded as either holy or medicinal, but it is included here to avoid any future confusion about a well on Newton Moor, and the genuine holy well (no. 10 below) on the other Newton tenement at Troon (cf. p.72 above).

3 Well at Peter James', Carwynnen

In an open space among several little holdings at Carwynnen, the best-known of which is sometimes named after a recent occupier (Mr. P. James), there is a small shallow well enclosed in an arched or covered edifice of rude granite blocks (pl. IX). It is shown here as an instance of a number of wells in the southern half of the parish, all of which are probably medieval in origin. There is a very similar one (4 *The Reens Well*) in the lower part of the valley called 'The Reens', just east of the road from Killivose to Treslothan, which once served a now-vanished farm called 'Rocks' or 'Rocks Farm'[5], and the writer remembers as a boy seeing yet another somewhere in the woodlands of Pendarves park.

5 Treslothan Well

The little spring in the central area of Treslothan village, hidden behind a battered iron door, is enclosed in a handsome Gothic arch, and would look more at home in a Breton hamlet than in a Cornish one. Despite its appearance of weathered antiquity, this is really Victorian, a tasteful shrine constructed at the same time as the model village of Treslothan. Visitors sometimes assume, wrongly, but understandably, that this is a holy well of great age.

6 Silver Well

No one seems to know where this picturesque name came from. The little natural spring so called lies immediately below, and on the west side of, the enclosed public footpath across the former Pendarves Woods at the Stennack—a footpath which runs from the lane behind the vicarage at Treslothan, across a stile into the field called Hound Close, and joins the road from Stennack to Carwynnen Water (Lower Carwynnen) opposite a modern bungalow. The site is now choked by brushwood resulting from tree felling operations, and few people except some elderly persons in the locality could even locate this spring. Thirty years ago, the writer can remember it being a 'lucky' well, into which pins had to be thrown for a wish, and it gave its name to Silver Well Lane, the upper part of the roadway from the Stennack to Lower Carwynnen.

7 *Pendarves*

There used to be a supposed wishing-well in the side of a bank below a small ornamental bridge, in one of the main drives in Pendarves park. This was noted in the last century by John Arthur[6], and the writer recalls throwing pins into this one, too, about 1935. It may still be known to children in Ramsgate and Killivose, though it never seems to have had any special name.

8 *Maudlin Well*

Just north of Roseworthy is the tenement of Cornhill, and in the valley bottom, on the Camborne side of the Connor stream where a large field meets the uncultivated moor by the river, there is a spring now enclosed in a modern concrete housing. On the 1840 Tithe Map, this appears as 'Maudlin Well' (field no. 435), miscopied as 'Moudlin Well' on one version. Henderson noted a version 'Medlenswell', but does not state where he found this.[7] It is hard to think of any Cornish word which could have given rise to this by way of corruption, and it looks as if this well was formerly ascribed to Mary Magdalene, sister of Lazarus and Martha.

9 *Sandcot Well*

In the extreme north-west corner of the parish, there is a small stream flowing on the south side of the B.3301 road, from opposite the small one-storey cottage called 'Sandcot' (below Pencobben) down to the Red River bridge, or Gwithian Bridge, which divides Camborne from Gwithian. The stream comes out from under a rock in an overgrown quarry, and issues with some force.

The writer is indebted to Mr. W. J. Furze, of Beach House, Gwithian, for the information that this was at one time thought to be a holy well.[8] The physical situation is certainly not against this theory, and it is interesting to note that there is no holy well otherwise known to be connected with the nearby chapel of St. Gothian, patron of Gwithian. This may be St. Gothian's holy well.

10 *Fenton-Ia*

The history and development of this site was fully discussed above, in chapter V. It is worth stressing again that this may have been a medicinal well. Edward Lhuyd merely comments that 'the well is call'd fenton Ia in the pish. of Cambron' (see Appendix A), but fifty years later, Dr. Borlase described it as 'a Well noted for Physical virtue', and again (Appendix B) as '. . . a rude Well noted for its Physical virtues'. It is a pity that we are not told what these virtues specifically were.

11   Fenton-Veryasek

The evidence for the existence of St. Meriasek's holy well in Camborne, a shrine of some renown, rests not only on the passages from *BM* discussed in chapter II, but on a wide range of independent accounts. The earliest is probably that of Nicholas Roscarrock, writing *circa* 1600[9], who says 'There is a well wch also bereth that name and it is called St. Marazaack's well.' Lhuyd does not appear to have regarded the well as worth noting (Appendix A), but it appears in his notes as his chapel no. 4 ('at Rhoszwern'—i.e., Rosewarne), and that some kind of structure was still visible about 1700 is confirmed by Tonkin.

Thomas Tonkin of St. Agnes, in his unpublished Parochial History of Cornwall, wrote, between 1702 and 1730, the following passage concerning Camborne:[10]

> 'I am inform'd that there is a walled Consecrated well in this Parish, called *Mearhagos* . . . and yearly the young People of the Parish frequent this well, drink of the water, and perhaps Cast some kind of offering in it, besprinkle themselves, and then for the future are reckoned true Parishioners and called *Meerhagicks*.'

Tonkin clearly shared an informant with William Hals who, in the published portion of his county history, stated this[11]:

> 'CAMBURNE, a Rectory. Is situate in the Hundred of Penwith, etc. For its modern name *Camburne*, which was not extant at the Time of the *Norman Conquest*, it signifies a *crooked*, or *arched Burne*, or *Well-pit of Water*, so named from that famous consecrated Spring of Water and wall'd Well in this Parish, call'd *Cam-burne Well;* to which Place Young People, and some of the Elder Sort, make frequent Visits, in order to wash and besprinkle themselves with the Waters thereof, out of an Opinion of its great Virtue and *Sanctity*, forsooth! And such as are thus sprinkled are called by the Inhabitants *Mer-raslcks*, *viz.* such as have been much sprinkled with Sprigs, Shrubs, or Branches, *viz.* the Shrubs, or Branches, of Rosemary or Hyssop, with which they are besprinkled. These again by others are also nick-named *Mearagacks*, alias *Meraragiks;* that is to say, Persons erring, straying, doing amiss, rash, fond, perverse, wilful, obstinate.'

This strange and much embroidered passage contains a good deal of hidden information. Tonkin's 'Meerhagicks', Hals' 'Mearagacks', and Lhuyd's spelling of the saint's name as 'Maradzock', all confirm that by the 18th century, in the last stage of spoken Cornish, the intervocalic -*s*- in Meriasek's name had become an English -*j*- sound. As Nance commented[12], the colloquial pronounciation would now be 'Mer-*aj*-ek' (probably with a strong penultimate stress). Hals gives at least two false etymologies; that of the name 'Camborne', taking 'burne' as a well or 'well-pit' (OE. *burne*, 'stream, brook, fountain, well'), an idea which was also expressed by Borlase (Appendix B); and an ingenious attempt to translate 'Mer-rasick' as a compound word instead of as a proper name. As he appears to think it means 'much sprinkled', presumably he saw it as C. *mur*, *meor*, 'great', or *meor a*, 'many, much' and an invented adjective '*rasick*', possibly intended as a lenited form of *crasyk* (? *crysek*), from ModC. *crys*, 'a shaking, a shiver' ? cf. W. *crynu*, vb. 'to shiver' and the Middle Ir. *cresach*, 'shivering'. 'Mearagacks, alias Meraragiks', on the other hand, he translates by a string of not wholly related adjectives, and it is hard to see what Cornish words, real or imagined, he had in mind here.

The special virtue of this well, as we know from *BM*, lay in the power of its water to cure insanity (lines 1005-8, 'Likewise the water from my well / I pray that it may be a cure / For a man gone out of his mind / to bring him back to his wits again'). This reflects an original facet of the Meriasek cult. At Stival in Brittany, an early medieval bell attributed to the saint is used to cure headaches and deafness, and at St. Jean-du-Doigt, a medieval silver reliquary in the form of a bust of the saint contains what is alleged to be a piece of his skull.[13] This 'head' motif is thus central to some lost tradition which seems, in this respect, to have been common to both Cornwall and Brittany. In Camborne, by a simple transference of ideas, those frequenting Fenton-Veryasek would be jocularly regarded as in need of this specific cure, and the name 'merajick' must, by Hals' and Tonkin's time, have become a local synonym for a hot-head or giddy fellow of any kind.[14]

It also seems clear from what Tonkin says that this well was in some way central to the life of Camborne; one suspects that the young people who frequented it 'yearly' did so in particular in early June, on the occasion of Meriasek's feast-day (p.129).

Neither well nor chapel are mentioned at all by Borlase, and all subsequent accounts derive either from Hals' florid passage quoted above, or (more recently) from a minor elaboration of Hals' remarks by Robert Hunt in his folk-lore collection.[15] The chapel may have been in ruins as early as the 16th century, even if some kind of structure—as Thomas Tonkin suggests—remained around the well itself until after 1700. In some form or other, the actual well was both known and identifiable until the last century, and gave its name to a house ('St. Maradox Villa') at the bottom of Tehidy Road, Camborne.

The well was not, as tradition sometimes asserts, inside the present wall around the grounds of Rosewarne House. It stood on the opposite (west) side of what is now Tehidy Road, probably within the front garden or gardens of the late 19th-century dwellings there. This is made clear from an interesting and unpublished paper by the late Thomas Fiddick, J.P., of Camborne, a precis of which is fortunately preserved in Canon Carah's notes. The paper, read to Camborne Old Cornwall Society on 15th June 1925, states[16]

'St. Meriadoc's Well, which existed until about 70 years ago' (i.e., 1850-1860) 'was then a wishing-well, and children dropped pins into it, and expressed some wish, hoping to have their desires fulfilled.

This well was inside a wall on the left of what is now Tehidy Road, going from the town, and just opposite St. Maradox Villa. It appears to have been drained dry by mine adits and pumping operations at Gustavus Mine. The water of the well was thought to have miraculous powers, and especially for the insane . . .'

An interesting account of 1872 comes from the Reverend John Bannister (vicar of St. Day, and author of *A Glossary of Cornish Names*, 1871). Reviewing Stokes' edition of *BM*, he wrote[17]

'At the foot of Fore Street also, east of the parish church, is a well still vulgarly called St. Merijick's and the first Friday in June (some say July) is Teeming-day in Camborne. Some fifty years ago, I am told by an old inhabitant (who when a youth learnt orally from his uncle, the Cornish numerals up to 20, which he can now, though upwards of 80 years, repeat fluently from memory), no one could pass up the street on this day without having a pitcher of water thrown at him. Something of the kind, though not quite so bad, is still kept up; and old Hals tells us that persons washing in Camborne well, for the relief of some maladies, were called Mereasicks, or Mearagasks. Though ignorant of St. Meriasek, he gives, as usual, some strange derivation for it, making it mean something like "sprinkled with rosemary".'

Bannister must be regarded as a reliable informant and this takes the life of the well a decade later than Thomas Fiddick states. 'Teeming-day' means 'Pouring-day', from the obsolete dialect word 'teem', to pour (out) water, preserved only in the (English) phrase 'teeming with rain'.

The famous well is now recalled only by a bronze plaque let into the wall of the former Rosewarne park, a short distance away on the opposite side of the street. Erected by the late Mr. James Holman, who bought Rosewarne in 1911, it commemorates the starting-point of Richard Trevithick's first run in his road locomotive in 1801— the birth of the modern railway system—and is dated 'Peace Day, July 19th, 1919'. It concludes: 'Also near this spot was the once famous Well of St. Meriadoc supposed to possess healing qualities of great virtue'.

12   *Bodryan Well*

Henderson[18] recorded a 'Bodryan Well' for both 1608 and 1650, as being in Camborne parish. Despite the most intensive search, the writer has been unable to find any other occurrence of this place-name, either with reference to a tenement or to a field. It may represent *bos* plus *dreyn*, 'thorns', 'house by the thorns', but this scarcely helps in locating it.

A note on the locations of the wells listed
The following is based on the new (1963) Ordnance Survey 6-in. revised edition; 'N.M.' indicates 'not marked'.

No.	Name		Location		Marked as
1	Vincent's Well		SW 67683776		N.M.
2	Newton Moor Well		SW 67103873		'W'
3	Peter James' Well		SW 65633728		'W'
4	The Reens Well		SW 65203834		N.M.
5	Treslothan Well		SW 65143784		N.M.
6	Silver Well		SW 65253744		N.M.
7	Pendarves	?	SW 64703812	?	N.M.
8	Maudlin Well		SW 61413986		'Spring'
9	Sandcot Well		SW 59304230		N.M.
10	Fenton-Ia		SW 65833815		N.M.
11	Fenton-Veryasek	?	SW 64604052	?	N.M.

NOTES

1. Fleuriot 1964, 172; Graves 1962, 319.
2. Graves 1962, 321.
3. From Latin *puteus*, 'well'.
4. MS. Henderson II, 293.
5. MS. Arthur.
6. *Ibidem.* This may have been once called 'Gilley Well'.
7. *JRIC* (*n.s.*) II.3 (1955), 70.
8. From the late Mr. Richard Johns, Gwithian (via Mr. Furze's brother). Mr. Johns lived at both Sandcot and Pencobben as a boy (*circa* 1890).
9. Quoted in Doble 1934, 40.
10. MS. Tonkin I. 155.
11. Hals 1750, 52.
12. Note in Doble 1934, 41.
13. Discussed and illustrated, Doble 1934, 34-37.
14. Cf. Cornish dialect 'mazed', which can mean (a) 'mad' (certifiably insane), (b) 'eccentric or peculiar', and (c) 'furious with, mad at (someone)'.
15. Hunt 1871, 426; his informant 'Lanyon' must have been Dr. Richard Lanyon of Camborne (see under Lanyon 1841 in the Bibliography, p. 196). According to William Bottrell, *Traditions and Hearthside Stories of West Cornwall* (*3rd series*), Penzance (1880), 155, 'Camborne people are now' (i.e., about 1880) 'frequently called Merry-Geeks'. It is uncertain whether this represents first-hand knowledge, or is mere literary borrowing.
16. MS. Carah 22, 53.
17. *RCG* 21 September 1872 (the writer is grateful to Mr. H. L. Douch for drawing his attention to this extract).
18. Henderson, *Topography of Penwith* (MS. at RIC).

X
FEASTS, FAIRS, AND MARKETS

Both feasts and fairs are ecclesiastical festivals which have subsequently assumed commercial or secular characteristics. 'What do you mean by Festivals?' wrote Robert Nelson in 1703[1], and he provided the answer; 'Days set apart by the Church, either for the remembrance of some special Mercies of God . . . or in Memory of the great *Heroes* of the Christian Religion, the Blessed Apostles, and other Saints.' The word 'fair', which we tend to associate with stalls and roundabouts, comes from the Latin *feria*, meaning, firstly, a pagan Roman festival or holiday, and later, a specifically Christian festival. When fairs tended to become linked with markets, they were still usually held during the period of a saint's feast, and took place in the precincts of that saint's church.

Two main feasts—of St. Meriasek and St. Martin—and a number of fairs have at one time or another been part of Camborne life. Most of these events can be shown to have had ecclesiastical origins. As the churchtown grew, and became a convenient market centre for a wide agricultural and mining district. the commercial aspect could, and in several cases did, replace the religious one almost entirely. The most convenient way to examine these events is probably to take them in the order of the calendar year.

The February Fair

Its history commences with a grant by letters patent dated 1st June 1708, to Robert Hooker of Camborne (then living at Rosewarne[2]) of three fairs to be held yearly in the churchtown for the buying and selling of cattle and all manner of goods and wares. Two of these fairs will be discussed below; the first was stated to be on February 24th, 25th and 26th, save that if any of these days should fall on a Sunday, then the fair would be on the Monday, Tuesday, and Wednesday following.[3] The grant was in trust for the use of the parish, one-third of the moneys so received to be for the church, and two-thirds for the relief of the parish poor.[4] This grant is also mentioned in the Glebe Terrier of 1727 (see Appendix C).

In practice, the profits of the fairs would be let, that is, a concession leased to one or more persons, who in their turn would recoup as much as possible by charging 'stallage and picage' (money for the right to erect stalls, and for the right to break ground in putting stalls up). By early Victorian times, when the churchwardens had succeeded the Hooker family as assignees, the profits were let for £10 per annum, £6. 13s. 4d. being duly distributed to the deserving poor.

The February fair underwent a change of date about a century after the grant of letters patent. In 1750, the Calendar (New Style) Act provided that 3rd September 1752 would be entitled the 14th September 1752, and all dates reckoned onward from it; this was in order to bring Britain into step with the Continent, and to adjust the British year to the Gregorian cycle.[5] Not everybody could understand this essential step, and the calendar change led to some rioting ('Give us back our eleven days!' etc.). A number of rural festivals were obstinately maintained by their devotees at the same point in the *solar* year, which made them now eleven days later in the (New Style) *calendar* year; thus, we find St. Peter's Feast being held on 10th July instead of 29th June, and an 'Old Christmas Day' on 5th or 6th January.

The Camborne February fair seems to have shrunk by the late 18th century to a one-day event. In 1779, it is recorded as *Cambron*; *Feb. 24th— Cattle*[6], and in 1792 as *February 29th* (error for 24th?)[7]. In 1805, both February 24th *and* March 7th are listed under Camborne as fairs for cattle[8], and this seems to be the last mention of the February event.

The March fair

Though it is now impossible to prove this, it looks very much as if the former February fair continued, after 1752, to be held on the same day, Old Style, which would be March 7th/8th/9th (New Style). After about 1805, a year in which fairs are recorded for *both* days, this fair seems to have been removed permanently to March. Subsequent records (see Appendix E) are all of this date.

This may have been a popular change. The first Friday in March, which can never be *later* than 7th March, though it may be any day in March before this date, was a traditional holiday for tinners under the name of 'Friday in Lide'[9], perhaps by association with the feast of St. Piran (patron saint of tinners) on March 5th. Camborne by the early 19th century was very much a mining parish.

Whitsuntide Fair

About 1590, Nicholas Roscarrock wrote (concerning St. Meriasek) 'There were three particular feasts kept in memorie of this Sainct. The first on 9 of November, the second on the Fridaie in Easter week *and in the Whitson week* as I have been informed . . . there is a feast besydes' (etc.).[10] Whether his information was genuine or not, and it seems to imply that 9th November, Good Friday, and a day in Whit-week were all festivals of St. Meriasek in addition to the main feast (7th June), the Camborne Whitsuntide fair was long held.

Subsequent references to it include 'a holiday fair in Whitsun week' (1814),[11] and a whole series from 1824 until quite recently (see Appendix E), all of which specify Whit-*Tuesday* as the day. This is of course a particularly favoured time for fairs throughout Cornwall; in a religious sense, Whitsuntide owes something of its popularity in the county to the fact that the Methodist Church locally regards Whit-Monday as one of its main occasions, specially associated (as in Camborne) with Sunday School treats and outings.

The eclipse of this Camborne fair is mainly due to competition elsewhere. As A. S. Oates wrote not long ago,[12] 'Helston's largest fair was
formerly held at Whitsuntide. Unfortunately it was discontinued many
years ago, probably because it was relegated from Coinagehall Street'
(Helston's main street) 'to the Lower Green . . . Camborne's Whitsun
Tuesday fair petered out about the same time; consequently Redruth
became the Whitsuntide metropolis of West Cornwall'. Again, Methodists
may have considered the fair unsuitable for their children; in 1849, the
Superintendent (Thomas Collins) arranged an alternative Sunday School
outing to Hayle, at which the children sang this, written for the occasion;[13]

> We rejoice and we have reason,
> We shall not attend the fair,
> We shall spend this happy season
> Breathing in the fresh sea air.

The Feast of St. Meriasek

This was a purely religious festival, with apparently no commercial
aspect. Its correct day, as held in the late 15th century, is given in *Bewnans
Meryasek* lines 4302-5 ('My festival shall surely be / In the month of June /
The first Friday / For ever, certainly'). A century later, Nicholas Roscarrock[10] gives the same information; 'there is a feast besydes kept in the
honour of this Sainct the first fridaye in June'. It is also given in two
15th-century Vannes missals and in the Treguier Breviary of that century,
according to Doble[14] (as the first week in June, June 3rd, and June 7th
respectively). Edward Lhuyd implies that it was still the main parish feast
about 1700; 'The parish day is the first Friday in June wch. is call'd
Maradzock day' (see Appendix A).

The feast now survives only in the official Calendar of the Diocese of
Truro, where June 7th is entered as the Feast of St. Meriadoc of Camborne.

St. Peter's Fair

The feast of St. Peter the Apostle occurs on 29th June, and was once
widely kept in Cornwall—particularly in fishing-ports, of course—as a
kind of alternative to the Midsummer celebrations on June 24th. In the
1708 Grant to Robert Hooker, this is the second of the three fairs; June
28th, 29th and 30th. After it had shrunk to a one-day event, it seems to
have been kept from 1779 to 1925, for which the dates are given in the
Appendix (E), and possibly later. By the 19th century, this had become a
cattle fair in the church-town.

A good example of how these ancient statutory fairs could get out of
hand, and how the opposition of the Church was aroused by the nature
of the proceedings, is afforded by the following extract:[15]

'CAMBORNE ST. PETER'S FAIR. The following has been sent to
us by a respectable correspondent; and we give it with one or two
slight alterations. We know not who the parties may be, whose
unseemly proceedings are referred to; but the author of the paragraph
allows us, if necessary, to give up his name.—At this Fair, cattle sold

slowly and at lower prices than have lately been current. A most disgusting exhibition took place, which we hope never to see repeated, being a rivalry between a merryman of one of the shews and a person on the opposite side of the street, who occupied himself with burlesquing—as we understand our Correspondent—the solemnities of religious worship. The worthy Rector' (Hugh Rogers) 'justly scandalized at these proceedings, interfered to put a stop to them; but without success, as the preacher, or whatever he was, who had set himself up as the rival of Jack Pudding, was supported by a host of followers. At length the showmen and their allies had recourse to a discharge of crackers, which so enraged the opposite party, that serious consequences would have ensued, had not a spirited gentleman on horseback, with the assistance of some other well-disposed persons, parted the belligerents and dispersed the crowd'.

The late Mr. T. C. Quintrell of Camborne, whose memories extended back to the 1870's, described[16] this fair as it was in his youth.

'Near the end of June came St. Peter's Fair, which lasted three days, and it may seem strange to our younger readers that it was held in the streets, and attracted large crowds each night. The horse fair was held in front of the Basset Arms at Basset Road, and potential buyers exercised the animals up and down the road. The donkey fair was held at the rear of the same hotel and Cross-street presented a lively appearance with the donkeys and shays so popular with the miners. In the Market Square, standings were erected for the sale of fruit, sweets and fairings, and ice-cream carts only seen on fair days.

The menagerie with a stage and a brass band outside, was erected in the Commercial Square, with sufficient space left on one side for the railway' (the tramway to Redruth), 'bus, and other horse traffic to pass. In Church-street booths were erected for small shows, peep shows, boxing booths, freaks of nature, small circuses, shooting galleries, and three-balls-a-penny shies . . . In Wellington-road the hobby horses and swings were erected with the usual musical accompaniment. The street itself was thronged with people, who occasionally had to make way for a passing horse and cart.

The passing of time has seen the end of these street fairs, provision for which is made at odd times in fields near the town.'

At an earlier date, the fairs—especially St. Martin's—probably took place in and around the churchyard, notably on the unenclosed portion of the glebe lands (see fig. 29) lying west of the church. In the Glebe Terrier of 1680, the rector, John Collins, states that 'There being a customary fair held in the churchtowne, much of the fair being held upon the ground belonging to the parson' (Appendix C). The idea that this ground had somehow become public property occurs in William Tuck's little book[17], where the writer voices a complaint that it 'has now been included in the glebe land' (i.e. after the Turnpike Road was built in 1839). In fact it had never ceased to be church property. The name 'Fair Field' still survives, though the site is built over. 'The first building erected in Cornwall as a health area office and clinic is at Camborne, in what was known as the Fair Field in Rectory Road.'[18] Fairs, in the sense of travelling commercial shows and circuses, were for the last thirty years or so held in another large open plot at the west end of College Street, but this, too, has now gone. 'Camborne will lose its circus and fair field by the Urban Council's purchase of the land formerly retained by the late Mr. Fred Rodda, of the Regal and Golden Lion hotels, for circus use.'[19] The property, always called 'Rodda's Field', was sold for £6200, and has subsequently been developed for housing. In the summer of 1966, a travelling circus and fair was obliged to pitch on a nearby building-site, causing some annoyance.

Camborne Feast and November Fair

Since the eighteenth century, the 'parish day' of St. Meriasek in June has been completely superseded by the major parish feast on St. Martin's day, 11th November, attached to which was the main fair of the year, often just called 'Camborne Fair'. Nicholas Roscarrock claimed that the 9th November was a feast of St. Meriasek, but this claim rests entirely on him and is not found anywhere else. Edward Lhuyd, about a century later, could record that 'the feast is kept on the 11 of 9ber. (November)', and that 'the feast day and fair day, St. *Martin*.' This is independently borne out. The churchwardens' accounts for the later 17th century refer constantly to a November event. There is a memorandum dated 18th November 1678 that the twelve men granted to Richard Williams and Christopher 'Pryear' (Pryor) the fair and market 'belonging to the said parish' on 7th November, and the usual market before and after, for seven years, with an option of a further seven; Williams and Prior were given the 'tollsery' of the said fair for cattle and horses, at what seems to have been £2. 3s. 6d. per annum. In 1680, this was reduced to £1. 13s. 0d., 'it being a Customary fair'. This probably reflects the fact that the churchwardens could not produce evidence that the fair was held under either a royal charter or right of prescription and that, strictly, they were acting outside the law in selling the franchise of it. In 1688 the fair was again let for seven years at £2. 3s. 7d., in 1694 for another seven years at £2. 3s. 6d., and in 1702 for yet another seven at £2. 4s. 6d.

It will be noticed that November *7th*, not 11th, is the date mentioned in 1678. In the Grant of 1708, the three-day fair was fixed for November 10th, 11th and 12th (Sundays excepted) thus linking it more closely to the parish (Martinmas) feast. That the fair was originally connected with this feast is an obvious assumption and is borne out by Lhuyd's comments. The various references to 'Camborne Fair' (Appendix E) include an early nineteenth-century group which give it as 'the second Tuesday in November' (i.e. from the 8th to 14th November). This seems to imply that, from about 1800 onwards, the fair tended to be on the day following Camborne Feast, which had similarly become stabilised as the Sunday (religious) and Monday (secular) nearest to November 11th.

The best-known description of Camborne Fair is probably Tobias Martin's poem of that name[20] first published in 1831 and no doubt written rather before that date (see Appendix E). Earlier accounts do not always make it clear whether the celebrations of Camborne Feast Monday or the general excitement of the Camborne Fair on the same or the following day are being described, and this scarcely matters, as they must have been in retrospect indistinguishable. Clearly a good time was had. In his reminiscences, recorded in 1896, Captain Charles Thomas of Tuckingmill stated;[20]

> 'At Camborne Feast there used to be cock fights, the cocks being steeled for the occasion. My grandfather' (another Charles Thomas, 1764-1820, also the present writer's great-great-great-grandfather) 'when a lad, more than a hundred years ago, made a bet on certain cocks at Camborne Feast'.[21]

It was also a family occasion. John Harris of Bolenowe, the 'Miner Poet', wrote of his boyhood in the 1820's:

> 'My grandmother Smith I well remember . . . For a long time we visited the farm-house at Beacon annually, at the parish feast, when we generally dined off roast goose . . . at such times my uncles would tell stories, as we clustered around the November log; we continued to go to the farm-house, on the annual feast day, until my brothers and sisters became too numerous for my grandmother's table'.[22]

A writer in the *Western Morning News* (November, 1921) described the Feast in his boyhood '—great hospitality, and the fullest enjoyment which could be compassed of the good things of life, not paying much, if any, regard to the origin of the festival in the consecration of the venerable parish church and its dedication to St. Martin of Tours, whose life was an eminent example of self-denial.'

Much of the tone of the feast was changed during the rectorship of William Pester Chappel (1858-1900), a progressive churchman who had already served as a curate in both Leeds and London. Finding the festival of the parish saint observed chiefly by excessive eating and drinking, and no doubt liable to be marred by such occurrences as that described earlier at St. Peter's Fair in 1840, he commenced a series of social gatherings and concerts. These appear to have begun in 1859 in a school-room, but in 1860 took place in the old Market Hall, and after 1866, in the new Assembly Rooms which replaced the hall. An account of the 1860 celebrations has survived. 'On Tuesday last, the social gathering of those who are interested in the work of the church in the parish was held in our large Market Hall.' More than 300 persons took tea, amid a welter of flags, banners, evergreens, and illuminated texts, at five o'clock. Anthems, a lecture on 'A journey over the desert to Jerusalem', a concert by the parish church choir, a hymn, and a final blessing, then took place, the audience of nearly 500 people finally dispersing.[23]

In recent years, Feast Monday has continued to be something of an event. In 1953, for instance,[24] 'Many Camborne people, old and young, have made their way back to the town for celebration of Feast weekend.' This was marked by two local shows—cage-birds and chrysanthemums— the (morning) Armistice Day service and the (afternoon) children's Feast service at the parish church, and a busy Monday. The local works all had a full-day holiday, and the town's shops all closed in the afternoon. The

Four Burrow Hunt met at the Basset Arms in the morning, and in the afternoon Camborne entertained Redruth at Rugby football, a traditional fixture, always played at Camborne. In the evening there were concerts at two of the Methodist Churches, the Feast Hunt Ball at Tonkin's Cafe, and the Camborne R.F.C. Supporters' Club dance at the Drill Hall.

A partial echo of the social evenings established by Canon Chappel in the 1860's is afforded by the introduction of a proper Feast Dinner. This commenced in 1956, through the initiative of the Rector (Canon Sandfield) and the Camborne Old Cornwall Society, and has since been held annually. 'Everyone in the town is welcome' claimed a newspaper report[25], though in practice the accommodation is limited. The main toast at the dinner is always 'The Parish of Camborne', proposed by the Rector.

Times change. Already in 1953, Camborne Chamber of Commerce wondered whether Camborne shops were really well advised to close for Feast Monday. 'Traders in Redruth had had the best day's business for months' said the (non-Cambornian) chairman[26]. 'It was purely detrimental to Camborne trade for such a thing to happen.' Older local traders were scandalised. 'They must recognise that there was something more in life than money-making' said a very prominent business man. Another thought that the Chamber was on dangerous ground in even discussing such a question.

After the 1961 Feast, however, the employees of the town's largest engineering works voted to abolish the Feast holiday and to add it to the Christmas break instead. In 1962, and subsequently, Feast Monday has been a working day. Today (1966) a bare handful of locally-owned shops, as opposed to chain stores, close for the afternoon, and only the hairdressers continue to observe the whole day as a holiday.[27]

Camborne Markets

Brief consideration must be given to this topic. Prior to 1802, trading appears to have been confined to the fixed shops, and on the market-day (which was then almost certainly Saturday) stalls would be erected all along Church Street and on waste ground by the churchyard. This practice did not finally die out until about 1939, and many Camborne people will recall the little canvas stalls with their hissing lamps, stretching from the town clock, along in front of the church, and round the corner into what is now Rectory Road.

In 1801-1802, the Basset of the day (Lord De Dunstanville) built a primitive market-house on the corner of the glebe land, by the main intersection of the churchtown. This is described[28] as containing nineteen butchers' stalls; and an eye-witness tells us[29] that 'there stood just in a central position a primitive erection or shelter for those who might bring their commodities for sale . . . it was simply a protection from the elements, its architecture being described as two sides of a square each about thirty feet in length, one side facing east, the other the south. Opposite the latter stood an inn known (as) . . . the Unicorn.' This is shown on the Tehidy Estate Map of *circa* 1805 (fig. 26). 'About fifteen years after' i.e. *circa* 1817, 'it received an addition, to meet the wants of the public'[30];

probably the extension of the northern ('south facing') wing westwards. During the late 1830's—in time to appear on both the Tithe Map (*circa* 1840) and J. S. Olver's plan of Camborne (*circa* 1845)—Lady Basset, Lord De Dunstanville's widow[31], built a much larger market on the same site. This was an elongated quadrangle, with a major entrance on the north side (now the facade of 'Knee's Arcade') and a minor one on the east (now the way into the Skating Rink). It contained fifty butchers' stalls, which, unlike the 1802 market, faced *inwards* to the centre of the market, not outwards to the streets (?), and encircled 'an area of considerable extent, for the use of persons selling boots and shoes, fruit and vegetables. Forming a part of one side of the quadrangle' (the eastern half of the south side) 'the same noble lady has built a spacious hall for the accommodation of the magistrates of the east division of Penwith.'[32]

In 1864, most of the roof of the market was destroyed in a storm, and it was decided to pull down everything and erect 'a handsome suite of buildings, to include a Market House, Corn Exchange, Town Hall, and Assembly Rooms.' This project commenced in 1866, the buildings being actually opened formally in September 1867. The cost of the building was borne by John Francis Basset, of Tehidy. The final area was 124 feet by 111 feet, using the same two entrances ('one in Penzance Street' (i.e., Church Street) 'and the other in Market Street') as the former market had possessed. The corner by the clock tower was rebuilt as Assembly Rooms, the ground floor to be the 'Town Hall', and magistrates' retiring rooms, the upper part a Public Hall. An excellent description of the old Market as it was about 1880 is given by the late T. C. Quintrell.[33] 'Butchers and pork hucksters' were on the ground floor stalls, with 'a gallery and clock at the western end for butter women. There was also a toy stall, a crockery stall, a florist's stall, and provision in wet weather for itinerant vendors of various wares generally known as cheap-jacks'.

The whole of the Market House block has undergone considerable change of use since then. Earlier this century, the western half—the old single-story market proper—had a superstructure added to it (containing, for example, most of the former Scala Cinema; pl. XV) though the fine granite front of 1866 is still intact. The Public Rooms at Camborne Cross, now Messrs, Holman Bros.' museum, replaced the old Assembly Rooms, and the Magistrates' Court has had a good many changes of venue. Saturday is still, nominally, market day in the town, though in practice this means very little, and there are no more stalls to be seen either in the market or in the streets around it.[34] The present cattle-market (Fridays) is on the south side of College Street, and has from time to time in recent years incurred criticism from such bodies as the R.S.P.C.A. for its dilapidated state.[35]

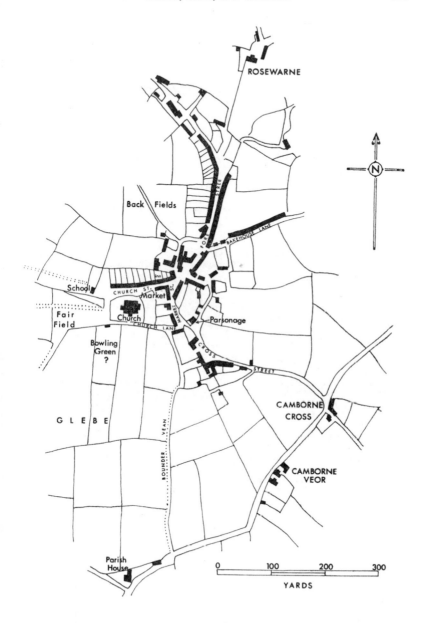

Fig. 26
Town plan of Camborne, circa 1805, from a Tehidy Estate Map. Street names have been added from slightly later sources.

NOTES

1. *Companion for the Festivals & Fasts of the Church of England.*
2. Cf. Lhuyd's note (Appendix A) that in 1700 'Rhoswarn' was 'Mr. Rob. Hwkers'.
3. *Coll. Cornub.*, col. 1581.
4. *Report of the Charities Commissioners relating to Cornwall,* 1819-1837 (Gray, London, n.d.—1839?), 436-7.
5. For explanation, see under 'Calendar' in any encyclopaedia.
6. M.U.B.T., 505.
7. *Coll. Cornub.*, col. 1584.
8. Cooke 1805, 17.
9. A. K. Hamilton Jenkin, *The Cornish Miner* (1927), 129.
10. Doble, 1934, 40.
11. Lysons 1814, xxxix.
12. *Around Helston in the Old Days* (1951), 33.
13. J. F. Odgers, *Early Methodism in Camborne; Wesley Chapel 1828-1958* (Camborne 1959), 83-4. The song, a lengthy one, was written by Thomas Collins himself.
14. Doble 1934, 44 n.2.
15. *RCG* 3 July 1840, p.2 col. 5.
16. *Cornishman* 6 December 1956.
17. Tuck 1880, 7; he calls this 'the Bowling Green', which was actually slightly further to the east (see p. 153).
18. *WB* 28 Feb. 1963.
19. *WB* 9 May, 1963.
20. *The Remains of . . . Tobias Martin* (Penaluna, Helston, 1831), 92.
21. Herbert Thomas, *Cornish Mining Interviews* (Camborne, 1896), 170.
22. John Harris, *My Autobiography* (1882), 3 ff.
23. *RCG* 16 November, 1860, p.4.
24. *Cornishman* 12 November, 1953.
25. *Cornishman* 6 November, 1958.
26. *Cornishman* 12 November, 1953.
27. Efforts are being made (1966) by the Chamber of Commerce to re-establish the Feast as a whole *week* of festivities, a carnival, etc. The last public holiday on this day was in 1961.
28. Lanyon 1841, 113.
29. Tuck 1880, 3.
30. Lanyon 1841, 113.
31. He died in 1835.
32. This petty sessional court, still held in Camborne, appears to have met in the town since at least 1790.
33. *Cornishman* 9 December, 1954.
34. The last 'nicey' (i.e. sweets) stall finally disappeared in 1940.
35. e.g., *Cornishman* 13 June 1963 ('Cinderella of Cornish markets; RSPCA Inspector criticises Camborne conditions', etc.)

XI

THE PARISH CHURCH

It is not the writer's intention to give here a complete architectural history of the parish Church of Camborne; the successive restorations would make any attempt to do so speculative in the extreme. The best guide to the church so far has been Miss Beatrix Creswell's now unobtainable booklet[1], but the latest of the more recent guides[2] should also commend itself to the enquirer.

Some possible origins of the church were briefly discussed in chapter IV, where it was suggested that the earliest place of worship in or around the present churchyard might have been an (?) 11th century chapel of the vill, or tenement, of *Cambron*. Whether this was the Chapel of St. Mary and St. Anne, some traces of which seem to have survived until the 17th century (p. 56), or another chapel ascribed to St. Meriasek, is not clear. The first proper *ecclesia* or full church, with parochial rights, and a burial-ground, is likely to have been, as elsewhere in Cornwall, cruciform in plan, with nave, chancel, north and south transepts, and a short tower over the crossing. This early cruciform stage has been inferred by most writers[3], perhaps from some definite traces seen in the 1878-79 enlargements. If it existed, it is unlikely to have been older than the 12th century, a date which would suit cross no. 1 (p. 86) which may be contemporary, and designed to mark the original churchyard's entrance.

The major re-building which took place was—again, as so often in Cornwall—in the latter half of the 15th century. The north aisle, whose width possibly indicates the extent of the north transept, the western tower, and the old (inner) south aisle, with an additional south transept which was presumably used as the vestry,[4] all belong to this phase. The tower, a handsome example of a style familiar throughout the county, has remained practically untouched. It is in three stages, the battlements being surmounted by pinnacles, rises to a height of 53 feet, and has narrow set-back double buttresses. Fig. 27 is a charming, but little known, sketch of the west face, drawn about 1850 by Charles Wickes (see also pl. XI).

The position of the former rood-screen and rood-loft is fixed by the remains of a stair in the north wall, level with the fifth pier from the west in the north arcade of the nave. The 15th-century arcades separating the nave from its two flanking aisles each have six piers and seven bays; and it is worth noticing that the foliage design on the capitals of the columns, best seen at the west end of the nave, is exactly repeated on the capitals from the former arcade at Gwithian (now built into the lych-gate[5]), and on some of those in the arcade on the south side of the nave at Gwinear. These instances are all so similar as to raise the presumption of the same hand at work, at much the same date—*circa* 1450-1470.

Further alteration of the interior took place at a date which is not otherwise recorded[6], but may be given by that carved on the stem or foundation-block of the pulpit—A.D. 1711. The rood-screen and rood-loft were apparently removed altogether; the 15th-century seating was replaced by box pews, the carved bench-ends being, one fears, very largely destroyed. At a slightly later date, if not now, there may have been minor alterations to the actual fabric as well.[7] Galleries were built at the west end, the main one being across the west end of the nave, spanning and partly concealing the tower arch, and carried on two granite columns; probably the same columns as those which now support an eastward extension of the Rectory, used as a billiard-room in Canon Chappel's day, and constructed in (?) 1862 or so.

There may have been minor western galleries across the ends of the two aisles. The following account describes their function:[8]

'Let us think what the parish church was like sixty or more years since. Outwardly its walls were much as now, excepting the new south aisle. Inside these walls it was filled with family pews which have been described as 'horse boxes', with seats on three sides and a door at the end. At the western end were three galleries, one over the tower entrance, in which the choir took its place in front of a small organ. The choir included many musical instruments and several singers with voices of great compass, and when music took its allotted part in the service, all the congregation turned its back to the parson, facing about towards the choir.

The other two galleries were for the use, one of the girls and the other of the boys of the Sunday-school. Well I remember, when a small boy myself, watching these boys raising their hands in trying to catch a sparrow that had found its way into church, and was flying to and fro over the gallery in its frightened attempts to escape.

The ceiling of the wagon roof, with its carved oak ribs, was very dilapidated and, like the granite pillars supporting it, was coated with many generations of whitewash, almost hiding all appearance of carving. The flooring was of slate, and over the centre of the nave hung a chandelier for lighting the worshippers whilst, to make some attempt at warming them, a huge stove stood also in the nave, the smoke from which escaped through an iron pipe taken through the roof.'

Some of these features are shown in pl. XII, a remarkable photograph taken in the decade 1850-1860 by Robert H. Preston of Penzance, which depicts the western (choir) gallery, the box pews, and the organ. William Tuck records that before this last improvement was introduced (not long before 1850?) the instruments used were 'Bassoons, Bass Viols, Flutes, Fiddles, Clarionets, etc.'[9], and that earlier still, before 1800, so he had been told[10]

'The musical part of the Church service was sung by men who used to wear leather breeches and buff gloves standing in front of the orchestra, and each beating time by giving a slap on his pantaloons thus emphasizing the tonic in the scale.'

Fig. 27
Camborne church tower, about 1850, drawn by Charles Wickes (from his
'Illustrations of the Spires and Towers of the Medieval Churches of England',
London, 3 vols., 1853-59).

In 1862, not long after William Pester Chappel had become Rector,
the entire church was renovated at a cost of £1,600. The galleries were
removed, the box pews were replaced by pine seating, the old 15th-
century wagon roof, which was no doubt riddled with worm, was replaced
with a pine one[11], and the dirt and whitewash of ages was cleaned out.

The work was entrusted to J. P. St. Aubyn, the architect of Penpons and numerous other churches, as the following rather cautious professional comment of 1859 makes clear[12]:

'*CAMBORNE*. This typal Cornish church, of three parallel and equal low aisles. is about to be enlarged and re-arranged by Mr. St. Aubyn. Unless he is compelled by the nature of the site we should have counselled an extension of the church eastwards or westwards rather than the addition of a fourth aisle on the south side. But granting this to be the only feasible plan, it has been here well carried out. The style is the usual late Third-Pointed of the district, with its four-centred arches and cradled roof. The roofs are all to be renewed, after the original fashion. The area is to be properly arranged and the chancel distinguished; but we observe the retention of one large pew. The eastern end of the added aisle forms a vestry which has a very good chimney that partly relieves the monotony of the exterior.'

This is probably a critique of the plans and elevations as submitted by the architect, since the extension described does not seem to have been commenced until 1878. The existing south wall and projecting south vestry were removed, an arcade copying those of the nave added on the line of the wall, a second or outer south aisle added beyond it, and a projecting porch and vestry added outside the new south wall, the former near the south-west angle, the latter at the south-east.

The only subsequent work of any scope has been the incorporation of this vestry into a large new church hall, of simple and dignified design, which was completed in 1963; and the recent cleaning and restoration of the whole of the interior, and some parts of the exterior, under the inspiration of Canon Sandfield.[13]

It is surprising that (apart from pl. XII and Wickes' drawing, fig. 27) no early depictions of this church seem to be known. The only ones that the writer has been able to find are: a very rough plan of the whole church, with dimensions, in pencil, apparently prior to the 1862-1879 work, a series of pencil sketches of such details as the tower arch, the capitals of the arcade, a piscina, etc., and some rather more careful ones showing details of windows and crockets, all by the Penzance artist and ecclesiologist J. T. Blight.[14]

The pulpit

After the *Leuiut* altar, discussed in chapter VII, the most interesting object in the church is probably the pulpit. This is not, as has been sometimes suggested[15], a composite affair constructed with panels from the former rood-screen, but a complete pre-Reformation pulpit on its own; nor can it really be supposed that its panels were ever bench-ends. There are six in all, the sixth being decorated with conventional ornament and forming the door; of the other five, four display various symbols of the Crucifixion (the Five Sacred Wounds, the Instruments, the Crown of Thorns, etc.), and the fifth the Royal Arms, with talbot and griffin supporters, the Tudor rose, and the Beaufort portcullis on either side. The character of this last panel points to the reign of Henry VII (1485-1509),

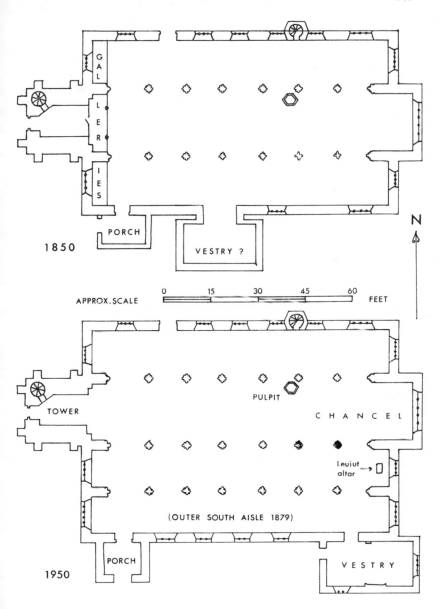

Fig. 28
Ground plans of Camborne parish church; top, after J. T. Blight's sketch,
bottom, after the drawing in Vincent 1959, p.7.

and divorces the actual pulpit from the date of 1711 carved on its stem. A very odd feature of this stem, which is a stout oak block taking the whole weight, is the presence of a carved and grotesque human face in flat relief, part of the rusticated foliage ornament which covers the block. On the analogy of Cornish bench-ends generally, a late 15th century date would be perfectly apposite for this, but it cannot be by any hand as skilled as that which carried out the pulpit panels. Pl. XIII, L, shows the Royal Arms panel from the pulpit; and pl. XIII, R, the face on the stem which, from its position, can only now be photographed at an oblique angle by someone lying on the floor under the choir stalls.[16]

The bench-ends

The fate of the bench-ends, removed in (putatively) 1711, is not in general known, but a few have survived; fourteen of them have been mounted as a frieze from ground-level, seven along each side, in the sanctuary, and two smaller ones, perhaps choir stalls, have been incorporated into a bench. These bench-ends belong to the latter part of the 15th century and, though little known and not very accessibly displayed, show that vigorous style of carving seen elsewhere in Cornwall at this period. Pl. XIV, shows three of them: a winged horse; another quadruped with a serpent, a fleur-de-lys and a tiny cross; and a grotesque face issuing from scroll foliage. Another (not shown) shows a mermaid playing a harp, surmounted by a 'memento mori' (skull and cross-bones); other display further grotesque animals and foliage.

Stoup

The stoup now built into the wall, just inside the south doorway, appears to be of Polyphant stone from north Cornwall. According to Miss Creswell, this was carefully removed in 1879 from what one assumes was a similar position in the previous, 15th-century, south wall[17]. According to Arthur Adams, it was 'found under the tower in the restoration of 1862'[18], which might be taken to imply that it was hidden below the west gallery in the wall by the tower arch. Pl. VIII shows this attractive little feature.

Piscinae

There are two piscinae, neither of them of special interest, in the south wall of the sanctuary. Whether both are in their original situations, and if so, whether this piece of wall is 15th-century or older, cannot be determined with any certainty.

The Marble Reredos

The massive reredos of Sienna marble was erected in 1761 by Mr. Samuel Percival, then the proprietor of Pendarves, at the very considerable cost of £300. It bears inscribed the Ten Commandments, the Lord's Prayer, the Creed, and the Holy name in Hebrew characters. A most distinguished ecclesiologist has written:

PLATE IX

Above: 'Clapper' bridge at Penpons (p. 18). Below: Well at Peter James' tenement, Carwynnen, 1960. (Photos: N. D. Thomas)

PLATE X

Vincent's Well, Bolenowe, Camborne, in 1961. (Photo: P. J. Fowler)

PLATE XI

Camborne parish church; the tower, from the south-west. (Photo: N. D. Thomas)

PLATE XII

Nave of Camborne church, looking west towards gallery: taken before 1862 by Robert Preston, Penzance.

PLATE XIII

Left: Camborne church, pulpit panel with arms of Henry VII. Right: grotesque
face carved on stem of pulpit. (Photos: J. V. S. Megaw)

PLATE XIV

Camborne parish church: above, former bench-ends, now in chancel (Photo:
J. V. S. Megaw). Below, left: sundial over south porch (photo: N. D. Thomas).
Right: blocked doorway into parish 'clink' (p. 154) with (arrowed) date of '1820'
on stone (photo: author)

PLATE XV

Above: south front of Camborne Rectory, built 1820-21 (photo: J. V. S. Megaw).
Below: Church Street, Camborne, looking east, 1965—the former Market
House and the clock tower in the centre (photo: Harry Parkinson, Camborne)

'This beautiful and refined piece of classical work is a rare example in stone of the type of 'altar piece', as it was called, which was usual in the better-appointed churches from the earlier 17th century, until the Gothic Revival and the Oxford Movement between them played havoc with things of this kind. These classical 'altar pieces' were nearly always made of wood.'[19]
The influence of these 'Sentences', as they were popularly known[20], was extended by the late 18th and early 19th centuries to the interior furnishings of some Cornish Methodist chapels, as Mr. John Probert has recently demonstrated[21].

King Charles' Letter

Hung on the wall of the belfry in the tower is a large board painted with what is known as 'King Charles' Letter', the formal acknowledgement by Charles I written to the people of Cornwall in 1643, thanking them for their adherence to the Loyalist cause. Dr. J. C. Cox, who has reminded us that 'in the great majority of cases the letter dates from the restoration of the Monarchy, the originals having been destroyed during the Commonwealth', has also provided a list of all those Cornish churches which possessed examples of this Letter, both panel-painted and in plaster, in 1912.[22]

The South Porch

The present south porch, which was built in 1878-9, employs the original 15th-century carved granite door surround, and the internal roof uses the surviving carved fragments from the wagon-roof taken down in 1862. Of special interest are the niche above the door, and the sundial on the exterior. The niche, or image bracket, may have been found in the previous south wall. It is tempting to relate this to a provision in Reginald Mertherderwa's will of 1447 (p. 91) for a lamp to be kept burning for a year before the image of St. Martin of Camborne.
The sundial (pl. XIV) is of slate, bears the date '1793', and includes the motto *Hora Pars Vitae* ('(Each) Hour is a Part of life') and, as at St. Blazey, a complicated table for correcting local time by Greenwich.[23] The break in the lower left corner has destroyed the maker's name, (*Jam*?)*es* . . . *er*; the lower right corner bears the word '*Philomath*', the final '*th*' being raised.[24]

Memorials

There are a number of memorial slabs and tablets within the church, mostly to the Pendarves family; lists and transcripts of these appear in several accessible publications.[25] The monument to Hugh Rogers, Rector from 1816 to 1858, on the north wall by the former rood-stair, is a fine example of the work of the Cornish sculptor Neville Northey Burnard, who died in circumstances of poverty,[26] was buried in the churchyard as a pauper, and has recently been properly commemorated by a handsome grave-stone.[27]

The Bells[28]

The 18th-century peal of six bells was re-cast by Rudhall of Gloucester in 1767, the first occasion of their renewed use being duly commemorated in the Churchwardens' Accounts:

'Paid expenses of the parishioners on the first time of ringing the bells, the 23rd December, 1767 . . . . £2. 7s. 0d.'

By 1882, the bells had again become unsound in various ways, and the whole peal was then re-hung; the work was undertaken by Taylor & Co. of Loughborough. Two new bells, a tenor and a treble, were added, and one of the old bells re-cast to make it in tune. The inscriptions on the various bells are given here, as they are not now generally accessible in print:

1. 'Peace and good neighbourhood'
2. 'Fear God Honnour the King'
3. 'T. Rudhall founder Glocester 1767'
4. 'Prosperity to this parish 1767'
5. 'Mr. Wm. Harris, Mr. Andrew Paull church wardens 1767'
6. 'I to the church the living call
   And to the grave do summon all. 1767'

The work of 1882 was accompanied by the suggestion—happily, not effected—that the church tower be raised 20 feet to accommodate the new peal.[29] In the end, the estimate given by Taylor's, of £156. 9s. 0d., exclusive of carriage, seems to have proved enough. The two new bells were both inscribed:

7, 8. J. Taylor & Co Bell founders Loughborough.
William Pester Chappel M.A. Rector
Joseph Vivian
Charles Budge   Churchwardens.

The Windows

Camborne church windows are not of any particular interest, with the exception of the large heraldic window at the east end of the inner south aisle, erected in 1864 by the Pendarves family, or rather by Mrs. Pendarves to the memory of her husband. The following reading of its very complex display is due to the late Mr. W. Treffry Hoblyn of Union Street, Camborne, a keen genealogist.

The window contains five main panels, given here from (the viewer's) left to right, reading down each panel:[30]

1. Five coats; *1*, Howard, Duke of Norfolk; *2*, Windham impaling Howard; *3*, Windham; *4*, Luttrell impaling Windham; *5*, Luttrell impaling Sacheverell.
2. Six coats; *1*, Luttrell, Abott on an escutcheon of pretence; *2*, Luttrell impaling Wraxell; *3*, Luttrell, Mapounder on an escutcheon of pretence; *4*, Wynne impaling Luttrell; *5*, Wynne, Brydger on an escutcheon of pretence; *6*, Wynne (1), Mapounder (2), Brydger (3), Wynne (4).
3. Seven coats; *1*, Gregory, Brydger on an escutcheon of pretence; *2*, Acton, Gregory on an escutcheon of pretence; *3*, Stackhouse,

Acton on an escutcheon of pretence; *4*, I Pendarves (1), Wynne (2-3), Pendarves, covered (4): II Stackhouse: III Stackhouse on a shield of pretence, quartered, Trist (1-4), Coryn (2-3): IV Pendarves covered (1), Wynne (2-3), Pendarves (4); *5*, Pendarves; *6*, Pendarves impaling Arundel; *7*, Courtenay (1-4), Redvers (2-3), impaling Pendarves.

4. Six coats; *1*, Williams, Courtenay quartering Redvers, of pretence; *2*, Stackhouse, Williams on an escutcheon of pretence; *3*, Stackhouse, Acton on an escutcheon of pretence; *4*, I Pendarves, Wynne, II Stackhouse, III Stackhouse, IV Pendarves, Wynne on a shield of pretence, Trist (1-4), Coryn (2-3); *5*, Courtenay (1-4), Redvers (2-3), Reskymer on a shield of pretence; *6*, Courtenay (1-4), Redvers (2-3), impaling Cosowarth.

5. Five coats; *1*, Pendarves impaling Prideaux; *2*, Pendarves impaling Hoblyn; *3*, Pendarves impaling Godolphin; *4*, Pendarves in lozence (for Mrs. Grace Percival, née Pendarves); *5*, Stackhouse impaling Pendarves.

The Church Plate

The earliest reference to this occurs in the Returns of church plate, which had been confiscated from 1549 to 1553 by Edward VI's orders, and was subsequently re-delivered to the churches by order of Mary Tudor.[31] The entry for *Cambron* specifies two chalices, with their patens, normally regarded as covers for the chalices, weighing 30 ozs. The metal is not specified but is almost certainly silver.

In 1683, the Churchwardens' Accounts contain this entry:[32]

'Memorandum. That Wm. Pendarves of Pendarves Esq. did present on good friday this year a guilded Chalice for the Administration of the holy sacrament to this parish, Mr. John Collins being then Rector. And there doth belong unto the sd parish another Chalice, which was formerly used and a silver saucer for the bread, and a Pewter flagon, Anno 1693.'

In the terrier of 1727 (Appendix C), the church plate is listed as one silver cup gilded with gold, and one silver salver, both weighing 20 ozs. and three-quarters troy weight; also one large flagon of pewter. This is substantially the same list as that of 1693, except that the 'another Chalice' of the latter year is not mentioned, and may have been disposed of. The silver salver, or saucer of 1693, may be the patent mentioned in the 1553 *Returns;* as only one chalice is described in 1693, one of the two 16th-century ones, noted in the *Returns* as being 'defacyd', may have been sent to the Tower for melting down.

A list of the present plate is given in the 1949 edition of the church guide,[33] though it is not quite clear whether either the 1553 chalice, or the one given by William Pendarves, still exist. The dated pieces are: a large silver paten with raised cable-moulding, hall-marked for 1708, and inscribed 'W. H. T. H. Churchwardens 1720'—(probably William Harris and Thomas Hocking); a tall silver flagon hall-marked for 1720, and inscribed 'Exdone G.C. 1727' (there is no clue as to who G.C. may have been), and a silver communion-cup said to be hall-marked for 1738. There are in addition two other chalices, one silver-gilt and one silver, and three patens, one silver-gilt and two silver.

Charities
A list of the various charities, some of them of an educational nature and discussed in the next chapter, is given on a board hanging in the church tower; the most adequate list occurs in the Report of the Charity Commissioners.[34]

NOTES

1. Creswell 1910, largely based on Thurstan C. Peter's notes.
2. Morton 1936; Morton 1949 (ed. Vincent); Vincent 1959.
3. e.g. Arthur Adams in *PZNHAS n.s.* III (1888-92), 205; the same, Camborniana 1897, 24; Creswell 1910, 11; Carah 1925, 30.
4. This seems to be shown in fig. 26, town plan of 1805.
5. Thomas 1964, 12, and pl. ii, lower left.
6. Cf. Adams, in Camborniana 1897, 25, who for some reason accuses Charles Basset, the Rector, and his curate Mr. Vigurs, of this 'Vandalism'.
7. There was apparently a small church-like structure in the garden at Lower Rosewarne, traditionally built from pieces ejected during some such alterations. From 1738 to 1775, John Trevenen, then curate, lived at Lower Rosewarne. Information from the present owner, Mr. Johnson Glanville, who recalls this from when he was a boy. Carah (1927, 13) notes an entry from the Churchwardens' Accounts, 1725: 'Paid Joseph Hocking for building the Loft, £26. 10s.'. Does this refer to the main gallery at the west end of the nave?
8. Anonymous article, *WMN* of (first week in ?) November 1921, entitled 'St. Martin's Feast'. Hugh Rogers is said to have been the first to introduce church Sunday Schools into the county.
9. Tuck 1880, 4.
10. *Ibidem.*

11. Apart from pieces in the south porch (p. 143), one is now the lintel of the north door in a two-storey barn about 50 yards up the road from 'Largiemore', Lower Rosewarne; information from Mr. Johnson Glanville.
12. *The Ecclesiologist* XX (i.e. vol. 20) (1859), 137.
13. Cf. *Cornishman* 11 November, 1965 ('Thriving Church his monument').
14. Blight SB I, fols. 30a, 30b, at Penzance Library.
15. Creswell 1910, 13 ('. . . it appears to have been constructed out of old bench-ends'); Adams, Camborniana 1897, 25 ('. . . saving some few of the panels of the rood-screen and converting them into a Pulpit'); and now Pevsner (!), *Cornwall* (Penguin, 1951), 40.
16. The writer is especially grateful to his friend and colleague Mr. J. V. S. Megaw for actually doing this.
17. Creswell 1910, 11.
18. *PZNHAS n.s.* III (1888-92) 205.
19. The late Dr. F. C. Eeles, *in litt.* 26 October, 1950.
20. Creswell 1910, 17: cf. entries in the Churchwardens' Accounts like 'expenses for cleaning the sentences', in 1774.
21. J. C. C. Probert, *The Architecture of Cornish Methodism* (Cornish Meth. Hist. Assn., Occas. Publ. no. 10, 1966) 16-19.
22. Cox 1912, 46-48.
23. Jean Crowley, 'Cornish Sundials: I', *CA* 2 (1963), 34-46 illus.
24. This has given rise to the current misreading of 'Th(omas) Philoma' as the imagined maker's name!
25. Creswell 1910, Vincent 1959, etc. The fullest and best list is in Polsue-Lake, vol. II, under 'Camborne'.
26. F. H. Davey, 'Neville Northy Burnard', 77 *RCPS* (1910), 248-280.
27. His unmarked grave was at last located by Canon Sandfield in 1953, and subsequently (through the efforts of Camborne Old Cornwall Society) marked by a slate headstone, donated as a tribute by the Delabole Slate Quarry.
28. This is based on a long MS. essay, Camborne Bells, written by the late Rev. A. A. Clinnick about 1925 (MS. Clinnick).
29. *CRP* 8 November 1960.
30. Some of this is explicable by the Pendarves pedigree, as in J. L. Vivian's *The Visitations of Cornwall* (Exeter 1887), 355; some of it refers to Mrs. Pendarves' own Devon family of Trist.
31. L. S. Snell, *Documents towards a history of the Reformation in Cornwall, 2; The Edwardian Inventories of Church Goods for Cornwall* (Exeter, 1955), 38.
32. Peter 1909, 381.
33. Morton 1949, 20.
34. *Reports of the Charity Commissioners relating to . . . Cornwall, 1819-1837* (London, 1837), 790.

XII

MISCELLANEOUS ANTIQUITIES

The Glebe Land

The glebe is that portion of land which is assigned to an incumbent as part of his benefice; in early centuries, the profit from farming the glebe was frequently the only method by which an incumbent could, over and above tithes in kind, support his family. The nature of the former Camborne glebe land can be defined from surviving terriers, those of 1601, 1626, 1680 and 1727, the full texts of which are printed as Appendix C below. Terriers (from the Latin *terrarium*, itself from *terra*, 'land') are descriptive inventories of glebe land and fields, of any buildings including the parsonage, of implements, of rights of tithe, and even, when these are demanded, of church fittings and customary payments. Such terriers were made from time to time at the order of the Bishop, copies frequently being retained in the parish chest, and they served among other purposes to define church rights and to prevent any improper encroachment upon ecclesiastical privileges. They constitute documents of the highest interest, not least in the field of agricultural history,[1] and have been surprisingly little employed in local historical studies in Cornwall.

It was suggested on p.15 that the glebe land may, in origin, have been the northern end of the early medieval tenement called *Cambron* (fig. 3), detached and allotted to the support of the church by the Bassets, as patrons of the living,[2] possibly in the 12th or 13th centuries. There appears to have been a belief, which finds explicit statement in the 1680 terrier, that the glebe land when originally given amounted to '40 acres'. The 'acre' here means the so-called Cornish acre, five of which equal six statute acres,[3] and 48 statute acres is close enough, bearing the inadequacy of early methods of mensuration in mind, to the real acreage, which appears to have been about fifty-one.

The most instructive aspect of the terriers is that which depicts the progressive enclosure of the glebe land, a process which shows in microcosm what was happening all over the county. The 1601 terrier mentions four fields, the external hedges of which stood on the adjoining lands. This is an important provision, which may suggest that the hedges had not been all that long erected; for 'hedge' here means, not a line of vegetation, but the Cornish hedge, which has sloping stone faces and an earthen core, and can be up to six or more feet across its base. The area of potential arable which would have been lost, had these hedges stood within the glebe boundary, would have been at least an acre.

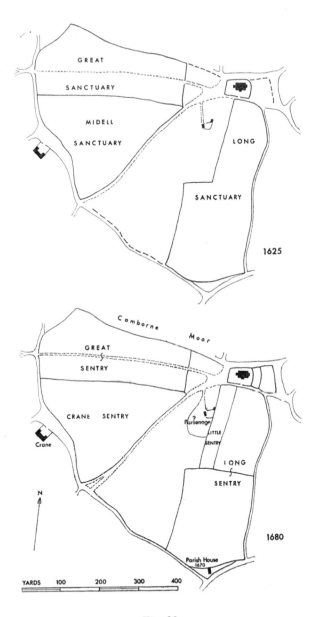

Fig. 29
Reconstructions of Camborne glebe lands from the Terriers (see Appendix C), 1625 and 1680.

The 1625 terrier names the fields as Great Sanctuary, Midell Sanctuary, and Long Sanctuary (fig. 29). The word 'Sanctuary', from French *santuaire* through Middle English *sentuarie*, is a common name for a glebe field, meaning no more than 'church ground', and is frequently corrupted (as in the 1680 terrier) to 'Sentry'. The sketch-maps, figs. 29 and 30, are in one sense reversed, since the location of these fields depends upon working backwards from 1840 and 1805[3], when it is possible to detect the obvious sub-divisions of the fields, and allotting the names in accordance with topographical clues (e.g., Crane Sentry must have stood next to Crane) and the acreages given in the terriers. One can see that the loss of a field as between 1601 and 1625 must be due to the 1625 Long Sanctuary representing a coalition of two earlier fields.

In 1680, the terrier, which is unfortunately physically defective and not all that clearly expressed, gives the fields with their individual extents. These add up to a total (checked from the 1727 figures) of 38.3 Cornish acres, which gives 45.9 statute acres—acceptably near the true total of just over 44 acres. 'Great Sentry' has been divided into two fields, probably only by the churchway footpath which traverses it, though the figure of '20 acres' is wildly out here; 'Midell Sanctuary' has become 'Crane Sentry'; and the Long Sanctuary of 1625 has again been split into two fields, which do together amount more or less to 8 Cornish acres (9.1 statute acres is the real extent). There is an additional field called 'Little Sentry', whose most probable position is also shown in fig. 29.

A greater attempt at accuracy has been made in the 1727 terrier (fig. 30). The fields are now all named and given extents which descend into fractions. Crane Sanctuary, and the Great Sanctuary (treated as undivided), still remain; there is a new enclosure called 'Parish Close'; and the Long Sanctuary has been split into 'Parsonage Croft', its northern portion, and a southern portion which is divided into Trezurthen Higher and Lower Sanctuaries. There is an implication, therefore, that between 1680 and 1727 the lower part of the Long Sanctuary had been re-named 'Trezurthen Sanctuary'; an odd name, which does not occur elsewhere in the parish, can hardly represent the place-name Treswithian in any of its older forms (see Appendix G), and may have been invented, though what Cornish word the second element represents is not clear. The position of the Bowling Green, which replaces the former Little Sanctuary, is to some extent independently fixed.[4]

The acreage as given in the 1727 terrier compares with the statute acreage, as taken from the corresponding pieces of land on the O.S. 25-inch sheet, in such a way as to suggest that the 1727 unit was 1.15 of a statute acre. This is near enough to the proportion of a Cornish acre (1.19 statute acres—an error of only 4 per cent) to show that Cornish acres were being used here.

Presumably most, if not all, of the glebe was cultivated. The 1625 terrier speaks of 'tillable lands'. An interesting point is that the eastern edge of the Long Sanctuary (after 1727, the Parsonage Croft and the two Trezurthen Sanctuaries) became fossilised at an early stage, because it was also the course of a right-of-way, track, or footpath, called 'Bounder

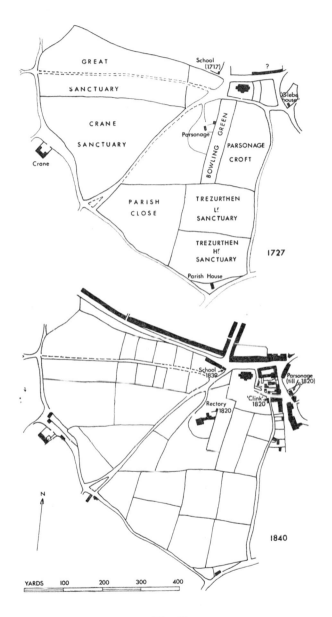

Fig. 30
Reconstructions of Camborne glebe lands from the 1727 Terrier (see Appendix C) and the Tithe Map, 1840.

Vean' (C. *bounder vyghan*, 'little lane'). Its perpetuation into the 20th century was due to its having formed the line of walls at the end of the gardens to the houses springing up along Basset Road or 'New Road'. Now this line, as shown in fig. 30, is not straight, as fields laid out *de novo* might be expected to give, but is really a classic series of shallow curves— the so-called 'aratral curves' resulting from prolonged ploughing of strips by teams of oxen[5], where a combination of features (slight slope of the ground, the lateral drag exercised by a heavy plough, etc.) can bring this about. This field-formation goes back to at least the 17th century and probably earlier, when it was in the highest degree unlikely that the incumbents, most of whom were absentees or pluralists, farmed the glebe themselves, and we cannot assume that this was always done by the curates. The series of shallow curves suggest that the whole Long Sanctuary area—and quite possibly the Great Sanctuary too—may have been laid out in strips (in Cornwall, *stitches* or *quillets*) for the inhabitants of the churchtown hamlet and its surrounds, as tenants of whoever farmed the glebe. The complete absence of any other traces of such bundles of stitches, almost invariably detectable in Cornwall as a concomitant of the medieval churchtown settlement,[6] is very puzzling.

The lower plan in fig. 30, which is taken from the Tithe Map, shows what had happened to the glebe by 1840; the inevitable sub-division into smaller fields, a process which led to still further sub-division and finally the sale of most of the glebe in the 1920's. Today (1966) it has almost all been developed for housing, the bulk of it the inter-war years Council Estate.

The Parsonage and the Rectory

It is doubtful whether many of the medieval rectors lived in the parish at all. The first terrier which mentions the 'mansion house' or parsonage is that of 1625; absence of any such mention in 1601 does not of itself imply that none then existed, since the rector, John Harding, was buried at Camborne[7] and presumably resided there as well.

The 1625 parsonage had, on its east side, 'more' land, which consisted of 'one house with a garden' ('house' here may be just 'house of office', i.e. a barn). In the 1680 terrier, John Collins describes his parsonage as being two-storied, with three chambers or upper rooms, and insofar as the defective text can be read, he claims the use of a barn, mowhay (rickyard) and garden, which must be the establishment mentioned in 1625. Collins' further references in this terrier to 'a stone house . . . a little meadow and garden hedged in out of the common' seem to refer to the same thing, as they are said to be in 'the towne place'. The phrase *townplace*, not yet extinct in Cornish rural usage, means all the area (sometimes paved, more often a sea of mud) around and behind the farm with its quadrangle of farm-buildings.

The indication is that the 17th-century parsonage was no more than a farmhouse with appropriate outbuildings. Its precise position is not known, but the odds are that it occupied more or less the site of the present rectory with its outbuildings, and it is shown there in figs. 29 and 30.

In the 1727 terrier, the parsonage is rather more fully described—we learn that it was 30 by 13 feet, which sounds tiny, but is no smaller than the majority of Cornish farmhouses today—and the size of the 'Garden and Mowhay' is given as a quarter-acre and 21 perches. We are also told of two other buildings, church property, but *off* the glebe; one is a two-storey house with two little gardens and a little meadow behind it, and the other is a single-roomed building of 'mud' (that is, cob-walled). The latter, as Mr. T. R. Harris points out to the writer, is almost certainly the school built under the provisions of Francis Basset's 1717 will, and discussed below. The former can perhaps be located with reference to later events. Joseph Vivian, who was born in 1835, states in his reminiscences (Appendix F) that the former parsonage house of Camborne had been 'a very mean house' (as the 1727 terrier might suggest) and that it was on the corner of Gurney's Lane and Commercial Street, a site subsequently occupied by a shoe-shop (Harris's Boot Co.). There is no reason to doubt this first-hand statement. The 1805 Tehidy map, fig. 26, shows in precisely this spot an isolated dwelling with a plot of ground behind it—the 'little meadow' of the terrier? It was probably occupied by curates, and according to T. C. Peter[8] may have been known as 'the Glebe house'.

By the early 19th century, the parsonage proper may have become either too small or too dilapidated for the times. Hugh Rogers, rector from 1816 to 1853, at first gives his address as 'Camborne Veor'.[9] The farm-house at Camborne Veor was a Basset property, and the rector was Lord De Dunstanville's nephew, so this is quite explicable. From 1821, however, the rector and his wife were 'at Camborne Parsonage',[10] and as Rogers in his *Reply* to the bishop during that year[11] refers to his rectory as 'an house very lately built under the Gilbert Acts', it must have been built about 1820.

Camborne Rectory is a large, solid house, constructed in rag masonry with granite coigns. It has a false front rendered in the most carefully cut Bath or Cotswold stone, giving an air of charm and dignity, and an impression of a style rather earlier than 1820. Comparatively few people outside the town—and not everyone within it—know what this building looks like, and as it seems only once to have been illustrated in print,[12] pl. XV, a frontal view, is included here.

The Bowling Green

By no means all the glebe was enclosed at once, and in 1680 the 'garden' on the glebe, by the parsonage (fig. 29) is stated to have been 'hedged in out of the common'. This may imply that the unenclosed parts of the glebe, criss-crossed by customary footpaths, were treated as common land by the parishioners—Tuck rather implies that this was still so in the first quarter of the 19th century[13]—but the 1827 reference to a 'bowling green' undoubtedly refers to a real green or rink where this game was played. As far as one can ascertain, it was near the churchyard (fig. 30), the rest of the former Little Sanctuary becoming eventually the rectory kitchen garden.

There is a reference in J. Harris Stone's well-known book[14] to this sport, which goes on 'At St. Ives, Marazion, and *Camborne* ... the bowling green was Corporation property'. This cannot strictly refer to Camborne, which had no charter, no Mayor, and no corporation, but it suggests that Mr. Stone had encountered a source of information which neither the present writer, nor any previous writer about Camborne, has been able to locate.

The Churchyard

Fig. 30 shows the enlargement of the churchyard. Up to 1727, and later, it retained what must have been the original 12th-century lay-out. The main entrance was on the south side, opposite the main (south) door of the church, and doubtless the churchyard cross, no. 1 (p. 86), stood just inside the gateway, in the base which is now occupied by cross no. 2 (p. 88) and which seems never to have left the churchyard.

By 1840 (fig. 30, lower) the first expansion has taken place; the Bowling Green has gone (and Tuck seems to imply[15] that it was no longer used as such in the 1820's, indeed that the very name had been transferred to the open ground west of it) and the northern end of Parsonage Croft has become added to the cemetery area. A note in the parish registers indicates that this enlargement took place in 1816. Today the graveyard has spread still further, in keeping with the enormous population expansion of the parish, and occupies the whole area marked as Parsonage Croft in fig. 30.

The Clink

The small building shown under this name in fig. 26 and fig. 30 post-dates the churchyard extension of 1816. It was used for some years as a 'clink' or parish lock-up for wrong-doers. The whole structure is rather unusual. It was built as an additional two-storey vestry, and the upper storey is still called the Vestry Room and was until recently used for the Parochial Church Council meetings. The ground floor was divided into two. The west side, facing the church-yard, has cut granite mullions and lintels, and inside were two rooms. One, with a door and two windows (now blocked) opened to the east, on to the lane, and the date '1820' is cut on one of the stones forming the door surround. This was the Clink. The other part, now a tool-store, was all that was available in 1906 for the headquarters of the local St. John Ambulance Brigade.[16] The Clink ceased to be used as such about 1858, when the police station in Moor Street was opened.

The former Church School

Under his will of 1717, Francis Basset of Tehidy left an annuity of £5 for teaching poor children of Camborne to read and write.[17] This sum was expended on the teacher's salary; from 1731 to 1739, for example, Richard Craze of Illogan was paid £1. 5s. a quarter for this office, and from January 1739, Ralph Williams. In 1779, the Tehidy accounts mention a payment to 'Henry Bond (schoolmaster) for teaching poor children at

Camborne half year to the 29th January last', and in 1786, James Gray had 'a years sallary for keeping the Free School in Camborne to the 6th June last, £5.'

The actual school building must have been provided by either Basset, or the parish, but on land owned by Basset. It may be identified with the building mentioned by William Tuck,[18] in relation to his 'walk-around' description of Church Street:

'Standing directly across the street, there stood an ancient-looking structure with its two windows facing the town toward Church Street. This antiquated building was of very early date . . . At the time of which I am writing, the early part of the present century' [i.e., *circa* 1820] 'this little sanctuary was occupied by a Mr. Reece for a school-room . . .'

The description implies that this school was the small building, shown in figs. 26 and 30, standing square-on to the west end of Church Street. This again carries the implication that it is the ('antiquated' and 'ancient-looking') building mentioned in the 1727 terrier as lying off the glebe land, and as being 'built with mud' (cob) and having 'a ground floor nor wainscotted nor ceiled'; which is borne out by Tuck's remark that is possessed only two windows.

Tuck continues:[19]

'It was not long after . . . this ancient school-room had to be removed to make room for the new road then projected from Camborne to Treswithian, and the name of Mr. Reece became a dead letter. It may be here mentioned that the above building was the property of the inhabitants, the freeholder' (Basset) 'having to compensate for it either by purchase or exchange—it was arranged that the late Lord De Dunstanville should provide similar accommodation close by it, which was known as the Bowling Green . . . I have however lately been told that it has now been included in the glebe land. The occupier of the new building was a Mr. John Thomas, who kept a school at one end, the other being used as a dispensary.'

The building was certainly demolished for the Turnpike, which ran straight through where it had stood, in 1839 if not before. The replacement building was a little to the south, and is shown in fig. 30, lower. It is described by Mr. John Arthur[20] in 1928, presumably from some older informant:

'The front of the house at the top of College Street from Mr. Harvey's shop to the Plough Inn was kept up on pillars. The upper room was overhanging the under rooms. The upper room was for many years a school kept by Mr. John Thomas.'

What is not certain is whether, in the early years of the 19th century, the school was still a free (Church) school, with a salary of £5 paid over by the churchwardens, and the pupils drawn from the illiterate poor; or whether economic considerations had brought about a change of character, only the actual premises remaining ecclesiastical (or parochial) property. One suspects the latter case. The name 'College Row' for the houses added west of the school, along a lane in the direction of Treswithian (fig. 30, upper), is found as early as 1819,[21] antedates the Turnpike Road by twenty years, and suggests that the 'Free School' of 1786 had been elevated to 'College' status.

Mr. Reece, who came from St. Austell, was appointed to 'Camborne New School', in 1818, to take charge of twelve boarders and a limited number of day pupils, and to teach English grammar, arithmetic, etc.[22] Either Tuck is at fault in associating Mr. Reece with the Church school, or there were two people of this name, or Mr. Reece had taught at the Church School up to 1818 and at 'Camborne New School' after that; but the two establishments do not sound as if they could possibly be the same, unless the Church school had radically changed its nature (the 'boarders' were presumably lodged in a house in the town?).

The idea that Mr. Reece had changed his employment has most to commend it, since his successor, Mr. John Thomas, appears to have been the master of the Church school in the 1820's. In a Directory of 1830, under 'Schoolmasters', Mr. Thomas' name appears, but not Mr. Reece's.[23] William Cock Vivian of Reskadinnick (1818-1918) interviewed at the age of 100,[24] gave a long account of how, having attended a dame's school kept by the wife of David Duckham, then the parish clerk, he was sent to Mr. Thomas' school, and this would have been about 1826-1830.

The career of Mr. John Thomas affords an interesting side-light on Camborne at this period, He was born a few years before 1800, a younger brother of Captain Charles Thomas of Killivose (the present writer's great-great-grandfather) and the son of a mine-captain at Dolcoath. In 1818, with his brother Charles, he was admitted as a local preacher in the Camborne circuit.[25] (There is some evidence[26] that Mr. Reece was himself a Methodist minister, which looks as if the master of the Free School was not required to be an Anglican.) According to John Harris,[27] Mr. Thomas was also (1825) a Sunday School teacher. His education came largely from private study and, as Dr. George Smith tells us[28]

'. . . he not only acquired a respectable acquaintance with mathematics, but became a tolerable linguist, knowing French, Latin, Greek, Hebrew, and I believe some other languages, and was for many years the master of the grammar school in Camborne.'

In addition to all this, he was a subscriber to the *Classical Journal*, possessing a set of bound volumes—which still exist—from the commencement in 1810; and with his sisters Mary and Eliza he wrote a deal of poetry in rather a melancholy vein.[29]

The post-1839 school, once Harvey's stores and later Kendall's, was extensively re-built in 1965 to provide a number of smaller shops, but the upper part, with its pointed 'chapel' windows, has been preserved. During this re-building, the 1839 granite pillars along the front, mentioned by John Arthur (above, p. 155), were revealed, and are shown in fig. 31, a sketch made at the time by Mr. Michael Tangye of Redruth.

The Charity School at Penpons

In 1760, Mrs. Grace Percival of Pendarves founded a school for twenty poor children, twelve being boys and eight being girls, between the ages

Fig. 31
Pillared front of the post-1839 successor to the old 'Church School', as revealed in re-building, 1965; sketch by Mr. Michael Tangye, Redruth.

of 7 and 14. These children were to be inhabitants of Camborne parish, preference being given to the Pendarves tenantry, and each child was to be presented with a Bible and prayer-book upon leaving. The master, who had a salary of £21 per annum and a free house, with liberty to take up to ten private pupils in addition, was to be 'a person of a religious and sober life and conversation, professing the religion of the Church of England'; and the rector of Camborne and squire of Pendarves were to act as managers and trustees.[30]

The endowment took the form of a tenement and houses in Penpons village known as *Parkanfenton*—this was somewhere between the present (Lower) Penpons and the Penpons Mill tenement—'with the dwelling-house then used as a school-house'—though how long prior to 1760 it had been a school is not stated.

The school, frequently referred to as 'Mrs. Percival's School', seems at most times to have been run by the parish clerks of Camborne. The first master is not known, but probably the second was John Gribble, parish clerk from 1780.[31] He retired in 1802, when he was 53, and the post was duly advertised in the *Sherborne Mercury* (to teach reading, writing, and arithmetic: salary £21, free dwelling-house, and other advantages, £35 in all[32]). David Duckham, parish clerk from 1824(?) to 1837, seems to have succeeded him, one of his earliest pupils being Charles Thomas, whose memoir[33] states that he was sent to the 'school of the parish clerk, at that time the best in the neighbourhood.' If we are to judge by this former pupil's superb calligraphy[34] and practical application in mathematics,[35] Gribble and David Duckham must have been fairly competent teachers.

Duckham's name also appears in 1830 as the master of a school in Camborne, [36] though according to William Cock Vivian this was really a dame's school conducted by Mrs. Duckham.

A subsequent master was a Mr. Whear, whose daughter, another amateur Sappho, was a friend of Charles and John Thomas and their poetry-writing sisters. Mr. John Arthur implies that the school at some stage moved from Penpons, and was conducted in a house at Ramsgate, a hamlet between Baripper and the Pendarves north lodge. [37] In the decade 1840-1850, it moved to Treslothan, somewhere near the present church, [38] and was finally closed in 1876, the Percival moneys then being applied by the Charity Commissioners to the maintenance of Camborne National School in College Street. [39]

The Parish House

The office of Overseer of the Poor was created in 1572 (14 Eliz. c.5), but it was the 1601 'Poor Law' (43 Eliza. c.2) which formed the basis of local poor-law administration. [40] It is likely that it was under the provisions of this act that a parish like Camborne, with a comparatively small poor-rate, was first obliged to provide a 'parish house' or poor-house, in which the destitute would have to be housed at the parish's expense.

According to Carah, [41] references in the Rate Book for Camborne from 1647 indicate that there was such an establishment at 'Gherry Water'; possibly near the modern Roscroggan, that is, down in the Red River valley beyond the hamlet of (Wheal) Gerry or 'Gurry'. In 1670, Basset of Tehidy conveyed a small plot of land, part of Camborne Veor and just off the south-west corner of the glebe, to the parish, [42] for a new alms-house, which was duly built in 1671 (cf. fig. 29 above).

This must have been a fairly substantial building, since the account for it [43] includes 60 feet of 'crests' (ridge-tiles) at £1—the crests (as in fig. 17 above) would have been 15 ins. long, so four dozen would be needed, at 5d. each. [44] The accounts are of some interest; '2 horse loads of hairs from Helston' (this was too much for Canon Carah, but probably refers to chopped horse-hair or cow-hair used in the lime plastering of the interior), and no less than 10,000 Delabole slates, at 11s. the thousand.

The exact location of this 'parish house' was pointed out some years ago by the writer, [45] unaware that it is in fact shown on Thomas Martyn's 1748 map (fig. 5; 'Alms house'). It is also referred to in the 1680 terrier as '. . . the Almshouse at the charge of the parish consisting of 3 houses of the parish . . . and a garden also hedged and with a half acre of ground in the highway' (Appendix C, p. 174). This suggests that the 60 feet of roof covered three small houses side by side.

Carah [46] has discussed at length the entries in the now-lost Rate Book (1647-1717) which refer to the administration of this building, and the treatment of the poor; it is sufficient here to say that, in comparison with the brutality which such accounts all too frequently display, the quality of mercy does seem to have been exhibited in Camborne.

In the early 19th century, when the parish had increased its population very considerably, the parish registers contain a number of cryptic entries

—mostly under *Burials*, some under *Baptisms*—which allude to an additional establishment. The normal formula is (burials) 'Eliza Tallack, of *Parish House*, 8 months, croupe'[47], or 'Thomas Edward of *Poor House*, aet. 54',[48] but in 1817, 1818, 1823, 1824, 1826, and 1832, there are also references to burials where the address is given as 'Penpons Poor House'.[49] No doubt it proved necessary to find this extra accommodation. Was it conceivably the former dwelling-house of Mrs. Percival's school, if the latter had really been removed to Ramsgate at this time (p. 158)?

The use of the Camborne parish house came to an end with the Act of 1834, the 'New Poor Law' (4 & 5 W.IV, c.76), which compulsorily amalgamated parishes into Poor Law Unions, under Boards of Guardians, and inaugurated the establishments known as workhouses. It is perhaps not generally known that, within the Redruth Union (which included Camborne), the first workhouse was not Barncoose, Redruth—now a geriatric hospital—but the large building on Camborne Hill known as Trevu, for many years the home of Dr. George Smith. The tender for its building was advertised on 7th March, 1834, and it was duly constructed; but with the inauguration of the Redruth Union in 1837, it was sold to Dr. Smith, though on some copies of the Tithe Map for the parish, it is actually marked as 'Workhouse'.[50]

The old Poor House was demolished at some stage in the 19th century, and a stable-block constructed in the same plot; for some years this was a livery-stable. In 1955, this was demolished, and the plot cleared, and subsequently built over.

The Parish Registers and Accounts

Camborne is fortunate in possessing an almost complete set of its Registers of baptisms, burials, and marriages, from their commencement in 1538. It is even more fortunate that, following the publication of the Marriages (1538-1812) in 1911,[51] the entire set has been printed up to 1837, the year in which civil registration commenced under the Births and Deaths Registration Act of the previous year.[52] This latter publication has the Marriages and Burials from 1538, but the Baptisms only from 1592, the earliest entry which can now be deciphered, and has been checked against the various 'Bishop's transcripts' at Exeter.

Physically, the Registers comprise fourteen volumes, kept in the church safe, of which Vol. VIII, Marriages from 1776 to 1790, is missing, and has been for some time.[53] Neither the Rev. Morton, nor his successor Canon Sandfield, was able to locate it, and its whereabouts remains a mystery.

The Churchwardens' Accounts for the parish were for many years in a poor condition, and the main volume was rescued from waterlogged destruction by the late Mr. Thomas Fiddick, J.P., of Camborne Cross. It was admirably repaired and rebound, but, perhaps in the absence of specific instructions, the sheets were not bound up in the correct order, and this makes the book infuriatingly difficult to use. It covers the period from 1675 to 1780, the phase which really saw Camborne transformed from a hamlet of medieval character to a nascent mining town. An analysis of certain aspects of it was published by T. C. Peter in 1909, and further extracts, enlivened by much human wisdom and local knowledge, by Canon Carah in 1927.[54] The book, whose considerable interest would probably justify the cost of re-binding correctly, and which even in these days might profitably be printed *in toto*, is now at the Royal Institution of Cornwall, Truro. There is a later book of Churchwardens' Accounts, dating from about 1810, still in the possession of the Rector.

A former Rate Book, which, as Canon Carah says,[55] 'is really the account book of the Overseers' (of the Poor), was until the 1930's in the possession of the late Mr. F. J. Stephens, of Reskadinnick. He made certain notes from it,[56] and fuller extracts were published by Carah,[57] but the book itself seems to have disappeared. In case the present possessor should, unawares, read this, it seems worth repeating the description; an old calf-bound volume 13½ inches by 9 inches, with the Royal Arms, the letters 'C.R.' (*Carolus Rex*) and the date '1647', and above this the words 'Camborne Parish', all impressed in gilt on the cover. The leaves are, or were, loose, and the binding broken. The book covered the period 1647-1717.

A number of minor documents are still held in the parish safe, or by the Rector, including a Tithe Map, and Tithe Apportionment Survey (the book, which in the case of Camborne was printed; Liddell, Bodmin, 1840). There are duplicates of these at the County Record Office, Truro, together with the originals of the documents printed here as Appendix C. 'A huge mass of the parish records was not so successfully dealt with, as it was sold for waste paper' wrote Canon Carah; also, an all too common story in Cornwall a generation ago.

NOTES

1. W. E. Tate, *The Parish Chest* (3rd edn., 1960), 126, rightly stresses this point.
2. Their patronage dates from at least the 13th century; the Inquisition concerning William Basset at Tehidy in 1303 shows that he had held the advowsons of 'Cambron, S. Ilogan, and S. Uny Rudruth' (*Calendar of Inquis. Post Mortem*, IV, Edw. I (1913), no. 245). The Thomas Basset who heads the list of rectors (Appendix D) was presumably a cousin or relation.
3. i.e., from the Tithe Map (1838-40), and the Tehidy Estate map of 1805, part of which is shown in fig. 26.
4. The best account of the Cornish acre is in *Notes and Queries; Antiquarian Lore of the West*, ed. J. H. Rowe, *WMN* c. 1922-1927, no. 445, by A. Pearse Jenkin; more accessible will be MacLean's *Trigg Minor*, II (1875), 339, 335, E. Smirke in *Report RIC* (1862), 18, 69, and W. F. Karkeek's essay in *Journ. Roy. Agric. Society* VI (1846), 457.
5. S. R. Eyre, 'The curving plough strip and its historical implications', *Agric. History Review* III (1955), 80 ff.
6. Well shown at, e.g., the neighbouring parish churchtown of Gwithian; for the best overall discussion, see P. Flatrès, *Géographie Rurale de quatre contrées celtiques, Irland, Galles, Cornwall et Man* (Rennes, 1957).
7. 25 November 1611 (*RPC* I, 102).
8. T. C. Peter, *Notes on the History of the Church in Redruth* (Camborne, 1899), 25; it is not absolutely clear whether this refers to Redruth or Camborne, but the context suggests the latter.
9. *RPC* II, 703, 713 (1817-19, the birth of his two children).

10. *RPC* II, 721, 729.
11. M. Cook, *The Diocese of Exeter in 1821: Bishop Carey's Replies, etc.*, Devon & Cornwall Record Society (1958), 8.
12. Creswell 1910, 23 (photograph of the front).
13. J. Harris Stone, *England's Riviera* (1912), 358.
13. Tuck, 1880, 7.
15. *Ibidem.*
16. *Cornishman*, 9 December 1954 (T. C. Quintrell's reminiscences).
17. Information from Mr. T. R. Harris, Camborne.
18. Tuck, 1880, 5-6.
19. Tuck 1880, 6.
20. MS. Arthur.
21. *RPC* II, 895.
22. Information from Mr. T. R. Harris.
23. Pigot, 1830, 138.
24. *CP*, undated cutting of 1918.
25. J. F. Odgers, *Early Methodism in Camborne: Wesley Chapel 1828-1958* (Camborne, 1959), 115.
26. *Bib. Cornub.* II, 670, under 'Theophilus A. Smith', who from 1818 to 1822 was educated at Camborne by 'Rev. Richard Reece'. The Index (*ibidem*, III, 1468) describes him as 'Wesleyan minister' and says he died in 1850.
27. *My Autobiography* (1882), 20 ('under the godly superintendence of Mr. John Thomas, who was a thoroughly educated man').
28. George Smith, *The Christian Warrior Crowned: a sermon on the death of Mr. Charles Thomas, etc.* (Camborne, 1868), 27.
29. MS. album in the writer's possession; typical titles are 'Parting Love', 'The Bequest', and 'Lines written at Pendarves on a Winter's Day, 1819'.
30. MS. Clinnick, essay on 'Education in Camborne'; cf. *Parl. Papers* (1872), XVI, and *ditto*, 1867-8, XXVIII, pp. 405-67, 520-527.
31. Tuck 1880, 4 ('The former schoolmaster was a Mr. Gribble').
32. *Sherborne Mercury*, advertisement, 19 December 1802 (reference kindly supplied by Mr. H. L. Douch).
33. Smith, *op. cit.* note 28, 19.
34. He copied out an entire treatise on punctuation, in copperplate and three different inks, at the age of 67, 'with the intention of improving his own calligraphy and style'.
35. Cf. his *Tables for ascertaining the value of tin stuff* (Redruth, 1836).
36. Pigot, 1830, 138.
37. MS. Arthur ('a house at Ramsgate, where there is an arch over the door of two cottages'—1928).
38. Information from Mr. T. R. Harris.
39. MS. Clinnick.
40. The account in Tate, 1960 (note 1 above), 187 ff., is, like much else in this classic work, the most convenient.
41. Carah 1927, 8.
42. Deed at RIC, Truro.
43. Carah 1927, 8-9.
44. Cf. the account for repairs to the Old Coinage Hall, Lostwithiel, in 1455 (*DCNQ*, vol. for 1916), when 'crestys' cost only 1½d. a foot.
45. Thomas, 1949.
46. Carah 1927, 8 ff.
47. *RPC* II, 948.
48. *RPC* II, 903.
49. *RPC* II, 890, 891, 902, 905, 907, 914, 933.
50. Cf. T. R. Harris, *CRP* 12 April 1960 ('How the Poor have been cared for in Camborne').
51. *Cornwall Parish Registers*, ed. W. P. W. Phillimore and Thomas Taylor; vol. XIX (1911), Marriages, Redruth, Camborne, and Boyton (II).

52. (Cited as *RPC*) *The Register of . . . the Parish of Camborne, Cornwall, A.D. 1538 to 1837*, ed. H. Tapley-Soper: Devon and Cornwall Record Society, Exeter (1945), 2 vols.
53. Cf. Phillimore and Taylor (note 51), 69; this volume was too big to fit in the safe; and see *RPC* I, v.
54. T. C. Peter, 'The Churchwardens' Accounts of the Parish of Camborne', *JRIC* XVII (1909), 381: Carah 1927, 11-20.
55. Carah, 1927, second part, 1.
56. Stephens, 1925.
57. Carah, 1927, second part.

XIII

MISCELLANEOUS ANTIQUITIES, CONTINUED

In this chapter, a number of minor features, all more or less ecclesiastical in their significance, can be examined.

Inscribed stones

The inscribed memorial stones of the post-Roman period are relatively common in Cornwall[1]—their context was briefly discussed in chapter III, p. 47—but none have survived from the parish. Two confusing instances must be mentioned. It has long been known that the doorsill of a barn in the yard of Callean farm, in the north of the parish, bears some form of lettering. This was photographed by Mr. J. V. S. Megaw and the writer in 1956, and the print, when turned upside-down, proved to read *C.H. 1729 I.H.* As an older name for Callean or Killahan was 'Harris's Killahan'[2], the initials must stand for an earlier member of this family, probably Christopher Harris and his wife (Joan?). The stone must originally have been a lintel for a doorway.[3]

A more likely instance of an early inscribed stone comes from Roskear, though it is now unfortunately inaccessible, and may be read only by some sharp-eyed worker in the future. In 1930, Mr. S. A. Opie wrote that[4]

'during some alterations in a building near Tuckingmill, between Camborne and Redruth, a stone was found with a deal of 'lettering' on one side. Mr. Jim Thomas of Camborne was quickly notified, but on arrival he found that the stone had been placed in the foundations. Part of the inscription was still visible, however, it ran down the face of the stone in the usual manner of our Romano-British and later inscriptions. Unfortunately the stone was built up before a copy was made, and here again we must await further building operations. The site was at the corner where the road from North Roskear branches from the main Redruth and Camborne road' [that is, at SW 659410?] 'and was formerly occupied by a wheelwright's shop under the name of Jenkin.'[5]

The caves at Weeth

During the earlier part of this century, two caves or tunnels, cut in the 'head' or thick gravelly deposits at Weeth, on the north side of the Gilly Road, were found. Various claims have been made as to their antiquity, and indeed it has been suggested that the longer example, a tunnel, may have been connected with an abortive, and unfounded, 'tradition' of a monastery at its lower end, on the lane from Rosewarne down to Reskadinnick.

One of the tunnels, which was in the back part of the former Treglinwith farm, is simply a dug cellar of 18th or 19th-century date—cruder examples, used for storing potatoes, can be found in the valley above Carwynnen, and in the valleys further west around Trencrom, in Lelant parish. The other does not however seem either so regular, or so purposeful, and while one end opens into a kind of pit, the other, which apparently goes *under* the Gilly road, is blocked and fallen away. The most likely explanation is that the tunnel, which goes down to the stream at Reskadinnick, was dug to accommodate a water-supply (through pipes?) in connection with engines erected on the Weeth by the engineer Sampson Swaine, for working the former Weeth mine; Swaine agreed in 1764 to pay the Bassets 'for leave of the pool and leats' in this area.[7] There is no evidence at all that this tunnel is of any great age, or has any ecclesiastical significance.

Coffin at Crane

In pl. III, which shows the discovery of cross no. 2 (the large cross from Fenton-Ia, now by Camborne church) at Crane, a stone trough can be seen lying just in front of the well. As no one seems ever to have exhumed this, it is presumably still there under the ground, though the well itself was sollered over a few years ago.

This is not, as is frequently stated in newspaper articles, a coffin. The chapel at Crane was a domestic oratory (p. 62) and it is inconceivable that, in view of its general date and the proximity of Crane to the parish church, a right of burial existed here. Nor, even if it did, would hollowed-out granite coffins be used. The object is a large domestic granite trough, as other contemporary photographs make quite clear; and, like another very large granite trough now in the garden at Lowenac,[8] would have been used for such purposes as salting-down the whole of a side of a pig.

The Pendarves copper coffin

William Pendarves (1689-1727), who was at one time M.P. for St. Ives,[9] and was knighted by Queen Anne, had made for him a coffin out of copper, enchased with arms and emblems, traditionally out of the ore raised from North Roskear mine. The story that he and his companions had the coffin filled with punch during their carousals may well be true, though it rests on the gossipy memoirs of Mrs. Delany, once the wife of his cousin Alexander Pendarves. Sir William was amongst those far-seeing Cornishmen who initiated the smelting of copper within the county, instead of sending the ores to Wales or Bristol, and given the flamboyance of this rather coarse period in English history, his action seems by no means incredible. He was buried at Camborne, at the age of only 37, in 1727, and the parish register states that this was 'in the Church'.[10] Either this entry is loosely phrased, or his remains were removed, since he subsequently lay in a subterranean vault on the south side of the church, which was disturbed in the 1879 expansions (p. 140). Arthur Adams, then the curate, notes with interest[11] that 'the Pendarves Vault was accidentally broken into, and in it I saw the very copper coffin . . . in it lay the perfect skeleton of the knight.' A newspaper report claimed that it was 'in excellent condition and still maintaining its high polish'.[12]

The site of the vault, and presumably the coffin, is now underneath the new Church Hall. Canon Sandfield, however, told the writer that a few years ago[13] it was still possible to squeeze through a small iron door in the stoke-hole of the boiler-house by the church, and to see the copper coffin in the vault at the end of the little aperture.

Coffin-rest

Directly outside the west door of the church tower, on the other side of the path, lies a long flat granite coffin-rest, a type of monument frequently encountered in Cornish churchyards. In the appropriate light, it is possible to see that a long-stemmed 'Gothic' cross has been incised on its upper surface, which suggests that this is a feature of the 15th century, if not earlier. The date '1815' has been boldly cut on the south-east side of this coffin-rest; apart from being the date of Waterloo, this seems to have no immediate significance.

Burial customs

In chapter VI, when discussing the function of the various crosses, it was pointed out that cross no. 3 had once stood at the junction of the former Crane Drive, or Crane Lane, and an old churchpath coming from Reskajeage and Menadarva; and that Dr. Mertherderwa's will of 1447 alludes to the habit or erecting such crosses to mark points where the dead could be temporarily rested, for prayers and for the relief of the bearers. As examination of the map, fig. 1, will show, there must frequently have been occasions when heavy coffins had to be carried several miles to the churchyard. A reference to this custom occurs as late as 1842:[14]

'In this part of Cornwall (the Camborne district) as indeed throughout the county generally, the bodies are borne at funerals, sometimes for several miles, to the church "underhand" as it is termed and not on the shoulders of the bearers. Napkins are passed through the handles, or under the coffin, for the convenience of this mode of carriage. Often the procession is heard chanting a psalm or hymn as it halts on the way to the church, which may be several miles distant from the dwelling of the deceased.'

The intense Cornish love of a really large funeral, with its combination of music, open emotion, and appropriate social display, is primarily a product of 19th-century Methodism; gone, perhaps fortunately, are the massive occasions[15] of the Victorian era, though the death of any prominent Methodist still calls for a funeral of decent proportion. It is interesting to reflect on the much quieter burials of bygone centuries, which clearly underwent little change from 1447 to 1842.

The Stocks

As a former instrument of correction, the stocks represent parochial rather than ecclesiastical antiquities, but are generally associated with the parish church or churchyard. Pl. IV, shows the present base of cross no. 2, with part of the chain by which the wooden stocks were formerly fastened to this heavy piece of granite.

It appears that at some stage, probably in 1864 when the Market House was built (p. 134), the stocks were removed from the churchyard. Mr. John Arthur noted in 1928[16]

'The old parish stocks . . . were kept under the town hall, the front of which was kept up on pillars, and the under-rooms set back some feet from the pillars. The parish stocks so I am told were kept between the pillars and the rooms. They were for many years kept upon the butter market, as it was called.'

As late as about 1858, a second pair of stocks were made, about the time that the police station was built in Moor Street; and it is perhaps unusual to find this so late. It is not known whether they were widely, if at all, used, and having been relegated to a loft over the stables in the yard, were eventually found and for some reason burnt.[17]

Parish stocks were, well into this century, not uncommon survivals; J. Hambley Rowe managed to elicit, in the 1920's, a list of twenty-seven parishes which still possessed examples, evenly distributed throughout the county.[18] The parish stocks of Gwithian, which are in quite good condition, have recently been illustrated.[19]

The Talcarn bequest

By his will dated 3rd July 1558,[20] John Talcarn, of Talcarn or Tolcarn(e) near Troon (see fig. 1), left certain properties, real and disposable, naming his two sons-in-law as executors. He had outgrown his native parish of Camborne, and become wealthy as a merchant in the City of London. Among the bequests was 'one crosse with the foote thereof being silver & gilte', which was left to 'the church of Cambron in Cornwayle, where I was born and christened' for the sake of his own and his wife's souls.

A few years later, the two sons-in-law (Thomas Argall and John Hornyolde) commenced, as executors, a suit in the Chancery Court against Richard Crane, of Crane, born about 1495 and at that time the head of the Crane family. They alleged that Richard Crane had improperly obtained possession of this cross, and was putting it to 'his own proper use and commodity', perhaps with the implication that it was now adorning the altar of the Cranes' private chapel (chapter IV). Richard Crane travelled all the way to London to answer this charge, complaining that he was 'an old man of 67'.[21] He stated that 'about a year ago' (1561) Thomas Argall delivered the cross to William Godolphyne, who delivered it to John Trevetheke, who delivered it to Mr. Crane 'being one of the best and chiefest of the said parish'. Richard Crane had then on the following Sunday in the parish church duly published and pronounced the gift of the cross, before all the parishioners, and it was immediately, by the consent of all, given into the safekeeping of the churchwardens, Nicholas Mathew and Alexander Luke. He claimed that the cross had ever since been kept to the use aforesaid and that the bill against him had been devised out of malice by the chief heir and eldest son, Justinian Talcarn, who 'hath by all waies and meanes sought to have the said crosse to his own use and commoditye, contrary to the will of his said father'.

The cross, which was probably very valuable by local standards, would have been a silver-gilt crucifix which could either stand on the altar upon its 'foot', or, with an ornamented wooden handle inserted into a hollow base, be carried in procession.

Whatever the real ins and outs of this obscure family quarrel may have been, the cross has not survived. The late F. J. Stephens cherished the romantic notion that it had, however, been secretly preserved in the parish well into the 17th century. He drew attention to certain entries in the old Rate Book, now lost (p. 160), relating to the bringing of 'the Kurse' (Cross) to persons *in extremis*, arguing that this was the same word as in the expression about 'Merry Kurse' (p. 37) which Henry Jenner thought meant 'Mary's Cross'. It is of course possible that it was somehow pre-served at least until the Commonwealth, but no other record of it exists.

NOTES

1. The fullest list (for Cornwall) occurs in *CIIC*, parts I and II.
2. As, for instance, the Tithe map (1838-1840).
3. *Cornishman*, September 1956 ('Camborne Mystery Solved', etc.).
4. *OC* I. 12 (1930), 18.
5. Kelly's *Directory* (1906 edn.) list 'William John Jenkin' as a wheelwright at Roskear. Mr. Jenkin was also from 1916 to 1945 the librarian of Camborne Public Library.
6. Report by Dr. C. A. R. Radford, *OC* II. 9 (1935), 16 ff.
7. Information from Mr. T. R. Harris, Camborne, from whom this suggestion comes.
8. This trough is 6 ft. by 3 ft. by 1 ft., with sides 6 ins. thick; it was formerly in a kitchen at Reskadinnick, and was given to the writer's father by Mr. F. J. Stephens, who could recall it being used for such a purpose.
9. In 1713, when he also gave a communion-plate to St. Ives church.
10. *RPC* I, 233, under 27th March 1726/7.
11. Quoted in Carah 1925, 32.
12. *Cornishman*, 10 October 1957 ('Copper Coffin').
13. *In litt.*, October 1950.
14. Cyrus Redding, *An Illustrated Itinerary of the County of Cornwall* (1842).
15. e.g., in Camborne, Dr. George Smith's in 1868: or that of Capt. Josiah Thomas (the writer's great-grandfather) in 1902, with 'a procession of 1500 people' (*Cornish Post*), all the mines closed, and a funeral oration by a venerable ex-President of the Conference.
16. MS. Arthur.
17. MS. James Thomas.
18. *Notes and Queries: Antiquarian Lore of the West*, in *WMN*, about 1923, item no. 25 and subsequent replies.
19. Thomas 1964, 16, fig. 5.
20. The will: P.C.C., Register Welles 53. The suit: Chancery Proceedings, series II, bdle. 3, no. 60, 29th May 1562. The writer is most grateful to Mr. T. R. Harris for allowing him to use his abstracts of these.
21. He died, aged 82 or so, in 1577 (*RPC* I, 90).
22. Stephens 1925.

XIV

THE DAUGHTER CHURCHES

The considerable increase in population during the late 18th and early 19th centuries, shown in such sources as the national ten-yearly census, meant that the churches and churchyards which had been designed to serve medieval needs became wholly inadequate to cope with both worship and burial. In Cornwall, the former aspect was admittedly relieved by the massive adherence to Methodism; but it must be remembered that many Methodist families have always chosen to be buried, if not baptised and married, at the parish church,[1] nor did they see anything inconsistent in attending either church or chapel as the occasion may arise. Physically, this is expressed throughout Cornwall by the extension of the parish churchyards, often seen as rectangular additions to an original circular or oval lan, and it will be noted that such additions commence in the period 1750-1800 rather than in the 19th century.

By the second quarter of the 19th century, numerous new ecclesiastical districts or 'parishes' were created in Cornwall. In some instances, this remedied such situations as that at Hayle, where the parish church was across the creek in the hamlet of Phillack, and the growing town possessed no established church of its own; or at Penzance, where the large church of St. Mary's, re-built on the site of the old free chapel in 1834, did not actually become an independent ecclesiastical establishment (free of the mother-parish of Madron) until 1871. In others, munificent land-owners had at their own expense constructed new churches to serve as chapels of ease, especially in the very large parishes where, by 1800, many people might be living and working several miles from the medieval churchtown, and these chapels of ease served as the centres of new districts.

Between 1840 and 1850, three new ecclesiastical districts were created out of the old parish of Camborne, and part of Illogan. They may be discussed in order of seniority. The locations of the three churches are shown above, in fig. 1.

Treslothan

The impetus for the foundation of this church, to serve Troon and the south-west portion of Camborne parish, came from the Pendarves family. Shortly before 1840, a site was chosen on the periphery of the Pendarves park. This may have been all that remained of the medieval tenement of Treslothan, a few cottages at the intersection of three or more lanes, unless indeed (p. 66 above) the medieval Treslothan really stood where Pendarves House was later built. The area was now re-modelled, and a 'model village' constructed, with a vicarage, a tenancy house opposite, a row of cottages in the line behind the vicarage, the village well (p. 121), and the new church itself, all executed in a kind of Victorian granite Gothic which is wholly un-Cornish but which none the less possesses a charm of its own.

The architect of the church was a Mr. Wightwick,[2] and the church itself, built in two years, was carried out in a Gothic idiom. It was consecrated in honour of St. John the Evangelist on 25th July 1842, as a Chapel of Ease. An interesting feature here is that, as was discussed earlier, there are grounds for thinking that the actual church site was already occupied by the ruins of St. James' chapel (p. 67), and that this expression of continuity was a deliberate one. In favour of this idea is the additional fact that the date of the consecration, 25th July, is not the Feast of St. John, but the Feast of *St. James*. Was this day deliberately chosen?

The ecclesiastical district of Treslothan was assigned to this church, with an area of 1950 acres, by an Order dated 4th July 1845, and the first Vicar and Perpetual Curate, George Bull, was inducted in 1846. The full list of vicars for this, and for the other two churches, is given below in Appendix D.

Treslothan Church is well worth a visit. It contains today the *Aegured* altar stone, mounted as a mensa in the south aisle (p. 103); the first Camborne font (p. 114), and a stone mortar which may have been used as a Methodist font (p. 118); the Treslothan cross (p. 93), standing outside the east end; and (in the vestry, visible upon application to the Vicar) a fine little Nottingham alabaster panel. This panel has nothing whatsoever to do with the pre-existing chapel of St. James. It was only placed in the church comparatively recently (early this century), and prior to that, had been at Pendarves House.[3] It represents the Adoration of the Magi (the Virgin, reclining on a couch, holding up the Divine Child) and is presumably one of a series forming a reredos over a Lady Altar. A note in an exhibition catalogue of 1923[4] states that it was 'brought from Italy some years ago' (information perhaps supplied by the Pendarves family), though another, equally likely, version is that it was given to the Pendarves family, for the church, by the St. Aubyn family of St. Michael's Mount (about 1840?). As there is a series of similar, and rather better, alabasters in the chapel on the Mount, some of which may well have been 'brought from Italy', this may be the true explanation.

Relief panels of this kind were made from alabaster obtained in Staffordshire and Derbyshire, and Nottingham may have been the main, if not the only, centre of carving. The late 14th and the 15th centuries form a more probable date than the 13th century, as has been suggested.[5]

The open-fronted Gothic structure which stands just by the south side of Treslothan church is the Pendarves mausoleum. Among those buried in the churchyard is John Harris of Bolenowe, the 'miner poet', a self-educated bard (1820-1884) whose worst productions are mere doggerel, but whose best can rank with those of Robert Burns.[6]

Tuckingmill

In the case of Tuckingmill, sometimes locally miscalled 'Roskear', the district preceded the actual church. The separate ecclesiastical district was gazetted by an Order of 3rd June, 1844, and was made up of an area taken out of both Camborne and Illogan, embracing a number of villages and scattered accumulations of dwellings which had vastly increased as a result of mining (e.g., in the Dolcoath—Crofty complex) and tin-streaming in the middle reaches of the Red River.

The church itself was begun in 1843, the architect being a Mr. J. Hayward of Exeter, who chose a simplified Romanesque or 'Norman' style. The work was undertaken at the expense of the Basset family of Tehidy, within whose demesne the new district lay. The church was finally consecrated, in honour of All Saints, on 7th July 1845, when a sermon was preached by the Rev. J. Punnett (of Plymouth?).[7] The first incumbent, Edward Crow, continued this tradition by publishing his own addresses (he was Vicar for five years) under the uncompromising title of *Plain Sermons*.[8] A later incumbent was Arthur Adams, well-known and popular in the area as a former curate of Camborne church.

The main treasure here, ignored by almost every writer on Cornish ecclesiology, is the magnificent early-to-mid-Norman font, which came from St. Derwa's chapel at Menadarva, *via* Tehidy (see p. 167). As Carah (1925, 35) points out, its style happily matches that of the building.

Penpons

The ecclesiastical district of Penpons or Penponds (both forms of the name are used, but the former is linguistically correct and has been preferred in this present book) was formed in 1846, to cover the western part of Camborne parish, and was gazetted by an Order dated 1st January, 1847. In the absence of a munificent landlord, the church itself was some while being built and was finally consecrated on 15th May, 1854, under the title of The Holy Trinity. The Rev. W. W. Butlin, who had been appointed as curate in-charge in 1850, became the first Vicar and Perpetual Curate.

In many ways this is the most interesting of the three daughter churches. As Appendix D shows, it is remarkable in that the first three vicars— W. W. Butlin, J. Sims Carah, and C. R. Coates—between them spanned just over a century, during which times Treslothan had nine, and Tucking-mill ten, incumbents. Secondly, Canon Carah (from 1896 to 1935) was responsible for transforming the church into a veritable museum, albeit an active centre of worship with distinctly High characteristics. Canon Carah was not only a local man—the families of Sims, or Sems, and Carah are widely represented in Camborne and Crowan parishes—but also an antiquary of considerable knowledge, whose interests were divided between the Church in Europe in the middle ages, and the entire past in Cornwall. As President for many years of Camborne Old Cornwall Society, and as the author of numerous works on local antiquity, he was instrumental in saving an enormous number of objects, and facts, which would other-wise have been sunk without trace. Cornwall has much to be grateful for, in remembering this modest, lovable, and faintly eccentric enthusiast.

Penpons Church was built in the Early English style by the Hon. J. Piers St. Aubyn, a man of only moderate imagination whose extensive restorations of Cornish churches have never commended themselves to the ecclesiologists. From about 1900 to 1934, Canon Carah, with the aid of his flock, set about transforming the interior of St. Aubyn's work. This cost them 'more than £2,500 . . . practically the whole cost has been borne by those who worship there.'[9] The details of the fittings and accessories, which include such things as a 16th-century Flemish alms dish (purchased in Antwerp by Canon Carah), a modern copy of a triptych by Memling incorporated in the pulpit, with the former Communion rail flung out of Camborne church, and various pieces of 15th-century Cornish bench-ends, are given in Canon Carah's book.[10] The most impressive aspect is undoubtedly the replaced seating. The 1854 deal seats were finally abandoned, and between 1929 and 1934, the entire church was equipped with 'a set of oak benches with carved ends after the old manner in Cornish churches.'[11] There are about sixty of these, nearly all paid for by members of the congregation at that time as memorials (e.g., one to Richard Trevithick's memory, given by three of his great grand-children), and as a conscious revival of a late-medieval feature, the whole scheme must be judged an astonishing success. A special tribute must be paid to the anonymous master-craftsman who carried out the work; for both the beautiful natural oak, and the actual carving, are of the highest quality. Nor are the bench-ends haphazardly placed; some illustrate aspects of the Creed, in a proper succession, others refer to local saints (like Derwa, Crewenna, Gothian, etc.), and to the Twelve Apostles. Quite a few act as 'spacers' and bear floral emblems, which include such local favourites as bluebells and the Royal Fern (*Osmunda regalis*, L.) The whole scheme is described in Carah's now very rare booklet.[12]

NOTES

1. In the case of meeting-houses or chapels not licensed for the solemnisation or registration of marriage or burial, it was of course necessary to attend the parish church.
2. See e.g., W. F. Collier's *Tales and Sayings of William Robert Hicks* (3rd edn., 1893), 14-18, for George Wightwick's fame as a *raconteur*.
3. Letter from Mrs. Alice Pendarves to Canon Carah, MS. Carah 22, 7.
4. *Catalogue of the Loan Collection at the Church Congress*, Plymouth, 1923; no. 305.
5. British Museum *Guide to the Mediaeval Room*, 52-54.
6. Cf. his collected *Wayside Pictures, Hymns and Poems* (London, Hamilton Adams & Co., 1874), and his *My Autobiography* (London, do., 1882).
7. J. Punnett, *The Church of England, diffusive of good, etc.; a sermon preached on the occasion of the consecration of . . . All Saints Tuckingmill* (Plymouth, 1845).
8. Edward Crow, M.A., *Plain Sermons* (London, 1848).
9. Carah 1925, 36.
10. *Ibidem*, 35-38
11. Carah 1934, 3.
12. See Carah 1934 in the Bibliography.

APPENDICES

A

EDWARD LHUYD'S NOTES ON CAMBORNE, 1700

This is taken from the Bodleian Library MS. Rawlinson D. 997, fols. 1 v and 2 r. The MS. is a small notebook written, with numerous abbreviations and contractions, in a spiky hand, and a peculiar style or orthography, which make the attribution to Edward Lhuyd almost certain. Lhuyd (c. 1670-1709, and at this time Keeper of the Ashmolean Museum) was visiting Cornwall in 1700, and the notebook, which deals with a number of Cornish parishes, is in the nature of field-notes made at the time.

In this transcript, the abbreviations have been expanded and the irregular punctuation ignored, but otherwise Lhuyd's spelling is faithfully reproduced.

(*Fol. 2 r*)   *CAMBRON*

From Dredruth 3, Helston 7, in the Hundred of Penwyth. 7 m. long from Gwidhian parish to Gwendan, broad about 2 m., viz. from St. Michels foot on the borders of Lygan to the borders of Gwiniar. 5 or 6 chapels all ruined, viz. one in the church yard *An*, 2 at Treslythan, 3 at Penpons, 4 at Rhôszwern, 5 at Manadàrva, 6 at Tredzothan. The feast is kept on the 11 of November. The parish day is on the first Friday in June which is called Maradzock day, & the feast day & fair day St. *Martin*. A Rectory, Mr. Charles Basset the present incumbent. The villages are, 1 Breppa, 2 Penpons, 3 Pendarvis, 4 Tredzothan, 5 Manadàrva, 6 Laeti, 7 Tshetòdn, 8 Trewn, 9 Rhoswârn, 10 Enterl, 11 Rhysgadzêg, 12 Rhoskîar, 13 Kilavôs, 14 Gear. The seats of the Gentry are; 5, Esqre. Arundels, 3, Esqre. Pendarvis, 9, Mr. Rob. Hwkers, Mr. Jn. Rhôswarn of Rhoswarn, 10 Mr. Jn. Herl. Other howses; 1 Pwl strong, 2 Trevỳrian, 3 Trevyrnw, 4 Condòro, 5 Pengìgan, 6 Crŵn. A cromlech in the parish. The house next which it stands is called Kerwìnin. 4 Rocks in the parish called the Gyant's bowls. Tredzothan commons. Rhoswarn common.

(*Fol. I v*)

Another chappel at Trewn called Ia. The well is called fenton Ia in the parish of Cambron.

Entrenchmenents here are called Plains. Hent's one called Plain an gwari where they use to act, but no one alive remembers it.

Notes

The various references to individual chapels are discussed above in Chapter IV. The spelling of names employs certain devices elsewhere used by Lhuyd. There are: *dz* for the sound of English voiced *j*, by 1700 the normal sound of intervocalic *s* in late Cornish ; the vowel *y* to represent an obscure vowel in Cornish, stressed or unstressed; the use of *w*, as in Welsh, for the short sound of *oo* (thus, *Hwker* for the surname 'Hooker'); and the use of two accents, one apparently to indicate stress ˋ , and the other (circumflex) to show vowel length. These are both used correctly in all instances and, apart from any other consideration, confirm that all the modern pronounciations of these names have not changed since 1700.

The following list may assist the reader to identify the places in question.

Breppa	*Baripper*	Pwl strong	*Polstrong*
Crwn	*Croon*	Rhoszwern	*Rosewarne*
Condoro	*Condurrow*	Rhoswarn	
Enterl	*Entral*	Rhoskiar	*Roskear*
Gwendan	*Wendron*	Rhysgadzeg	*Reskajeage*
Gwidhian	*Gwithian*	Tredzothan	*Treswithian*
Gwiniar	*Gwinear*	Treslythan	*Treslothan*
Kerwinin	*Carwinnen*	Trevyrian	*Trevorian*
Kilavos	*Killivose*	Trevyrnw	*Trevornow*
			(*Roskear*)
Laeti	*Laity* (*Troon*)	Trewn	*Troon*
Lygan	*Illogan*	Tshetodn	*Chytodden* (*Troon*)
Manadarva	*Menadarva*		

The persons named by Lhuyd help to confirm the date. Charles Basset was Rector from 1684 to 1709. John Hearle died in 1706; William Arundell of Menadarva in 1708; John Roswarne in 1714.

B
WILLIAM BORLASE'S NOTES ON CAMBORNE, 1750

The following extract comes from Borlase's unpublished *Parochial Memoranda*, the material for a parochial history of Cornwall which he intended to compiile. It represents fol. 16 of British Museum MS. Egerton 2657, and has been transcribed from the microfilm of this MS. at the R.I.C., Truro.

CAMBRON als CAMBOURNE

1. Passing up from Treslothan through some of the most ancient Stream-works I have seen, now lying in a common called the Stenak about a mile above Pendarves, we turned to the left towards a small village call'd Chitodn (various Chi-dun, i.e. house on the Hill, the 'd' corruptly inscribed) and passing forwards about a bow shot turned to the left hand and there found a very clear stream of water, cross wch. we came to a rude Well noted for its Physical virtues, 'tis called Fenton

Er signifying (as I conjecture) the New Well. A few paces distant stood a Cross, about 3 yds from wch. was a chapel, the walls of wch. are still partly standing. The Retirment of this place, the chapel, Well & cross, & a plentiful cascade of pure water about 10 paces from the chapel falling down into a hollow valley, with a most solemn noise, makes me imagine this to have been the habitation of some holy Hermit. The Cross is very singular, and may be seen in the Church Monuments, p.65, fig. This Chapel, etc., are on the tenement of Treun.

2. In the Tenement of Caerwynen, in a field adjoyning to the Moor, half a mile to the S.E. of Pendarves, stands a very entire Cromlech called the Giant's Quoit—it stands upon 3 stones which inclose an area 5 ft. 3 inches wide & 7 ft. long—the covering stone is 12 ft. 3 long by 11 ft. 6 wide being nearly square and no more than 1 ft. thick at a medium.

3. Edwd. Sheffield Eccles. Paroch. de Cambourne 1525. This is the proper spelling—see Cam & Bourn.

4. In this Parish there was the Chapel of St. James: The Chapel of St. Ye and St. Derwe: the chapel of St. Margaret and St. Anne.

5. In Redman's Reg: (Ex. Bp. circ 1490) fol. 24 the Church of Cambourn is styled Eccles. Paroch. Sti. Meriadoci de Cambourn.

6. In a grant to John Cogh of one third part of the Manor of Tehidy to Wm. son and hr. of Sr Wm. Basset, Sept. 15 1343, 17th of Ed. 3, it is called 'Advocatio Ecclesiae Sti. Martini de Cambron . .' See the original among the family deeds of Tyhydy.

7. De Sancto Birino see Capgrave fo.xxxviii . . . Qu. an Cam a prefix to this St. qu.?

8. Camborn, or -bourne (corruptly written Cambron) takes not it's name from a Saint but is a parish so nam'd from a crooked Spring or brook wch. gives rise to the principal river of the parish call'd Conar which receiving all the other little side-brooks and traversing the whole extent (nearly) of the parish from E. to W. carries them all into the Northern ocean near a place call'd, formerly, Conarton of high [illegible] as the chief domain of the Hundred, now Gwythian church-town. Note that borne or bourne signifies a spring and the Saxons denominated places situated on Waters (says Risdon, Surv. MS. pa.119 & 134) by affixing the termination of borne—as Eaborne, Willeborne, Winterborne . . . Cam in British signifyes crooked or winding, so Cam-hel the River Alan, etc.: Camborne is therefore a crooked winding spring or brook . . . but Cambron, a crooked hill. In this parish is Manor House of Conarton, a principal Manor of the Arundels of Lanheren als. Lanherne—this Manor in the time of the Conquest gave name to the whole Hund. now called Penwith—see Domesday—the Domain is called Roseworthy; i.e. the Valley lying upon the water or River, Ros-worth-uy . . Nikenor as printed in Leland, I take to be erroneously printed—it should be Nikonor, i.e. the River or water of Conor or Conar—'n-uy-Conar-Dour Conor, says Ld.

9. Menadarva, in this pish . . . (The entry ends at this point).

C
SELECTION OF EARLY PARISH DOCUMENTS

1. Glebe Terriers

Terriers for the years 1601, 1625, 1680 and 1727 (the latter with a copy made 1779) are preserved in the County Record Office, Truro (acc. no. 11) where they were deposited some years ago by the Diocesan Registrar.

TERRIER OF 1601

Rectoria de Cambron   *5 die mensis Octobris 1601*

The psnage of CAMBRON is given by mr. James Basset Esquier, beinge 39 acres in the valewe, havinge belonginge to the said parsonage fower feeldes contayning by estimation 34 ackers of ground; being bounded upon the south side with the high waye, upon the north syde with the groundes of Mr. Nance, upon the west side with the groundes of Mr. Crane, and upon the east side with the high waye and the groundes of Mr. Treweeke, about all which grounds the parson is to have ground for to make all his hedges upon the grounds of Nance, Crane, and Treweeke. Implements: none were found by me John Harding nowe parson there.

TERRIER OF 1625

Penwith . Cambron

We haue belonging to our Psonage a Mantion House with all houses of office belonginge to the same, no bocks, implements, tenemts, portion of Tythes, other than the Tythes of our pish, anciently Dew and accustomed to be paid for the said Rectory.

Three clooses of tillable lands called and knowene by the names of the Great Sanctuary, the Midell Sanctuary and the long Sanctuary, contayning by estimation xxxvii akers of land or thereabouts, bounding one the north Side wth the lands of Sr. Thomas Dimes [?] Knight and one the East side with Lands of Frances Basset Esquire and one the Soath and West with the Lands of Richard Crane gent. there is more belonginge unto the siad [*sic*] psonage one the East side of the said psonage one house with a garden.

TERRIER OF 1680

(Note; *This is badly torn, about an inch and a half missing from the right margin of the sheets. A few obvious additions have been supplied in brackets*).

A dwelling House and a Court before itt with a . . . Mansion House built and covered with stone, Consisting [of] A Parler, 3 chambers and an under . . . outhouse, and to me the use of a large Barn cover'd . . . out house, . . . a mowhay [and a] Garden . . .

[There is] a field formerly called the Great Sentry now divided into two fields about 20 acres of land: also a field commonly called Crane Sentry, another field called the Long Sentry now divided into two fields . . . contayning about 8 acres also Little Sentry . . . contayning about an acre or more. Also there belongs with it . . . in the towne place, a stone house . . . of a little meadow and garden hedged in out of the common [contayning] an acre of land or thereabouts, as also common . . . In both towne places and adjoining both the higher and lower and . . . into it, whense that piece of land called Camborne Moor. The hedges round about all the land [are] not mixed with others . . . but joyned towards the east side with the lands of Francis Bassett Esqe and part at the highway on the other with the lands of Lawrence Calle gent towards the south and west and on the north with the lands of Sir Jhn. Roll knight of the Bath.

In that pt joyning to the highway [lies] the Almshouse at the chardge of the parish consisting of 3 houses [of] the parish and inhabited. And a garden also hedged and with a half acre of ground in the highway. Both the house and garden adjoining to the hedge of the glebe land wch was done by the behest of the patron ffrancis Basset esq and the psent incumbent John Collins, the said patron making a deed whereof the poor yearly . . . of the parish belonging to the pish.

There being a customary fair held in the churchtowne belonging to the parish much of the fair being held upon the ground belonging to the parsonage and against the Hedge. That belonging, the minister or his assignes have part in and part out of the property of the faire by the [reason?] thereof.

The psent incumbent hath been informed that the whole parcell of land given to the church at first was 40 acres. This he conceives may be. The ground with church, chchyard, garden and all doth still amount to the same.

JCllins Rector ibidem   *Richard Williams*
       1680   *Richard Durn*   *Churchwardens*

TERRIER OF 1727

A terrier of the Parsonage of Camborne in the County of Cornwall and Diocese of Exeter drawn up pursuant to his Lordship's directions, and delivered to the Archdeacon's registration at his Easter Visitation held at Helstone in the sayd county in the yr. of our Lord 1727.

The Parsonage House of Camborne is a stone building covered for the most part with Reed, consisting of 30 ft in length, 13 ft in breadth and 12 in height. It contains three ground rooms floored with earthe one of which is a little linney covered with slate and three chambers not wainscotted, nor ceiled, floored with deal. The Glebe contains the following fields:

	acres	perch
The Great Sanctuary	$9\frac{1}{2}$	$17\frac{1}{2}$
Crane Sanctuary	9	3
Parsonage Croft	$4\frac{1}{2}$	$\frac{1}{4}$
Parish Close	6	7
Trezurthen Higher Sanctuary	$3\frac{1}{4}$	17
Trezurthen Lower Sanctuary	$4\frac{1}{4}$	10
Bowling Green	1	10
Garden and Mowhey	$\frac{1}{4}$	21

All the field are arable or pasture enclosed and bounded with earth hedges. The whole is bounded on the east by an estate of John Pendarves Bassett Esq. called Camborne Veor, on the south and west by an estate of Mrs. Grace Hookers called Crane; on the north by an estate of John Roll of Stevenstone Esq called the Withs; the whole contains 38 acres 4 perch.

There are two other houses lying off the Glebe Land already described, one built of stone consisting of two ground rooms, floored with earth and two chambers floored with deal, neither wainscotted nor ceiled, behind which are two gardens and one meadow containing one quarter acre and 13 perch; the other built with mud contains one ground floor nor wainscotted nor ceiled.

The Surplice fees are this: for Easter offerings two pence, for marriages 2 shillings and sixpence, for Churchings sixpence, for burials and mortuaries we know of no custom of paying anything. All Tithes are due to the Rector in kind. To two parts in the great and small tithes of two estates called Hellow and Pencobben, John Pendarves Bassett Esq pretends a prescriptive right, demised by a lease of three livrs to William Harris of the said parish, gentleman.

Eevery 7th colt is due to the Rector, but 4d hath been generally received and is at present in lieu of it: every seventh calf, but the parishioners object to it. Every 7th lamb and fleece, the Rector paying to the parishioner 6d; if eight, 4d; if nine, twopence. Every seventh pig, carrying on the number till they come to ten. For every lamb and fleece under the number seven the Rector received two pence.

The furniture of the church consists of a surplice, one large Bible, two Common Prayer books, a book of Homilies, a pulpit-cloth and cushion of purple broadcloth trimmed with gold lace. Two linen cloths for the font and reading desk, one communion table cloth of purple broadcloth trimmed with gold lace, one linen cloth for the communion table, one linen napkin, one silver cup gilded with gold, and one silver salver, both weighing 20 oz and three-quarters troy weight. One large flagon of pewter. We have three bells in good order.

The profits arising from a fair called St. Martin's fair. held on the 11th of November yearly, has time out of mind been appropriated to the repairs of the church and still continues to be so; but the patent obtained from the Crown some years since for holding that, with two other fairs of their own purchasing, lies now in the hands of Mrs. Grace Hooker who refuses to deliver it up.

The churchyard is repaired by the parish.

The Clerk's salary is £3 a year, the sexton's two; the first appointed by the rector, the second by the rector and parishioners.

Robert Newcombe, Rector

Jas Daniell, Churchwarden	X *Johnson Bryant—the sign of*
John Harris	*Thos Hockin*
Wm. Harris	*Henry Tresahar*
Thos Tresahare	X *Francis Hockin—the sign of*
John Davey	*Johnson Vivian*

2. Statement of the Parish Bounds, 1601

We have perambulated the bounds & limits of our Parish aforesayd accordynge to the Canon and we fyndd them to be bounded with the parish of Crowan on the east syde from the Forrest gate with the high way to Carvolthe and from thence with the water or river to Bearepper bridge and from Bearepper bridge with the river Eneeis Cusven unto an old tynne worke called Polmidoe. And from Polmidoe with the Parish of Gwythian with the river and neere the river unto Gwythian bridge. And from Gwythian bridge by a path and a bancke unto the north sea cliffe and by the cliff unto a hedge called Keazek vres and from Keazek vrez unto the river under Treslothan Mill and by neere the said river with the Parish of Illuggan unto the foresaid Forrest gate.

Notes Certain of these names also occur in the statements of bounds for Gwithian and Illogan. *Eneeis Cusven* appears to mean 'alongside Coswin' (C. *yn-nes Coswyn*, 'nigher to C.'), Coswin (sawsen) being the tenement in Gwinear on the opposite bank from Penpons. The 'old tynne work' (tin stream) called Polmidoe must have been just below Roseworthy (? C.*pol medhew* 'soft pool', i.e. 'muddy pool'). For the 'bancke unto the north sea cliffe', see p.10 above. The hedge called *Keasek vres* (C.*ke segh vras*, 'great dry hedge') still exists and is discussed in *JRIC (n.s.)* V.1. (1965), 12 ff., *s.n..* 'Treslothan Mill' must be where Keeve Mill later stood; the connection, if any, with the Manor of Treslothan is not certain.

3. A later statement of the Parish Bounds, 1613 (?)

In CRO, Truro. This is undated but by analogy with other parishes should be about 1613. Of the signatories, Tonkin was churchwarden up to 1624, Brea died in 1623, Rosewarne in 1619. and Treskillard in 1626.

Penwith/Cambron

We have perambulated the bounds and limits of our parishe afforesaid accordinge to the Canon and Wee fynde them to be bounded with the parishe of Crowan on the East syde to the forest gate with the highe way to Carvolthe And from thence with the water or river to Bearepper Bridge, and from Bearepper bridge with the river unto an old Tynn worke called Polmidoe. And from Polmidoe with the parishe of Gwythian with the river and neere the river unto Gwythian bridge. And from Gwythian bridge by a pathe and a bancke unto the northe sea cliffe, by the said Cliffe unto a hedge called Kea [zek Vres?]. And from Kea [zek Vres?] unto the river under Treslothan Mill and by neer the said river with the parishe of Illuggan unto the foresaid forest Gates.

Wardens	Robert Tonkin	The Signe of William Brea
Sydemen	Walter Roseward	
	Humphrye Treskillard	

D
INCUMBENTS OF CAMBORNE AND THE DAUGHTER CHURCHES

1. *Camborne*

A list of the Rectors appears in Morton 1949, 21, and in Vincent 1959, 21. It does not altogether tally with a much fuller account in Creswell 1910, 21-27, which bears every sign of having been compiled by T. C. Peter. The late Mrs. Rolfe, whose work on Cornish incumbencies is well-known, unfortunately never completed her Camborne list, but the entries have as far as possible been checked against her notes.

The sources are from the 16th century the parish registers and accounts, and before that mostly Registers of the Bishops of Exeter, with other public records. In giving dates below, the 'Lady Day' year prior to the mid-18th century has been ignored: e.g. 1st February 1381 (in our sense) was part of 1380, written 1st Feb. 1380/1. The names of curates in the 17th and 18th century, insofar as they can be discovered, are appended.

Thomas Basset	? -1308	
John de Newland (?Neuband)	1309-1311	Resigned
William de Benetfelde	1312-1331	Resigned
William Bloyou	1331-1334	Died
Stephen de Penpel	1335-1361	Exchanged
John Coghe	1361	Died?
John Lucas	1361-1384	Died
John de Kirby	1384	Ejected by law?
Robert Neville	1385?	Resigned
Benedict de Canterbury	1387-1426	Died
Serlo Tregona(n)	1426-1427	Resigned
Walter Robyn	1427	Resigned
Richard Chichester	1427-1431	Exchanged
John Kelly	1431-1448	Died
John Cobbe	1448-1449	Resigned
John Pascowe	1449-1493	Died
Thomas Gilbert	1493-1500	Resigned
Alexander Penhylle (Penhale)	1500-1501	Exchanged
John Nans	1501-1507	Died
Edward Sheffield	1508-1522	Resigned
John Walshe	1522-1537	Died
John Waren?	1537-1540	Died
Philip English?	1540-1545	Died
George Rowe?	? -1572	Resigned
Richard Richardson	1572-1584	Died
Benet (Benedict) Hockin	1584-1596	Died
John Harding	1596-1611	Died
John Fleming	1612-1617	Died

John Rowe (ejected 1647?)	1617-1664	Died
John Collins	1664-1684	Died
Charles Basset	1684-1709	Died
William Smith	1709-1714	Died
Robert Newcombe	1715-1771	Died
John Basset Collins	1771-1790	Died
John Basset	1790-1815	Died
Hugh Rogers	1816-1858	Died
William Pester Chappel	1858-1900	Died
George Brereton Hooper	1900-1934	Died
Douglas Edward Morton	1934-1945	Resigned
George Frederick Sandfield	1945-1965	Died
Arthur Basil Etheredge Brown	1966	

Curates

Richard Healle (Hearle?)	1603-1610?
Edmund Orchard	1613-1617?
George Phippen	1617-?
Thomas Warner	1659-1674
James Tredenham	1693-1702
Joseph Vigurs	1703-1711?
John Trevenen	1738-1775
John Penrose	1776-1777
John Richards	1778-1815

Parish Clerks of Camborne

Hauton Hocking	c. 1660-1701
Francis Hocking	c. 1701-1730
? ?	?
Benjamin Glanvill	c. 1760-1780
John Gribble	1780-1824
David Duckham	1824-1837
John Duckham	1838-?

Parish Register
(under the Act of 24 Aug. 1653; see *RPC* I.118)

John Beard	1653-1660

2. *The Daughter Churches*

Treslothan

George T. Bull	1846-1894
H. H. Mills	1894-1906
H. W. Sedgewick	1906-1910
W. T. Haydon	1910-1923
H. E. Roberts	1924-1926

C. T. Richards	1927-1930
H. C. Baxter	1930-1940
A. H. Mock	1940-1942
D. C. Atwool	1943-1948
W. R. Newton	1948-1952
R. Whalley	1952-1961
W. Q. Lash	1962-1963
P. L. Eustice	1963-

Tuckingmill

Edward Crow	1845-1849
E. M. Pridemore	1850-1853
C. Jenkyns	1853-1874
T. R. McW. Bampfield	1875-1880
W. H. Hodge	1880-1883
Arthur Adams	1883-1904
H. Wright	1904-1923
J. Haworth	1923-1933
Albert Cocking	1933-1936
John Britton	1936-1945
R. S. Macdonald	1945-1961
G. M. Calder	1961-

Penpons

W. W. Butlin	1850-1896
James Sims Carah	1896-1935
C. R. Coates	1935-1952
R. M. Burlton	1952-1963
C. J. Alliston	1963-

(Details for the last three lists were kindly supplied by the Truro Diocesan Registry).

E
CAMBORNE FEASTS AND FAIRS

The tables below show the dates of the year on which the various fairs (pp.127-133) have been held in the last few centuries. The very latest instances are unrealistic, as they may represent copyings from earlier lists. The following references are used in addition to those which appear in the Bibliography (p.196 ff).

C.Alm.	*The Cornish Almanack, Camborne* (defunct).
Cooke	*G. A. Cooke's British Traveller's (Pocket) Directory* (1805).
DNC	Anon, *Description of England and Wales*, 10 vols. (1769), vol. II (Cornwall); for Newbery and Carnan, London.
Doidge	*Doidge's West Country Almanack* (Plymouth).
Kelly	Kelly's *Post Office Directory for Cornwall* (various edns.).

Old February Fair

1708	Feb. 24/25/26	Grant to R. Hooker (see p.127)
1769	Feb. 24	DNC, 213 (oxen, sheep, hop, cloths)
1779	Feb. 24	MUBT, 505 (Cambron: cattle)
1792	Feb. 29	Coll. Cornub., 1584
1805	Feb. 24 *and* March 7	Cooke, 17 (cattle)

March Fair

1805	Feb. 24 *and* March 7	Cooke, 17 (cattle)
1814	March 7	Lysons 1814, p.xxxix
1824	March 7	Drew II, 140
1878	March 7	Coll. Cornub., 1588
1884	March 7	Symons 1884, 17
1888	March 7	Coll. Cornub., 1584
1900	March 7 (Wed.)	Doidge 1900, 56
1906	March 7	Kelly 1906, 60
1925	March 7	CCG, and Doidge 1925
1927	March 7	C. Alm. 1927, 111
1933	March 6 (Mon.)	Doidge 1933, 52

Whitsuntide Fair

1814	In Whit-week	Lysons 1814, p.xxxix
1824	Whit-Tuesday	Drew II, 140
1830	Whit-Tuesday	Pigot 1830, 138
1878	June 11	Coll. Cornub., 1588
1884	May 30	Symons 1884, 17
1900	Whit-Tues., June 5	Doidge 1900, 56
1906	Whit-Tuesday	Kelly 1906, 60

| 1925 | June 2, Whit-Tuesday | Doidge 1925, 52 |
| 1927 | Whit-Tuesday | C. Alm. 1927, 111 |

St. Peter's Fair

1708	June 28/29/30	Grant to R. Hooker (see p. 127)
1769	June 29	DNC, 213 (oxen, sheep, etc.)
1779	June 29	MUBT, 505 (Cambron: cattle)
1805	June 29	Cooke, 17 (cattle)
1830	June 29	Pigot 1830, 138
1824	June 29	Drew II, 140
1878	June 29	Coll. Cornub., 1588
1884	June 29	Symons 1884, 17
1888	June 29	Coll. Cornub., 1584
1900	June 29 (Friday)	Doidge 1900, 56
1927	June 29	C. Alm. 1927, 111
1933	June 28 (Wed.)	Doidge 1933, 52

Camborne (Martinmas) Fair

1678	Nov. 7	1678 Ch'wdns. Accts. (see p.131)
1700	Fair day S. Martin	Lhuyd (Appendix A)
1708	Nov. 10/11/12	Grant to R. Hooker (see p.127)
1769	Nov. 11	DNC, 213 (oxen, sheep, etc.)
1779	Nov. 11	MUBT, 505 (Cambron: Cattle)
1792	Nov. 11	Coll. Cornub., 1584
1805	Nov. 11	Cooke, 17 (cattle)
1814	Nov. 11	Lysons 1814, p. 54
1814	2nd Tues. in Nov.	Lysons 1814, p.xxxix
1824	2nd Tues. in Nov.	Drew II, 140
1830	2nd Tues. in Nov.	Pigot 1830, 138
1884	Nov. 13	Symons 1884, 17
1888	Nov. 11	Coll. Cornub., 1588
1900	Nov. 12, Mon.	Doidge 1900, 56
1906	Nov. 11	Kelly 1906, 60
1927	Nov. 11	C. Alm. 1927, 111
1933	Nov. 10	Doidge 1933, 52

Tobias Martin's Poem on Camborne Fair

Captain Tobias Martin, of Wendron (1747-1828), wrote numerous poems, which were published with a life of their author as *The Remains of . . . Tobias Martin* (Helston, 1831: 2nd edn., 1856). His description here therefore takes us back to the end of the eighteenth century.

CAMBORNE FAIR

Crowds of people mix'd together;
Ladies dress'd to suit the weather;
Laborers in dirty frocks;
Gentlemen with powder'd locks;
Wretches calling for damnation;
Parsons preaching reformation;
Forward youths return'd from College,
Boasting of their wit and knowledge;
Handicrafts, Jews, *mumpers*, peddlars,
Spendthrifts, gamesters, dancers, fidlers;
Landlords busy at their calling;
Waiters skipping; drunkards bawling;
Wanton girls, and silly boys;
Infants pleas'd with gew-gaw toys;
Coaches passing thro' the throng;
Cripples singing mournful song,
How they suffer'd amputation,
Limbs lopp'd off to save the nation;
Darken'd by the nitrous grain,
Others their hard fate complain.
This and more, had you been there,
You'd have seen at Camborne Fair.

Postscript, November 1966

Due largely to the efforts of Camborne Chamber of Commerce, there was a considerable revival of Camborne Feast in November, 1966 (see p.133 above). This is fully described in the *Camborne Festival Magazine*, a special (48 pp.) issue of the monthly parish church magazine for November, two thousand copies of which were quickly sold. In addition to Feast Services on Sunday, 13th November, and the Feast Dinner on Monday 14th, there were both a carnival and a cage-bird show on the preceding Saturday, and an entire week of events until 20th November, including concerts and athletic events. See also *WB* for 17 November 1966, pp.13 and 16; *Cornishman*, same date, p.11.

F

JOSEPH VIVIAN'S REMINISCENCES, 1924

The very interesting letter which follows was copied by the writer from the original, in the possession of the late Mr. W. Blewett, Cross Street, in 1946. It was written, in response to a request from Canon Carah, by Mr. Joseph Vivian of St. Maradox Villa in 1924, when he was aged 89 (he lived until 95). Joseph Vivian was one of the nine children, including his centenarian brother William Cock Vivian (1819-1919), of Capt. Joseph Vivian, mine agent, of Reskadinnick, and his wife Nanny.

Saint Maradox, Camborne
29 Nov & 3 Dec 1924

Dear Mr. Carah,

I am going to try to answer your questions of 26th as far as is in my power and you may be sure that it will be done with the greatest pleasure if of any assistance to you . . .

To begin with the Mail Road, it ran over the ancient county road on which I have seen in the last century several of the old mile stones standing in their original position, but which I fear have all disappeared.

This County Road entered the parish at between the Hotel at Tucking-mill and Bickford Smith & Co's Fuze Works, turning to the right over the road leading past the rifle ground to Wheal Gerry, down what has always been known in my days as the Eastern Lane, which crosses what is known now as Tehidy Road at Parcan Bowan, thence by the Gilly Road to the Cornish Daws at Treswithian. Its direction then was pretty much the same as now, but bending a little to the right and running to Roseworthy over the old road still in existence past Wheal Room. At Roseworthy (the old name of which Mr. Symons, my uncle and great antiquarian, used to say was Resurrey, the prefixes Res meaning a ford as of course you know) into the Parish of Gwinear. My relatives, Mr. Joseph Vivian and John his brother who carried on the Roseworthy Hammer Mill, used to live one in Gwinear and the other in Camborne, the latter at Rosehill in the Ferns. In Gwinear the road went up the hill to Connor downs and on to Angarrack, not to Loggans. From Angarrack it went up the hill on the Phillack side and on to Guildford. It then passed by Copperhouse to St. Erth Bridge. There was no port of Hayle say before the 19th century. Mr. Henry Harvey of Gwinear commenced with a small brass foundry there and really created the port. Copperhouse was much more ancient and there the firm of Sandys Vivian and Co. had extensive engineering works and a large trade in coal, etc. They built the suspension bridge which now spans the Avon below Bristol. They built it however to span the Thames at Hungerford as the Hungerford Bridge, but after many years being found unequal to the traffic it was sold to Bristol and erected in its present position.

From St. Erth Bridge the county road passed on by the position of the St. Erth Railway Station to Marazion, breaking off on the right to Penzance which was formerly of far less importance than Marazion or Market Jew. I believe there are still extant many old maps of Cornwall from a survey made early in the 18th century which will, I believe, confirm the foregoing direction of this road. There used to be one of these maps at Reskadinnick and it should be there still but I rather think has not well been preserved. Mr. F. J. Stephens may know of it.

To go back to the bringing of the mails to Camborne, they were carried up from Parcanbowan through Fore Street to the Church town and thence westward along the Gilly Road. Until the making of the great Turnpike Road there was no road through the Church Town. Trelowarren Street was built alongside the Turnpike Road and chiefly by miners who had luck as tributers in the Dolcoath Mine, North Roskear, etc.

Dolcoath was resuscitated toward the end of the 18th century and North Roskear was opened early in the 19th. Simon Vivian, my father's uncle, who died about 1840 aged 95, remembered the Churchtown when it contained only forty houses, chiefly in Fore Street. There was no Trelowarren Street, but a short lane close to the site now occupied by the Commercial Hotel, which had not then been built. This lane was called Baker's Lane. A very little man called Goldsworthy, but nic-named Little Tuppeny, had a bakery in it which gave the name.

There was no College street or road to the west there, and the Parsonage was a very mean house situate where the Harris Boot Shop now stands. A description of this clerical residence may be found in the Parish Church-wardens' book, which also contains a statement of the boundaries of the Glebe. To the Northwest to it stood the Weeth estate, owned at the date of the record by Mrs. Elizabeth Roll of Stevenstone in Devon. Before the Turnpike Road was made through the Churchtown the exit from Crane was in the Gilly Road, almost opposite to the Farmhouse of Mr. Mounce, and this exit was known as Crane Gate, one of the old gateposts still being in situ. But when the Turnpike Road was made the exit from Crane was on it, just above the cemetery, and thence forward the name Crane Gate on the county road lost its significance and has been almost forgotten.

Referring to St. Erth Bridge alluded to before, I may mention that the late Dr. Gurney of Camborne who died about 1854 remembered as a boy staying with his uncle the Vicar of St. Erth [*Samuel Gurney: 1803-1833*] and seeing a coasting vessel discharging coal at that bridge. But when the Turnpike road was laid across the estuary [*1825*] it cut off navigation above that point, which the building of the railway many years later still further restricted. But the river has become so silted that it is now hard to realise that any sea-going vessel could ever have reached St. Erth churchtown. This reminds one of the fate of Tregoney, said to have been a seaport at the time of the Roman occupation.

Three very ancient houses in the parish; foremost would be Menadarva, then Mr. Harry Glanville's Rosewarne, and last Crane, all of them showing so plainly the solidarity of construction characteristic of the middle ages.

There was formerly a well at Crane and by it a roadside cross, and a Mrs. Dennis of Troon, who was born at Kehelland and used with her companions to go to school at the Churchtown told me some forty years ago that when they passed the cross they used to curtsey to it. The road to Kehelland was through the fields by the still remaining footpath.

I believe that the road from the Market Place ran through Cross Street to Camborne Cross and turned off there, passing by Camborne Veor, which four hundred years ago was the residence of Mr. John Vivian's forefathers, and on past the old poorhouse to the top of Beripper Lane, whence it branched off towards Pendarves and Boteto and on to Helston. Crane Lane opened into this road at the point now occupied by Tregenna. Vounder Vean (otherwise 'little lane') from Polgwartha [*Gwealgwarthas*] and Penponds joined the road close by the railway bridge, as it is now, which was constructed by the West Cornwall Railway Co. about 1852 or near it.

With very kind regards, Yours sincerely, JOSEPH VIVIAN.

(Two paragraphs, one purely social, the other dealing with the West Cornwall Railway, have been omitted.)

G
CAMBORNE PLACE-NAMES RECORDED BEFORE 1600

The stress placed throughout this book on the value of place-name evidence makes it desirable to include the following analysis, which embraces all the main tenement names and some of the natural features. There are a few other names—e.g., Cogegoes, Gwealgwartha, Vellan-saundry, Carwynnen—which almost certainly originated before 1600, but have not been recorded that early. The year 1600 forms a convenient horizon, since it is doubtful whether any new Cornish names, other than field- or cliff-names (*JRIC* (*n.s.*) V.1 (1965), 12-36) were evolved after the 17th century—cf. Nance, *OC* VI.1 (1961), 20-26. Most of the early forms given here are taken from Henderson's MS. Topography of Penwith (RIC, Truro), with additions from other records; forms marked (*RPC*) are from the 16th- and 17th-century Camborne parish registers, some-times in the guise of territorial surnames, but of special value as giving clues to contemporary pronunciations.

The phonetic equivalents, which are given in conventional form, are the current 'received' versions now in use by natives of the parish. The inverted r (ɹ) represents the west Cornish sound which Daniel Jones (*The Phoneme*, 2nd edn., 1962) aptly described as 'South-Western English r-coloured vowels', and not a full retroflexed r.

In the interpretations, some of which are tentative, the writer owes much to discussions with the late R. Morton Nance. The abbreviations *Fl.*, *Gr.*, and *LCB* refer to the Bibliography entries (below) under Fleuriot 1964, Graves 1962, and LCB, respectively. 'P.n.'=personal name.

The positions of all the places mentioned, except for *Chibettow*, which is lost, are shown on fig. 1, the sketch-map of the parish.

BARIPPER	(bə'ripə, bripə) 1397 *Beau Repere*, 1420 *Beaurepper*, 1530 *Berepper*, 1548 *Berypper*, 1577 *Beripper RPC*, 1835 *Baripper RPC*. French; *beau repaire*, 'good lodging'.
BALROSE	(bæl'rouz) 1571, 1617 *Balrosa*, 1827, 1838 *Balrose*. C.*bal*, 'mine, tin-work', and a second element which may be C.*rôsow*, 'wheels', if not just Eng. 'rose' or its C. equivalent *rosen*, coll. pl. *rôs*.
BEJAWSA	(bə'dʒɔ:zə) 1397 *Bosowesowe*, 1419 *Bossousou*, 1589 *Bossowsa*, 1725 *Bojasa*, 1801 *Bejosah*, 1884 *Bojosah*. C.*bos*, 'dwelling', and a p.n. *Sausou*, for which cf. OB. *Sauso* 1050 (*LCB* 164), apparently derived from *saus*, 'Saxon'.
BOLENOWE	(bə'lenou, blenə) 1397 *Bolenowe*, 1429 *Bollenowe*, 1538 *Bolenowe*, 1600 *Bollenowe*, 1838 *Bolenna*, 1884 *Bolenno*, *Bolenowe*. C.*bos*, 'dwelling', and a p.n. *Lalanou*, cf. OC.*laian*, 'faithful, religious' (*Gr.* 139); perhaps as a masc. noun, *laian*='a religious, a hermit' (*Gr.*).
BOSPEBO	(bəs'pi:bou) 1590 *Bospubo*, 1838 *Bosplbo*, 1884 *Bospebo*. C.*bos*, 'dwelling', and a p.n.? **Pabo*, **Pebo*, not otherwise known, rather than C.*pŷber*, 'piper, (bag-)pipe player', or even *pŷbow*, OC.**pibou* (*Gr.* 121), 'pipes'.
BUSHORNE(S)	(bə'zɔ:ɹn) 1530 *Boswronen*, 1600 *Boswrannen;* 1540 *Bossohorn*, 1610 *Bussorne*, 1723 *Boshornes*, 1833 *Bushorne*, 1884 *Bushornes*. The final s is intrusive and normally omitted. The first two forms recorded by Henderson, like the unidentified place 1540 *Rosevronen*, seem to be something different (with a p.n. **Bron-an*, **Bran-an*?) The series from *Bossohorn* is C.*bos*, 'dwelling', and p.n. *Eu-hoern*, for which cf. *LCB* 139, *Eu-hoiarn*, *Heuhoiarn* 843. OC.*hoern*, OB.*hoiarn*='iron' (*Gr.* 333, *Fl*.213); the first element (*Fl*.168) may mean something like 'excellent'.

BOSWIN   (bɔz'wɪn) 1397 *Boswyn*, 1530 *Boswyn*, 1591 *Buswin RPC*, 1600 *Boswydden*, 1831 *Beswidden*, 1838 *Boswyn, Boswydden*, 1884 *Boswin*. The *d* shows Late C. final *-n > -dn*. C.*bos*, 'dwelling', with either *gwyn*, 'fair, white', or the p.n. Gwyn, OC.**Guyn* (*Gr*.209), OB.*Uuin* (*LCB* 175).

CALLEAN   (Ka'li:n, Kɑɹ'li:n) 1316 *Kellian*, 1530 *Kyllyen*, 1562 *Kellean*, 1695 *Collean*, 1713 *Kileehan*, 1768 *Karlean*, 1790 *Killahan*, 1829 *Carlean RPC*, 1838 *Killahan*, 1884 *Carlean*, 1887 *Callean*. The present double form is due to imitation of names in *Car-*, especially as *Carlenno* (1838). C.*kelly*, OC. *kelli*, 'grove, little wood' (*Gr*.306), with dimin, suffix *-an* (*Fl*. 63).

CAMBORNE   ('Kæmbɔ:ɹn) See p.13 above for this name.

CARN C.   (Kɑɹn 'Kæmbɔ:ɹn) 1592 *Carne Camborne*, 1810 *Carne Camborne*, 1884 *Carn Camborne*. C. *carn*, see below, plus Camborne.

CARN ENTRAL   See under ENTRAL, and also p.14 above.

CARNLUSSICK   (Kɑɹn'lusɪk) 1540 *Carlusyk*, 1625 *Carnelusack*, 1819 *Cairn Lissick*, *Calissicks RPC*, 1838 *Carnlusack*. C.*carn*. 'rock pile, rocky hill-top', cf.*Gr*., 64, and p.n. *Loiesic*, from ? OC. **loies*, OB.*loes* (*Fl*., 245), and adjectival termination *-ic* (*Fl*.217); 'he who pursues, or chases out'?

CARNMOGH   (Kɑɹn'mou) 1380 *Carn Vogh*, 1530 *Carnemough*, 1625 *Carnemoghe*, 1826 *Cairn Mough*, 1838 *Carnmowe*, 1884 *Carnemough*. C.*carn*, 'rock pile, etc.', and *mogh*, pl. 'pigs', *Gr*.255-6, *Fl*.258.

CHIBETTOW   (*dʒə'betə?) 1600 *Chibettowe*, 1625 *Chibettowe als Chifettowe*. Late C.*chy*, 'house'; the second element is perhaps a p.n., OB.*Bidoe*, in compounds like *Iarn-bidoe* 845, *Mat-uedoe* 913 (*LCB* 109), *Hedr-uedoe*, 13th cent. (LCB 213); or from an OC.**betou*, like OB.*betiuou*, pl. (*Fl*.82), '?victims of a plague' (OB.*bat*, 'plague', *Fl*. 80).

CHINGWITH   (tʃiŋ'gwi:θ) 1583 *Chyangweath at Tolcarne vean*, 1625 *Cheyangweth*, 1838 *Chingwith*. Late C. *chy*, 'house', and either C. *y'n gwŷth*, 'in the trees', or *an gwŷth*, 'of the trees', with elision of the first two syllables.

CHYANDOUR   (*dʒæn'dauɹ) 1581 *Chyndowre*, 1600 *Chindower*, 1623 *Choyndower RPC*, 1622 *Jandower RPC*, Late C. *chy an dowr, chy'n dowr*, 'house of (at) the water'.

CHYCARNE   (tʃai'kɑɹn) 1537 *Chycarne RPC*. 1600 *Chicarne*, 1688 *Checarne*, 1835 *Chicairne*, 1838, 1884 *Chycarne*. Late C. *chy carn*, 'house (at) the rock-pile, hill-top'.

CHYTODDEN (tʃai'tɔdn) 1530 *Chywarton*, 1542, *Chiverton RPC*, 1600 *Chyton*, 1625 *Chiwarton als Chiverton*, 1835 *Chytodden*, 1884 *Chytodden*. The variants *-ver* for *-war* suggest the early forms had the last syllable stressed; with the change *ton > todn > todden*, the stress becomes penultimate. Late C. *chy*, 'house', and probably *wor(th) ton*, 'at the green'; C.*ton*, an uncertain word, not apparently OE.*tun*, but related to W.*ton*, 'surface'? Ir.*tonn*, OB.*tonnenn* (Fl. 315)?

CONDURROW (Kən'dʌrə) 1397 *Condorowe*, 1430 *Condorowe*, 1812 *Condurra*, 1829, 1838, *Condurrow*, 1838 *Condorrow*, 1884 *Condurrow*. OC.prefix **con* (*Gr*.99), in the sense of 'meeting of' (cf. OB. words in *com-*, *Fl*.114), and C.*dorow*, 'grounds, lands', *via* OCo.**doerou* (*doer*, 'ground, earth', *Gr*.35), rather than C.*dowrow*, 'waters'.

CRANE (Krei:n) 1283 *Kaervran*, 1331 *Carran*, 1380 *Kaerwran;* 1313 *Carhain*, 1335 *Carren;* 1397 *Caran*, 1417 *Karan*, 1420, 1460 *Caran*, 1510 *Karan*, 1570, 1600 *Crane*, 1620 *Crahan*, 1790, 1838, 1884 *Crane*. The two earliest series here refer to the same place, but represent OC. *kaer Uuran*, 'earthwork, or round, of Bran' (OB.*Bran*, *LCB* 111, a p.n. meaning 'raven, crow'), and OC. *kaer hên* (*Gr*.76), 'the old earthwork'. The post-1397 forms seem to descend from the latter, since 1620 *Crahan* must indicate a lengthened vowel as in *hên*.

ENTRAL ('ɛntrəl) 1380 *Entrall*, 1583, 1591, and 1597 *Entrall*, 1790 (Carn) *Entral*, 1838, 1884 *Entral*. The second element is probably C.*hal*, 'marshy ground, moor, in the dialect sense'—see *OC* VI.9 (1965), 393. The first has never been explained, but cf. the numerous instances of the name Antron (? **antr-*, *ûn*). Hantertavis (Mabe) and Hentergreen (Launceston) probably have C. *hanter*, 'half (of)'; initial H is similarly kept in the hundreds of names in Hendra (*hên tre(f)*, 'old homestead'). **Antr* suggests some meaning like 'part of' or 'middle of', and one might cf. OB. *entr*, *intr*, *Fl*.161, (pointing to an OC. **entr*?), literally 'between', but with the sense of 'within', followed by a noun (*hâl*, (*g*)*ûn*) in the singular?

GEAR (gi:əɹ) 1470 *Keyr*, 1504 *Gayr*, 1516 *Gere*, 1530 *Keyr als Engeire*, 1558 *Angeire*, 1600 *Geare*, 1838 *Gear*. The series shows confusion between the unaccompanied noun, and the mutated form following the article *an*, but this is from C.*kêr*, OC.*kaer*, in the particular sense of 'earthwork, fortified residence' (cf. *CA* 3 (1964), 38, for examples).

190   APPENDICES

GOONZOYLE (gu:n'zoil) 1560 *Gonan Soyle*, 1622 *Gonesoyle*, 1665 *Goon an soyle*, 1715 *Goonsoyle*, 1790 *Goonzoyle*, 1838 *Goonzoyle*. C.*gûn an*, 'downland, etc.', of the', with what must be a noun—possibly for C. *soul*, 'stubble' (*zoul*, Lhuyd).

HELLOW (he'lou,e'la) 1580 *Hellow*, 1600, 1649 *Hellowe*, 1620 *Enhellowe*, 1790, 1838, 1884 *Hellowe*. C.*hallow*, 'marshes, moors' (cf. OC VI.9 (1965), 393.

KEEVE (Ki:v) 1567 *Keve RPC*, 1569 *Kywe RPC*, 1600 *Kieve*, 1612, 1665, 1838, 1884 *Keeve*, 1887 *Kieve*. This is strictly the name of a mill and a stream-work, and seems to be C.*cüv*[*a*], 'tub, vat', a loan from OE.*cyf*.

KEHELLAND (Ki'elən) 1297 *Kellihellan*, 1335 *Kellihellan*, 1530 *Kelyhelland*, 1558 *Killihellan RPC*, 1768 *Kehellan*, 1790 *Kellihelland*, 1827 *Cahellan RPC*, 1838 *Kehelland*, 1884 *Killehelland, Kahellan*. C.*kelly*, OC.*kelli*, 'grove, little wood', and *hellan* for *hên lan*, 'the old enclosure' (not necessarily ecclesiastical—see p.48 above).

KILLIVOSE (Kili'vouz) 1480 *Kyllyvos*, 1547 *Killivose RPC*, 1566 *Kellyvos*, 1790, 1838 *Kellivose*, 1884 *Killivose*. C.*kelly*, OC.*kelli*, 'grove, little wood'. and C.*fôs*, 'trench, rampart, wall' (cf.Lat. *fossa*).

LAITY ('lei:ti) 1530, 1600 *Layty*, 1610 *Laytye*, 1835 *Laity RPC*, 1884 *Laity*. C.*leth-ty*, 'milk-house, dairy' (cf. OC. *lait*, 'milk', Gr. 375; and OB. *Laedti* (*laeth, ti*) LCB 143).

MENADARVA (menə'dɑ:ɪvə) 1285 *Mertherderwa*, 1297 *Merderderwa*, 1447, 1530 *Mertherderwa*, 1551 *Marthaderva RPC*, 1600 *Menedarva*, 1622 *Menethderva* (mill), 1670 *Menadarvy*, 1790 *Menaderva*, 1838, 1844 *Mena-, darva*. This begins with C.*merther* (< Lat.*martyr*[*ium*] cf. W.*merthyr*) in the sense of 'chapel or shrine containing relics', and the p.n. *Derwa*, cf.p.52 above. The shift of the first element after 1600 may be to C.*meneth*, Late C.*mener*, 'hill'.

NEWTON ('njiutən) 1420, 1430, 1662 (*RPC*), 1790, 1837 (*RPC*), 1838, 1844 *Newton*. From Middle English: 'the new farm, or homestead' (*scil.*, as a 15th-century extension of Troon or Trewoon?)

PENCOBBEN (pen'kɔbn) 1530, 1580 *RPC Pencom*, 1535 *Pencombe*, 1600 *Pencobne*, 1630 *Pencombe als Pencobine*, 1727, 1748, 1837 (*RPC*), 1884 *Pencobben*. C. *pen*, 'end. head, top', and C.*cum*, 'coombe, little valley', with the intrusive *b* of Late Cornish.

PENGEGON (pen'gɛgən) 1301 *Pengyen*, 1426 *Pengygen* vill, 1600 *Pengegan*, 1700 *Pedengiggall* (Gascoyne, fig.4), 1713, 1746, 1790 *Pengigan*, 1838, 1884 *Pengigan*. C.*pen*, 'end, head, top', and (ignoring the 1301 form

PENDARVES as a mis-spelling) a noun *gygen*, cf.W.*gagen* ('cleft, chink, rift, slit'; Pughe). (pən'daɹvis) 1530 *Pendyrfos*, 1548 *Pendyrfos*, 1592 *Pendarvas RPC*, 1600 *Pendervas*, 1790 *Pendarvis*, 1610, 1620, 1790, 1838, 1884 *Pendarves*. C.*pen.*, 'end, head, top', followed by C.*dyr fôs* (for *an dyr fôs*?) 'the three (*tyr*, fem. form) ramparts or walls'; but with the proviso (see p. 66 above) that this may not have originated as a place-name within this parish.

PENPONS (pen'pɔnz) 1302 *Penpount*, 1397, 1419, 1450 *Penpons*, 1838 *Penponds*. C.*pen*, 'end, head, top' and C.*pons*, OC.**pont*, *pons* (*Gr.*314), 'bridge'.

PELLUTES (pəl'u:ts) 1530 *Penelutys*, 1540 *Penhalewtyes*, 1610 *Pennalutus*, 1625 *Penhaluts*, 1768 *Pelewtes*, 1790 *Pollyteys*, 1830 *Pelutes RPC*, 1830, 1838 *Perlutes*, 1838, 1884 *Pellutes*. C.*pen*, 'end, head, top'; C.*hâl*, 'marsh, moor'; and possible (on the strength of the 1540 form) C. *a-ugh ty* 'above the house', if the final *s* is intrusive.

POLSTRONG (pul'strɔŋ) 1302 *Polstronk*, 1540 *Polstronk*, 1581, 1600, 1637 *Polstrongo*, 1790 *Polstrong*, 1838, 1884 *Pulstrong*, C.*pol*, 'pool', and C.*stronk*, strong, 'filth, dirt, mud', cf.B.*stronk*. In this sense it may be 'that which draws in, sucks in'; cf. *Fl.*308, s.v. *strocat*.

PONSPRETTAL (pɔnz'prɪtal) 1335 *Ponspretal*, 1536 *Ponsprettal*, 1790 *Ponsprettal*, 1833 *Pons Brittal*, 1860, 1926 *Ponsprittal*. C.*pons*, 'bridge', and a word which is less likely to be C.*brythel*, OC.*breithil*, 'mackerel' (cf.W.*brithyll*, 'trout') than perhaps an OC.**bruit-il*, formed from OC.*bruit* (*Gr.*210) cognate, as Sir Ifor Williams has suggested (*BBCS* XI, 94-96) with W.*brwyd* in the sense of 'variegated, blood-stained, discoloured . . .' Is **Bruitil > Brital, Bretal*, the lost name of the Red River, so-called from the red-brown tin waste which has stained it for centuries?

RACE (rei:s) 1250 *Le Res* (?), 1473 *Reys*, 1516 *Ryse*, 1768, 1830 *The Race*, 1838, 1884 *Race*. From OE.*ræs*, 'stream, water-course'?

RESKADINNICK (reskə'dınık) 1569 *Riskadenake RPC*, 1591 *Roscadenick*, 1677 *Ruskedenack*, 1832 *Ruskadennic RPC*, 1884 *Roskadinnick*, 1901 *Reskadinnick*. Probably C.*res*, 'ford'—a stream passes this house— and a p.n. **Catinic, Catinoc*, cf. *LCB* 115, 195 (*Katheneuc*, 1448), 'war-like, etc.', ultimately from OC., OB., *cat*, 'battle'.

RESKAJEAGE   (rɛskə'dʒɪg, rɛskə'dʒi:g) 1235 *Ruschedek*, 1236 *Roskedek*, 1252 *Roskediec*, 1283 *Roskadechic*, 1316 *Roskadaek*, 1335, 1447 *Rescasek*, 1362 *Reskegek*, 1530 *Reskeseke*, 1554 *Riskaieake RPC*, 1649 *Reskaseage als Rescajeage*, 1838 *Reskajeage*. Probably C.*ros*, 'spur, high ground' (rather than C.*res*, 'ford'), and a p.n. which three early forms suggest may have been *Cadioc* (cf.*LCB* 195, Cadioc, 1236) rather than *Catic* (*LCB* 115), both meaning 'warrior'.

ROSCROGGAN   (rəs'krɔgən) Partly in Camborne, partly in Illogan. 1598 *Riscroggan*, 1634 *Rescroggan*, 1687 *Roscroggan*, 1884 *Rosecroggan*. C.*res*, 'ford', and C.*crogen*, 'shell' (dialect 'croggan', a limpet-shell).

ROSEWARNE   (rəz'wɔ:ɹn) 1283 *Rysuharn*, 1304 *Risehoern*, 1317 *Roseuhoern*, 1400 *Rosowhorn*, 1420 *Resuhorn*, 1473 *Rysworn*, *Reswern*, 1510 *Reyswern*, 1539, 1591, 1677, 1790, 1838, 1884 *Rosewarne*. C.*res*, 'ford' (alternating with C.*ros* 'spur, high ground'?) and a p.n. *Eu-hoern*, OB.*Eu-hoiarn*, for which see 'Bushorne' above.

ROSKEAR   (rɔs'ki:ɹ) 1304 *Risker*, 1325, 1512 *Resker*, 1530, 1600 *Reskere*, 1790, 1850 *Reskeare*, 1700, 1838, 1884 *Roskear*. C.*res*, 'ford', and C.*kêr*, 'earthwork, fortified homestead, round' (cf. 'Gear' above); the original name of the river-crossing at Tuckingmill?

TOLCARN(E)   (tɔl'ka:ɹn) 1338 *Talkarn*, 1530 *Talcarne*, 1558 *Talkarn*, 1573 *Talcarn*, 1790 *Talcarne*, 1838, 1884 *Tolcarne*. This name contains C.*tal*, lit. 'brow', but here 'front (of)', cf.*Gr*.42, *Fl*.310, and C.*carn*, 'rock-pile'.

TOLGARRACK   (tɔl'garik) near Godrevy and Reskajeage. 1541 *Tolgarake*? 1600 *Tollgarracke*, 1699 *Tollgarrack*, 1790 *Tolgarrack*, 1884 *Tolgarrick*. C.*toll*, 'hole, pit', OC.*toll*, 'hole', *Gr*.125, and C.*carrek*, 'rock'. This farm stood in a small quarry.

TOLGARRACK   (tɔl'garik) near Roskear and Tuckingmill. 1250 *Talgarrek*, 1331, 1530 *Talgarrek*, 1538 *Talgarake RPC*, 1830 *Tolgarrac RPC*, 1838 *Tolgarrack*. C.*tal*, 'front (of)', and C.*carrek*, 'rock'.

TREGLINWITH   (tri'glɪnwiθ) 1495 *Treylenwer*, 1517 *Treglenwere*, 1583 *Treglenwith*, 1628 *Treglinwith als Treglenwere*, 1667 *Treglenweth*, 1838 *Treglinwith*. The ending -with is due to infection from Weeth, Withes, the neighbouring tenement. C.*tre(f)*, 'homestead', and *clünwer*, 'green pasture'; from *clün*, OC*clun (? cf. Domesday *Clunewic*, *clun* and *ewic*, C.*ewyk*, 'hind, deer'), meaning 'pasture, meadow', and C. *gwer*, 'green'.

TRESLOTHAN (trə'slɔθən) 1282 *Treselwithian,* 1283 *Treselwethen, Tresulwythen,* 1317 *Tresulwethen,* 1343 *Tresulwithan,* 1530 *Treslothan,* 1748, 1838 *Treslothan.* C.tre(f), 'homestead', and a p.n. *Sulwythen.* This is a combination of the prefix *Sul-*(<Lat. *sol.,* 'sun': *LCB* 165), and *Uueten, Uuethen,* as in *Cat-uuethen,* 1051 (*LCB* 173-4), from OB.*uueith, uuethen,* 'battle' (*Fl.*189).

TRESWITHIAN (trə'swɪθjin, 'dʒeθən, 'dʒʌθən) 1292 *Trevaswethan,* 1313 *Trevaswythan,* 1430 *Treveswethan,* 1517, 1658 *Treswethan,* 1591 *Trevasweathen,* 1677 *Treswethen,* 1700 *Tresothan* (Gascoyne), *Trejothan* (Lhuyd), 1790 *Treswithian,* 1838 *Treswithian.* The last form is by analogy with place-names like 'Gwithian'. C.*tre(f),* 'homestead', and a p.n. *Maswythen, Mat-uuethen,* for which cf. LCB 174, *Mat-uueten* 913. From OC., OB. *mat,* 'good' (*Gr.*101: *Fl.*251), and *uuethen,* 'battle'.

TREVORNER (trə'vɔːɪnə, trə'vəːɪnə) 1588, 1768 *Trevornowe,* 1830 *Trevornow,* 1838 *Trevorner,* 1834 *Travernow,* 1884 *Vorner,* 1890 *Trevarno,* 1950 *Treverno.* C.*tre(f),* 'homestead', and probably *vornow,* metathesis of (lenited) *bronnow,* from C.*bron,* 'breast, hill-front, hill'.

TREVORYAN (trə'vɔrjən) 1316 *Treworian,* 1520 *Treworyan,* 1544 *Treverrian RPC,* 1538, 1586 (*RPC*) *Treworrian,* 1614 *Trewerrian,* 1700 *Trevorian,* 1748, 1884 *Trevorian,* 1838, 1900 *Trevoryan.* C.*tre(f),* 'homestead', and a p.n. *Uuorien* (*Uuor-gen, LCB* 178, 132) with elements *uuor,* OC.*gur, Gr.*106, 'man', and termination *-gen* (*Fl.*174).

TROON (truːn) 1430 *Trewon,* 1530, 1543 *Trewone,* 1688, 1748, 1838, 1884 *Trewoon,* 1700, 1750, 1838 *Treun,* 1920 *Troon.* C.*tre(f),* 'homestead', and lenited form of C.*gûn,* 'downland'.

H
THE POPULATION OF CAMBORNE

A 'Census' of 1768 (CRO AD 55/24)
'The Number of Persons Resident in Camborn Parish as taken 1768 by Benjamin Glanvill'

In the Church Town	226
Camborn Cross	14
Camborn Veor and Beacon Lane	92
Camborn Vean	11
In and about Carnamoah	39
Condurrow	40
The Newton and Tolnewton	45
Chycarne	10
Bolenoe	27
Entrell etc.	116
Pengigan etc.	112
Roskear etc.	47
Tuckingmill, Skewbuds, Trevornowe and Whl. Crafty	64
Wheal Gerry etc.	28
The 3 Rosewarnes	82
Camborn Moor, Whl. Kitty, and Weeths	84
Reskedinick	25
Kieve Mill, Belly ache, and Roselewy	26
Balrose, Helloe, and Pencobben	14
Gwellenvellen, Roskejeage and Karlean	40
Carlenoe and Menedarva	29
Trevorian, Bushorn, Rosegrowse and New Downs	96
The Fern, Nancemellin and Kehellan	79
Merrymeeting and two Polstrongs	46
Gwelgwarthas, Little Kehellan, and neighbourhood	57
Gunsoyle, Craness, Croan, etc.	48
Treswithan, Kieve Lane, Parkholly, and Race	106
Crane, The Alms House, Penpons and Bejawsa	237
Berepor	98
Park pelew, Penventon, Gear, Pendarves and Mill	95
Stennack	60
Carwinin and Carwinin Carn	63
Treslothan	59
Killavose Moor and Reanvarah	36
Killavose	38
Knave-go-by and Tolcarne	38
Troon and Troon Moor	70
Chytodden	28
Pelewtes and Croft Michell	35
Buswidden	26
Laity	8
	2494

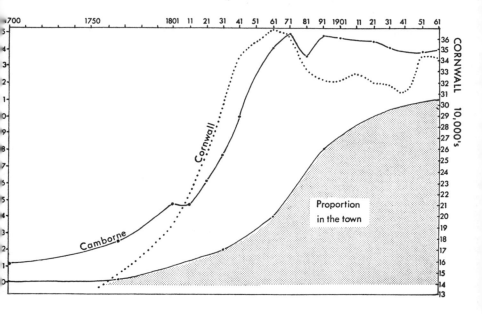

Fig. 32
The population curve of Camborne parish.

Comments

This extremely interesting document, to which Mr. H. L. Douch kindly drew the writer's attention, reveals—apart from the surprisingly high total for 'Church Town'—the truth of the old tradition that Penpons and its surrounds was once as big as the village of Camborne. It also shows the beginnings of the progressive urbanisation of the parish, which is better displayed in fig. 32. This is a graph showing the population rise of Camborne over the last two and a half centuries (the figure for 1700 is calculated, going back in ten-year averages, from the parish registers), contrasted with, on the one hand, the population rise for the county as a whole (the dotted line), and on the other, the proportion of the population of Camborne living in the town, as opposed to the outlying villages. Some of the figures are estimates—there was, for example, no national census in 1941, and only a set of estimated figures for 1939—but the general trend is clear enough. The almost explosive rise of the Cornish up to the peak in the 1860's was followed by the massive emigrations to the overseas mining fields, emigrations reflected in the subsequent decade in the Camborne figures (see Courtney's statistical discussion of this in *JRIC* XIII (1897), 211 ff.).

BIBLIOGRAPHY AND ABBREVIATIONS

Adams 1957   J. H. Adams, 'The Medieval Chapels of Cornwall', *JRIC (n.s.)* III.1 (1957), 48-65.

Ant.J.   *The Antiquaries' Journal* (Society of Antiquaries, London).

Arch.J.   *The Archaeological Journal* (Royal Archaeological Institute, London).

Baird & White   Major R. D. Baird and Lady White, *Cornish Crosses* (typescript notebooks with photos., RIC, Truro).

BBCS   *Bulletin of the Board of Celtic Studies*, Cardiff.

Bib. Cornub.   *Bibliotheca Cornubiensia*, 3 vols., 1874-1882. compiled by G. C. Boase and W. P. Courtney.

Blight SB   MS. Sketch Books containing drawings and notes by J. T. Blight, also H. A. Crozier and others, Penzance Library.

Blight 1856   J. T. Blight, *Ancient Crosses and other antiquities in the West of Cornwall* (Penzance, 1856).

BM   *Bewnans Meryasek;* a miracle play in Cornish, 'The Life of Meriasek', written *circa* 1480-1500 (?); see Stokes 1872.

Borlase 1754   William Borlase, *Observations on the Antiquities . . . of . . . Cornwall* (Oxford, 1754, 1st edn.).

CA   *Cornish Archaeology* (Journal of the Cornwall Archaeological Society, annual), 1962 onwards.

Camborniana 1897   *Camborniana; stories of our parish, its people and its past*, ed. Charles Rowe and W. Bartle Symons (for Camborne Students' Association); Camborne, 1897.

Carah 1925   J. Sims Carah, *The Parish of Camborne* (Camborne, 1925).

Carah 1927   J. Sims Carah, *The Parish of Camborne, part II, with Camborne Rate Book 1647-1717* (Camborne, 1927).

Carah 1934   J. Sims Carah, *The Carved Bench-ends of the Church of . . . Penponds* (Camborne, 1934).

CCG   *The Cornish Church Guide* (Truro, 1928).

CIIC   R.A.S. Macalister, *Corpus Inscriptionum Insularum Celticarum*, I (Dublin, 1945), II (Dublin, 1949).

Coll. Cornub.   *Collectanea Cornubiensia*, compiled by G. C. Boase (Truro, 1890).

Collins 1912   J. H. Collins, *Observations on the West of England Mining Region* (Penzance, 1912).

Cornishman   *The Cornishman Newspaper*, Penzance (weekly).

Cox 1912   J. C. Cox, *County Churches; Cornwall* (1912).

CP   *The Cornish Post and Mining News*, Camborne (defunct).

CR   *The Cornish Review*, ed. Denys Val Baker (first series, 1949-1952, ten parts).

Creswell 1910   Beatrix F. Creswell, *Notes on the History of the Parish Church of Camborne* (Plymouth, 1910).

CRO   Cornwall County Record Office, Truro.

CRP   *The Camborne-Redruth Packet* (Falmouth; defunct).

Davies 1939   W. LL. Davies, *Cornish Manuscripts in the National Library of Wales* (NLW, Aberystwyth, 1939).

DCNQ   *Devon and Cornwall Notes and Queries* (quarterly).

Doble 1926   G. H. Doble, *St. Gwinear, Martyr* (King's Stone Press, n.d.—1926): Cornish Saints No. 9.

Doble 1934   G. H. Doble, *St. Meriadoc, Bishop and Confessor* (Truro, 1935: originally *Truro Diocesan Gazette*, 1934): Cornish Saints No. 34.

Doble 1935   G. H. Doble, 'The Christian Origins of Camborne', *JRIC* XXIV (1935), 233-236.

Drew 1824   (F. Hitchins and) Samuel Drew, *The History of Cornwall*, 2 vols. (Helston, 1824).

Fleuriot 1964   L. Fleuriot, *Dictionnaire des gloses en vieux Breton* (Paris, Libr. C. Klincksieck, 1964; colln. linguistique no. 62).

FOCS   Federation of Old Cornwall Societies (acting as publishers).

Fowler 1961   David C. Fowler, 'The Date of the Cornish *Ordinalia*', *Mediæval Studies* (Toronto), XXIII (1961), 91-125.

Gilbert 1817   C. S. Gilbert, *Historical Survey of the County of Cornwall*, 3 vols., Plymouth Dock (1817).

Gough 1789   Camden's *Britannia*, ed. Richard Gough (London, 1789), vol. I.

Graves 1962   E. Van T. Graves, *The Old Cornish Vocabulary* (Univ. Microfilms Inc., Ann Arbor, Michigan, 1962).

Hals 1750   William Hals, *The Complete History of Cornwall; Part ii . . . Parochial History* (Exeter, 1750).

Henderson 1925   Charles Henderson, *Parochial History*, pp.51-222 of CCG (see above).

Henderson 1935   Charles Henderson, *Essays in Cornish History* (Oxford, 1935).

Henderson Top. Penwith   Charles Henderson, (MS.) *Topography of Penwith Hundred*, R.I.C., Truro

Hunt 1871   Robert Hunt, *Popular Romances of the West of England* (2nd edn., one vol., London 1871).

JBAA   *Journal of the British Archaeological Association* (London).

Jenner 1928   Henry Jenner, 'King Teudar', *Tre Pol and Pen* (London Cornish Assoc. annual), London, 1928.

JRIC   *Journal of the Royal Institution of Cornwall* (Truro); vols I-XXV (1863-1942), vol.I n.s. (1946) onwards.

Lacy I, II   *The Register of (Bishop) Edmund Lacy, 1420-1455; Registrum Commune*, vol. I (1963), vol. II (1966), ed. G. R. Dunstan (Canterbury and York Soc., with Devon and Cornwall Record Soc.).

Langdon 1896   A. G. Langdon, *Old Cornish Crosses* (Truro, 1896).

Lanyon 1841   Dr. Richard Lanyon, 'Statistics of Camborne',
                     9th Ann. Rep. R.C.P.S. (1841), 99-117.
LCB   J. Loth, *Chrestomathie Bretonne* (Paris, 1890).
Lysons 1814   Rev. Daniel Lysons and Samuel Lysons, *Topo-
                     graphical & Historical Account of the County of
                     Cornwall* (=*Magna Britannia, III*), London (1814).
Med. Arch.   *Medieval Archaeology* (Journal of the Society for
                     Medieval Archaeology, London).
Michell 1948   Frank Michell, *Notes on the History of Redruth*
                     (Redruth, 1948).
Misc.   Penzance Library, Morrab Gardens: *Volume of
                     Miscellaneous Prints, Extracts and Drawings.*
Morton 1936   Rev. Douglas E. Morton, *The Story of Camborne
                     Parish Church* (B.P.C., Gloucester, 1936).
Morton 1949   Reprint of Morton 1936, ed. Rev. James Vincent.
MS. Arthur   MS. notes on various aspects of Camborne, *penes*
                     Mrs. Gladys King, Camborne.
MS. Borlase 41   MS. 8vo. notebook of Dr. William Borlase, labelled
                     (41) and 'Excursions 1751-1758'; no. 149 in the sale
                     catalogue (Sotheby's, 1887) of the Laregan library,
                     at R.I.C., Truro.
MS. Carah 22   MS. bound notebook of Canon J. S. Carah, con-
                     taining essays on Camborne and partial text of Carah
                     1925, at Lowenac, Camborne.
MS. Clinnick   Series of MS. essays on Camborne, c.1920-1930, by
                     Rev. A. A. Clinnick, formerly curate, at Lowenac,
                     Camborne.
MS. James Thomas Notes on Old Camborne, by James Thomas, c.1880(?)
                     -1920, *penes* Mr. W. E. Wallace, Penpons.
MS. Russell   MS. notebook on Old Camborne ('Barber Russell's
                     album'), c.1870-1900, by the late Mr. S. T. Russell, at
                     Lowenac, Camborne.
MS. Tonkin   Thomas Tonkin of Trevaunance, *Parochial Antiquities
                     of Cornwall*, three MS. volumes at R.I.C., Truro.
MUBT   *The Modern Universal British Traveller* (?author),
                     chap. viii, 'Cornwall', pp.489-508 (London, 1779).
OC   *Old Cornwall* (Journal of the Federation of Old
                     Cornwall Societies—St. Ives, Marazion).
Penaluna   *An Historical Survey of the County of Cornwall . . .
                     a New edition etc.*, W. Penaluna, 2 vols., Helston
                     (1838).
Peter 1903   Thurstan C. Peter, *The History of Glasney Collegiate
                     Church* (Camborne, 1903).
Peter 1909   T. C. Peter, 'The Churchwardens' Accounts of the
                     Parish of Camborne', *JRIC* XVII (1909), 381.
Pigot 1830   J. Pigot & Co.'s *National Commercial Directory of . . .
                     (England) and the whole of south Wales* (London,
                     1830.)

Polsue-Lake — *A complete parochial history of the County of Cornwall* ('Lake's Parochial History'), edited & compiled by J. Polsue, 4 vols. and appendices (Lake, Truro, 1867).

PSAS — *Proceedings of the Society of Antiquaries of Scotland* (Edinburgh).

PWCFC — *Proceedings of the West Cornwall Field Club* (Camborne, 1953-1961); replaced by *Cornish Archaeology*.

PZNHAS — *Transactions of the Penzance Natural History and Antiquarian Society*, Penzance (new series, 1880-).

RCG — *The Royal Cornwall Gazette* (Truro).

RCPS — *Annual Reports* of the Royal Cornwall Polytechnic Society (Falmouth), from 1833.

RHR — The Registers of the Bishops of Exeter, edited by F. C. Hingeston-Randolph; various dates, cited by relevant bishop, and page in printed volume.

RIC, R.I.C. — The Royal Institution of Cornwall (Truro).

RPC — H. Tapley-Soper, ed., *The Register of . . . the parish of Camborne*, 1538-1837, 2 vols., Devon and Cornwall Record Society (Exeter, 1945).

SM — *The Sherborne Mercury* (Sherborne).

Stephens 1925 — F. J. Stephens, 'Contributions to the early history of the parish of Camborne' (various typescript lectures, etc.), at R.I.C., Truro.

Stokes 1872 — Whitley Stokes, *Beunans Meriasek, The Life of St. Meriasek, a Cornish drama* (London, 1872).

Symons 1884 — Richard Symons, *A . . . Gazetteer of the County of Cornwall* (Rodda, Penzance, 1884).

Thomas 1949 — A. C. Thomas, 'The Glebe Lands of Camborne', *116 Ann. Rep. R.C.P.S.* (1949), 22 ff.

Thomas 1950 — A. C. Thomas, *Some Notes on the Folk-Lore of the Camborne District* (Camborne, 1950).

Thomas 1958 — C. Thomas, *Gwithian: Ten Years' Work, 1949-1958* (Camborne, 1958).

Thomas 1963 — C. Thomas, *Phillack Church, an illustrated history of the Celtic, Norman, and Medieval Foundations* (B.P.C., Gloucester, 1963).

Thomas 1964 — C. Thomas, *Gwithian: notes on the church, parish, and St. Gothian's chapel* (Redruth, 1964).

Tuck 1880 — William R. Tuck, *Reminiscences of Cornwall—Camborne* (Netherton & Worth, Truro, n.d. but *c.* 1880).

VCH I — William Page, ed,. *The Victoria History of the Counties of England: Cornwall, vol. 1* (London, 1906).

Vincent 1959 — Rev. James Vincent, *A Short Guide to Camborne Parish Church* (Graham Cumming, Ramsgate, 1959).

WA — *The Western Antiquary* (Plymouth).

WB — *The West Briton* (Truro, weekly).

WDM — *The Western Daily Mercury* (Plymouth, defunct).

WMN — *The Western Morning News* (Plymouth, daily).

INDEX

A

NAMES OF PERSONS, PLACES, AND AUTHORS CITED IN TEXT

(exclusive of the Appendices)

SUBJECT INDEX

B